VERTICAL READINGS
IN DANTE'S *COMEDY*

Vertical Readings in Dante's *Comedy*

Volume 3

edited by
George Corbett and Heather Webb

OpenBook
Publishers

http://www.openbookpublishers.com

Digital material and resources associated with this volume are available at https://www.openbookpublishers.com/product/623#resources

ISBN Paperback: 978-1-78374-358-2
ISBN Hardback: 978-1-78374-359-9
ISBN Digital (PDF): 978-1-78374-360-5
ISBN Digital ebook (epub): 978-1-78374-361-2
ISBN Digital ebook (mobi): 978-1-78374-362-9
DOI: 10.11647/OBP.0119

Cover image: Fra Angelico (circa 1395–1455), The Last Judgement circa 1450, Gemäldegalerie, Berlin. Photo by Anagoria https://commons.wikimedia.org/wiki/File:1450_Fra_Angelico_Last_Judgement_anagoria.JPG, public domain.

All paper used by Open Book Publishers is SFI (Sustainable Forestry Initiative), and PEFC (Programme for the endorsement of Forest Certification Schemes) Certified.

Printed in the United Kingdom, United States and Australia
by Lightning Source for Open Book Publishers (Cambridge, UK).

Contents

Acknowledgements

We owe a particular debt to the wonderful community of students, academics and members of the public in Cambridge who have supported the lecture series, 'Cambridge Vertical Readings in Dante's *Comedy*' (2012–2016). We are also grateful to those who, following the series online, have contributed to this scholarly endeavour and experiment. The project has benefited from broad collaboration from the outset. Each public lecture was preceded by a video-conferenced workshop between the Universities of Cambridge, Leeds and Notre Dame on one of the three cantos in the vertical reading.

There are many people who have helped us during the different stages of the project. We are deeply grateful to you all and we regret that, in these brief acknowledgements, we can only thank some of you by name. Apart from the contributors to this volume, we would like to thank Pierpaolo Antonello, Elizabeth Corbett, Mary Corbett, Robert Gordon, Ronald Haynes, Claire Honess, Robin Kirkpatrick, Anne Leone, Vittorio Montemaggi, Helena Phillips-Robins, Federica Pich, Chiara Sbordoni, Nan Taplin, and Matthew Treherne. Finally, we would like to extend our particular thanks to Simon Gilson for his support, advice and encouragement on this project from its inception.

The master and fellows of Trinity College generously hosted the series and offered accommodation to the speakers. The series would not have been possible without the generosity of our sponsors: Trinity College; Selwyn College; the Italian Department, University of Cambridge; the Cambridge Italian Research Network (CIRN); and Keith Sykes.

Open Book Publishers has enabled us to build upon the growing public audience of the video-lectures by making all the volumes free to read online. We would like to thank especially Alessandra Tosi, Bianca Gualandi, and Lucy Barnes for their work in enabling an excellent peer review process, their meticulous comments on the manuscript, and for their help in preparing the bibliography and index, as well as Corin Throsby for the cover design.

Editions Followed and Abbreviations

A. Dante

Unless otherwise stated, the editions of Dante's works may be found in: *Le Opere di Dante*, ed. by F. Brambilla Ageno, G. Contini, D. De Robertis, G. Gorni, F. Mazzoni, R. Migliorini Fissi, P. V. Mengaldo, G. Petrocchi, E. Pistelli, P. Shaw, and rev. by D. De Robertis and G. Breschi (Florence: Polistampa, 2012).

A.1 Vernacular works

Inf.	*Inferno*
Purg.	*Purgatorio*
Par.	*Paradiso*
Conv.	*Convivio*
VN.	*Vita nova*

A.2 Latin works

DVE.	*De vulgari eloquentia*
Mon.	*Monarchia*
Questio	*Questio de aqua et terra*
Epist.	*Epistole*
Ecl.	*Egloge*

B. English translations

Unless otherwise stated, the translations of Dante are adapted from these readily available and literally translated English editions:

B.1 Vernacular works

The Divine Comedy of Dante Alighieri, ed. and trans. by Robert M. Durling; introduction and notes by Ronald L. Martinez and Robert M. Durling, 3 vols (Oxford: Oxford University Press, 1996–2011).

The Banquet, trans. with introduction and notes by Christopher Ryan (Saratoga, CA: Anma Libri, 1989).

La Vita Nuova, trans. by Mark Musa (Bloomington, IN and London: Indiana University Press, 1962).

Dante's Lyric Poetry, trans. by Kenelm Foster and Patrick Boyde, 2 vols (Oxford: Oxford University Press, 1967).

B.2 Latin works

De vulgari eloquentia, ed. and trans. by Steven Botterill (Cambridge: Cambridge University Press, 1996).

Monarchy, ed. and trans. by Prue Shaw. Cambridge Texts in the History of Political Thought (Cambridge: Cambridge University Press, 1996).

The Letters of Dante, trans. by Paget J. Toynbee, 2nd edn (Oxford: Clarendon Press, 1966); for the political epistles, however, *Dante Alighieri: Four Political Letters*, trans. by Claire Honess (London: Modern Humanities Research Association, 2007).

Dante and Giovanni del Virgilio, trans. by Philip H. Wicksteed and Edmund G. Gardner (New York: Haskell House Publishers, 1970).

In most instances, the translation [in square brackets] follows the original passage. Where the sense of the original passage is clear from the main text, the original passage (in parentheses) follows the paraphrase. Discussion is always with regard to the passage in the original.

Notes on the Contributors

Piero Boitani teaches Comparative Literature at 'La Sapienza' and the Gregorian University, Rome, and at the University of Italian Switzerland, Lugano. His books include *The Shadow of Ulysses: Figures of a Myth* (1994), *The Bible and its Rewritings* (1999), *Winged Words: Flights in Poetry and History* (2007), and *The Gospel According to Shakespeare* (2013). He won the Feltrinelli Prize for Literary Criticism in 2002, the De Sanctis Prize in 2010, and the Balzan Prize for Comparative Literature in 2016.

Theodore J. Cachey Jr. is Professor of Italian at the University of Notre Dame. He specializes in Italian Medieval and Renaissance literature, especially Dante, Petrarch and Boccaccio. He has authored and edited several books, as well as numerous essays and book chapters. He is founder and co-editor (with Zygmunt G. Barański and Christian Moevs) of the William and Katherine Devers Series in Dante and Medieval Italian Literature.

George Corbett is Lecturer in Theology, Imagination and the Arts in the School of Divinity, University of St Andrews. Prior to this, he was Junior Research Fellow of Trinity College and Affiliated Lecturer of the Department of Italian, University of Cambridge. He is the author of *Dante and Epicurus: A Dualistic Vision of Secular and Spiritual Fulfilment* (2013), and was the co-organiser, with Heather Webb, of the 'Cambridge Vertical Readings in Dante's *Comedy*' lecture series (2012–2016).

George Ferzoco is based in the Department of Religion and Theology, University of Bristol (where he also occasionally teaches in the Department of Italian). Most of his research is in the field of medieval religious culture, especially in relation to education, the creation of saints' cults, and sermon literature. He has co-edited volumes on Catherine of Siena and Hildegard of Bingen.

David F. Ford OBE is Regius Professor of Divinity Emeritus in the University of Cambridge and Fellow of Selwyn College. His writings include *Meaning and Truth in 2 Corinthians* (1987), *Self and Salvation* (1999), *Christian Wisdom* (2007), and *The Drama of Living* (2014). He has a particular interest in inter-faith relations and was Founding Director of the Cambridge Inter-Faith Programme. His current research includes work on: the Gospel of John; theology, modernity and the arts; religion-related violence; and contemporary worldviews.

Peter S. Hawkins is Professor of Religion and Literature at Yale Divinity School. In addition to his work on Dante — *Dante's Testaments* (1999), *The Poets' Dante* (2001), *Dante: a Brief History* (2006) — he has published on biblical reception and contemporary American fiction, most recently in *The Bible and the American Short Story* (2017), co-written with Lesleigh Cushing Stahlberg.

Elena Lombardi is Professor of Italian Literature at Oxford, and Fellow of Balliol College. She is the author of *The Syntax of Desire. Language and Love in Augustine, the Modistae and Dante* (2007), *The Wings of the Doves. Love and Desire in Dante and Medieval Culture* (2012), and *Imagining the Woman Reader in the Age of Dante* (forthcoming).

Ronald L. Martinez is Professor of Italian Studies at Brown University. With Robert M. Durling, he published a monograph on Dante's *Rime petrose* (1990), and an edition of Dante's *Divine Comedy* with English translation and commentary (1996–2011). Recent publications include essays on Boccaccio's *Decameron*, Petrarch's Latin poetry, Renaissance spectacle, Ariosto's *Lena*, and Dante.

Catherine Pickstock is Professor of Metaphysics and Poetics at the Faculty of Divinity, University of Cambridge, and Fellow of Emmanuel College. She is author of *After Writing* (1998), and *Repetition and Identity* (2014), and co-author, with John Milbank, of *Truth in Aquinas* (2002). She is currently completing two monographs, *Platonic Poetics* and *Aspects of Truth*.

Janet Martin Soskice is Professor of Philosophical Theology at the University of Cambridge. She is the author of *Metaphor and Religious Language* (1984), *The Kindness of God* (2008), and *Sisters of Sinai* (2009). She is the editor, with Diana Lipton, of *Feminism and Theology* (2003) and, with David Burrell, Carlo Cogliati and Bill Stoeger, of *Creation and the God of Abraham* (2010).

John Took is Emeritus Professor of Dante Studies at University College London. Among his publications are volumes on Dante's general and literary aesthetics, on the minor works, on Dante's theology and phenomenology and on the *Fiore*. He is at present at work on an intellectual biography of Dante and a book about why Dante continues to matter.

Heather Webb is Reader in Medieval Italian Literature and Culture at the University of Cambridge and Fellow of Selwyn College. She is the author of *The Medieval Heart* (2010), *Dante's Persons: An Ethics of the Transhuman* (2016), and articles on Dante, Catherine of Siena and others. She was co-organiser, with George Corbett, of the 'Cambridge Vertical Readings in Dante's *Comedy*' lecture series (2012–2016). She is co-editor, with Pierpaolo Antonello, of *Mimesis, Desire, and the Novel: René Girard and Literary Criticism* (2015).

Rowan Williams is Master of Magdalene College, Cambridge, and was previously Archbishop of Canterbury and Professor of Divinity, Oxford. He is the author of many books on theology and spirituality, and also several studies on the borderlands of theology and literature, including *Dostoevsky: Language, Faith and Fiction* (2008), and *The Tragic Imagination* (2016).

Introduction

George Corbett and Heather Webb

This third volume concludes the cycle of vertical readings in Dante's *Comedy*. In the introduction to the first volume, we surveyed the critical history of approaches of this kind, and outlined some interpretative justifications for such a reading of the poem.[1] In the second volume's introduction, we were able to reflect on the variety of methodological approaches and interpretative insights which had emerged in the course of the thirty-three public lectures (2012–2016) upon which the three published volumes are based.[2] The chapters contained within the three volumes convey, we think, a palpable sense of the opening of a discourse, and it is with excitement about new directions that we introduce the final volume of our series. The possibilities for vertical readings are indeed many and, as we have noted from the outset, each reading contained in these volumes offers only one possible thread of connection between the three cantos in question. As these threads of connection emerge, others come into view as well. Vertical readings are intentionally generative of further vertical, but also of 'diagonal' and 'horizontal', readings. They stress the desirability of seeking out resonances and retrospective patterns, of attending to links between

---

1 See *Vertical Readings in Dante's 'Comedy': Volume 1*, ed. by George Corbett and Heather Webb (Cambridge: Open Book Publishers, 2015), pp. 1–11 (esp. pp. 1–8), http://dx.doi.org/10.11647/OBP.0066

2 See *Vertical Readings in Dante's 'Comedy': Volume 2*, ed. by George Corbett and Heather Webb (Cambridge: Open Book Publishers, 2016), pp. 1–12 (esp. pp. 3–6), http://dx.doi.org/10.11647/OBP.0100. For videos of the public lectures, see 'Cambridge Vertical Readings in Dante's *Comedy*', https://sms.cam.ac.uk/collection/1366579

http://dx.doi.org/10.11647/OBP.0119.01

canticles and of heeding the poet's calls (particularly in the *Paradiso*) to pause and admire our changed perspective.

The third volume contributes in particular to the further opening of another discourse, which is born of the productive dialogue with theologians. Dante Studies in Britain, but also internationally, has begun to turn with increasing urgency to a renewed sense of Dante's *Comedy* as a theological poem.[3] From Robin Kirkpatrick's translation and theological commentary on *Inferno, Purgatorio* and *Paradiso* (2006–2007) to the collaborative volumes *Dante's Commedia: Theology as Poetry* (2010), *Reviewing Dante's Theology* (2013) and *Le teologie di Dante* (2015), to single-author studies such as *Conversations with Kenelm: Essays on the Theology of the 'Commedia'* (2013) and *Reading Dante's 'Commedia' as Theology* (2016), scholars have set out explicitly to make the case for avowedly theological re-readings of the poem.[4] Many more works of recent scholarship have made arguments that situate themselves, moreover, within these considerations. At an institutional level, each of the public lectures in our Cambridge series was preceded by a video-conferenced workshop between the Universities of Cambridge, Leeds, and Notre Dame, providing an additional forum for such discussions. The lecture series also coincided with the interdisciplinary investigations *Dante and Late Medieval Florence: Theology in Poetry, Practice and Society* (2012–2016) and *Dante's Theology* (2013) directed by scholars then working in these universities.[5]

---

3   Theological readings of Dante in Britain are, nonetheless, nothing new. In his wide-ranging survey, Nick Havely even makes the case for a potential reception of Dante as 'poeta theologus' in Cambridge as early as thirty years after the poet's death. See Nick Havely, *Dante's British Public* (Oxford: Oxford University Press, 2014), pp. 10–15. A current research project *Dante e la teologia secondo gli antichi commentatori della 'Commedia' (1322–1570)* is contributing to the reappraisal of this early 'poeta theologus': see *Theologus Dantes: Thematiche teologiche nelle opere e nei primi commenti*, ed. by Saverio Bellomo (forthcoming).

4   Dante, *Inferno, Purgatorio, Paradiso*, trans., ed. with comm. by Robin Kirkpatrick (Harmondsworth: Penguin, 2006–2007); Dante's *Commedia: Theology as Poetry*, ed. by Vittorio Montemaggi and Matthew Treherne (Notre Dame, IN: University of Notre Dame Press, 2010); *Reviewing Dante's Theology*, vols 1 and 2, ed. by Claire E. Honess and Matthew Treherne (Oxford: Peter Lang, 2013); *Le teologie di Dante*, ed. by Giuseppe Ledda (Ravenna: Angelo Longo, 2015); John Took, *Conversations with Kenelm: Essays on the Theology of the 'Commedia'* (London: Ubiquity Press, 2013); Vittorio Montemaggi, *Reading Dante's 'Commedia' as Theology: Divinity Realized in Human Encounter* (New York: Oxford University Press, 2016).

5   Matthew Treherne was principal investigator of the AHRC project *Dante and Late Medieval Florence: Theology in Poetry, Practice and Society*, with Simon Gilson and Claire Honess as co-investigators. In 2013, Anne Leone, Christian Moevs, Vittorio Montemaggi, and Matthew Treherne organised a two week symposium at the Tantur Ecumenical Institute

In envisaging the third volume, it was natural for us, therefore, to turn to theologians with a particular interest in Dante, to Dante scholars who have paid intense attention to theological concerns, and to Dante scholars, such as Peter Hawkins, who are also theologians. The discipline of theology is, of course, home to many different methodological approaches, faith perspectives and focal concerns, and this is one of the reasons why the increasing conversation between Dante scholars and theologians is so productive, with each theologian suggesting his or her own understanding of the enterprise of theology and of how that might be enriched by a close engagement with Dante's poem. This volume presents, then, theologians' interpretations of the poem alongside readings that emerge from the context of literary studies. This dialogue elicits new perspectives on the *Comedy*, a poem that, in systematically surpassing conventional boundaries, demands interdisciplinary investigation.

It seemed especially appropriate, given the 'matter' of the last eleven conumerary cantos, to foreground this dialogue with theology in the third volume. The end of each canticle strains towards ineffable theological truths, whether the vision of Lucifer, the mysteries of the procession in the Earthly Paradise and Beatrice's 'difficult' language, or the final vision of God. The cantos nearing those ends thus bear a burden that is both theological and poetic. As he tends towards the ungraspable and inexpressible, Dante draws upon Scripture as heavily as he draws upon his poetic predecessors, ancient and contemporary. The eleven scholars of this volume all engage with this immense scriptural and inter-textual richness, raising challenging questions about the reversals and recalls between the depths of damnation, the penitential ardours of Purgatory and the heights of Paradise.

In exploring the corporeality of the canto Twenty-Threes, Peter Hawkins brings together two worlds of discourse: the sacred, theological, and liturgical (animated more by his own 'Anglican imaginings' than by Dante's 'Latin mass') and feminist and queer studies. He emphasises the literary representations of the body across the three cantos, and establishes a contrast between the female and maternal aspects of *Purgatorio* and *Paradiso* xxiii, and the 'world of men' of *Inferno* xxiii (with Virgil, nonetheless, as 'mother' to Dante). He also registers numerous other lines of correspondence, weaving together the themes of exile and exodus, and the life of Christ, through the three cantos: his cross (*Inf.*, xxiii), his

---

in Jerusalem entitled *Dante's Theology: An International Summer Seminar on the Theological Dimensions of Dante's Work*, with Robin Kirkpatrick as a respondent throughout.

passion (*Purg.*, xxiii), and his salvific role as Wisdom incarnate (*Par.*, xxiii). Hawkins provides a critical meditation on the interpretative enterprise as a whole, from his 'vertical reading *avant la lettre*' in 1980 on the cantos Twenty-Fours to Twenty-Sixes to his work in the series now, and presents a reading which gives 'both predictability *and* surprise their due'.

Janet Soskice opens her reading of the Twenty-Fours by contextualising the practice of vertical reading within early Rabbinic practices of Midrash (of setting different texts alongside each other with copious commentary) and of the mediation of Scripture in medieval Christianity through glossed bibles, liturgy, architecture and art. In layering his own received authorities, Dante creates 'his own poetic midrash', and thus invites us to read his text in a decidedly con-textual way, as we do in *Vertical Readings*. Soskice traces a line of desire through the Twenty-fours, beginning with what she identifies as the threat of Dante's despair in *Inferno* xxiv, countered by the salvation he finds in Virgil, drawing him through poetry towards the good. *Purgatorio* xxiv then shows a turn from the misuse of poetry in the *tenzone* with Forese towards a poetry of truth that re-orients the desire it conveys. In *Paradiso* xxiv we see Dante confessing his faith amongst the 'tongues of God' and it is here that he finally takes up the title of poet, within the context of graced writing and speaking.

As George Ferzoco highlights, the number twenty-five has particular theological significance with regard to the liturgical year and salvation history, the Annunciation (25 March) and the Nativity (25 December) being but the most notable instances. Ferzoco draws an archaeological analogy — of gently excavating along a narrow trench — to describe his approach to reading the three cantos through the significance opened up by the number twenty-five. After a concise literal synopsis of relevant features of each of the three cantos in turn, Ferzoco argues that Dante's use of the 'rarest rhymes' at the beginning of each of the three Twenty-Fives provides a compelling reason to believe that the poet intended and invited his reader to recognise them as structurally aligned. In the next section, Ferzoco shows how the Twenty-Fives are characterised by various kinds of changes: in *Inferno* xxv, the peculiar shift in narrative structure, the metamorphoses of the thieves, and a changing of 'the poetic gods' from Ovid to Dante; in *Purgatorio* xxv, the shift from pagan Virgil to a Christianised Statius, and the various stages of the human soul through the phases of 'nascence, life and afterlife with its changing bodies'; in *Paradiso* xxv, the graduation of Dante in his examination on hope, the pilgrim virtue.

Elena Lombardi's chapter interrogates Dante's theology of love and desire through the canto Twenty-Sixes. These conumerary cantos, she suggests, act like magnets in the structure of the poem as a whole: Ulysses' proto-humanist desire for wisdom in *Inferno* xxvi is contrasted with the celebration of St John's *caritas* or divine love in *Paradiso* xxvi, while erotic and poetic excesses are interrogated on the terrace of the lustful in *Purgatorio* xxvi. Tracing the 'tri-headed alias for the poet-traveller' (Ulysses, Dante, Adam), the chapter focuses on the shared themes of language, desire, and transgression in the canto Twenty-Sixes. Lombardi frames her account with two examples of 'a richly allusive reuse and repetition' of rhyming words, of the kind that K P Clarke discusses in his reading of the canto Tens, noting that 'the deployment, reuse and repetition of a rhyme word offers the reader a point of privileged intertextual access, acting like a lightning rod that runs vertically along the entire length of the poem'.[6] Lombardi points out the 'reverberation' between the rhyme 'riva / viva' in *Inferno* i and *Paradiso* xxvi and concludes her account with the reverberating 'guardo / tardo / ardo' rhyme that appears in both *Purgatorio* xxvi and *Paradiso* xxvi. Through these resounding rhymes, Lombardi traces a central concern in the poem: the theorisation of desire and transgression as a metaliterary conceptualisation of the nature of poetry and language.

Ronald Martinez's reading of the canto Twenty-Sevens unveils new perspectives on Dante's political theology, in relation to the twin powers of Church and Empire (with an original reading, for example, of the crown and mitre in *Purg.*, xxvii), as well as in relation to Boniface's usurpation of spiritual and temporal power. Martinez considers temporal cycles as an underlying theme for the Twenty-Sevens and analyses *Purgatorio* and *Paradiso* xxvii as major thresholds in the pilgrim's journey; this brings him, in turn, to his principal theme of containment. As Martinez highlights, *Inferno* and *Purgatorio* xxvii are dominated by the image of containers of fire, while *Paradiso* xxvii features a humble flowerpot, itself made of fired earthware. Martinez examines many different aspects of containment (astronomical, geographical, physical, causal, metapoetical), before exploring, more explicitly, the subjects contained. The chapter provides close readings of each of the cantos in turn, as well as of the many parallels drawn out between them.

---

6 See K P Clarke, 'Humility and the (P)arts of Art', in *Vertical Readings: Volume 1*, pp. 203–21, http://dx.doi.org/10.11647/OBP.0066

Where Ferzoco investigates the cultural importance of the number twenty-five in relation to the liturgical calendar, Theodore J. Cachey takes as his point of departure the numerological and theological significance of twenty-eight. He argues that the two perfect numbers of the poem, six and twenty-eight (which equal the sum of their divisors), play a key role in the macrostructure of the three canticles: while the Sixes progressively map the human community in geographical space (city, peninsular, inhabited world), the Twenty-Eights map the world cosmologically (*mappamundi*, terrestrial sphere, entire cosmos). Cachey also demonstrates how the 'perfect Twenty-Eights' resonate among the Fourteens, providing a broader system of references. His interpretations of *Inferno* and *Purgatorio* in terms of cartography are substantiated with, and illustrated by, different kinds of medieval maps, and Cachey shows how Dante's poem itself makes considerable contributions to medieval cartography. He presents Dante's description of the nine rings of Paradise as, in cartographic terms, a kind of 'mandala of the cosmos': 'a diagram, chart or geometric pattern that represents the cosmos metaphysically and symbolically'. In conclusion, Cachey argues that the mapping programme discernible within the Twenty-Eights is a fundamental pillar that lends credibility to the poem's wider truth claims.

John Took begins his chapter by considering verticality in terms of the 'layered structure of [Dante's] mature spirituality'. In his view, Dante's intellectual development was characterised by successive encounters organised on 'the plane [...] of the horizontal: first nature then grace, first philosophy then theology, first reason then revelation'. In the *Comedy*, then, the '*horizontality* of human experience' is arguably resolved in terms 'of its verticality, of the *height and depth* of that experience'. In light of this broader theological paradigm of 'verticality', Took then addresses the three canto Twenty-Nines. *Inferno* xxix, the canto of the counterfeiters and impersonators, is notable for 'the systematic dismantling in human experience of every kind of trust and concern', the burlesque tone and comic style reinforcing the 'indignity of it all'. The twenty-ninth canto of *Purgatorio* is concerned, by contrast, with 'a commingling of nature and grace at the still centre of personality' which 'affirms one way of loving over another'. *Paradiso* xxix, then, opens up 'a fresh model of the universe, an alternative way of seeing and understanding it'. Took suggests that, in this canto, God is presented not as '*containing* everything' but, rather, as 'subsisting at the centre of the universe [...] the infinitesimal focal point of all being whatever'. All three Twenty-Nines, on Took's reading, share a common core concern: each is preliminary with respect to the soul's movement 'into God' and, more specifically, each canto suggests a different kind of resolution of 'the many and the one in the moment of ultimate homecoming'. Where the saints realise their potential as *capax Dei* and are characterised by '*in-Godding*', the infernal counterfeiters settle for '*in-selfing*' ('the installation of self at the centre of its own universe').

Piero Boitani draws out the vertical ascent through the Thirties on two levels: first, from falsehood to the divine revelation of truth and, secondly, with regard to the transformation of poetry, from the high style of tragedy, through the 'sublime' use of liturgy, to the language of ineffability. Where Lombardi counterpoises Ulysses and Adam, Boitani reads Ulysses and Beatrice as Dante's two 'ancient flames' representing, respectively, his passion for knowledge and his love for Christian wisdom. Boitani works through the references to the Last Judgment across *Purgatorio* xxx and *Paradiso* xxx, and presents the former as foreshadowing figurally the latter. The reunion of Dante and Beatrice in *Purgatorio* xxx constitutes, for Boitani, 'the hinge of the entire poem, where Dante's past and present join hands and where human and divine meet'. Boitani shows how this encounter is fulfilled in the proclamation of Beatrice's beauty in *Paradiso* xxx, even as the poet declares himself vanquished. The difficulty in speaking of Beatrice, Boitani claims, is the same difficulty the poet will declare in the last canto when writing about God.

Catherine Pickstock suggests that the *Comedy* 'expresses a poetic theology as the most appropriate for a religion of the God-Man of the Incarnation', and reads the poem as liturgical, in that 'it inhabits what it is about, and takes up its own time in doing this'. Comparing the speculative and all at once grasp of vertical reading to the divine viewpoint of a creative God who looks downward and outward from Himself, Pickstock interprets this as undercutting the narrative journey from darkness to light of the horizontal reading. Her chapter works through each of the three canto Thirty-Ones narratively in turn from this divine viewpoint. Pickstock's reading of *Inferno* xxxi focuses on the obfuscation of sight and hearing, as well as the paradoxically homeopathic role of the region for the pilgrim ('purification by filth, liberation by enchainment'), which leads to the uncovering of evermore 'gigantic paradoxes'. She cumulatively develops through her vertical reading of the three cantos themes of God's own mediation of Himself, of occlusion and veiling, of the struggle for mediation, and of the drawing together of the disparate.

In his 2010 essay, 'Dante as Inspiration for Twenty-First-Century Theology', David Ford analyses seven key areas in which contemporary theology might learn from Dante: these are genre, the moods of faith, the relation of Christian theology to non-Christian sources; the primacy of a 'middle distance' narrative perspective, the immersion of theology in the contingencies of history, the relation of scripture to philosophy, and the desirability of twenty-first-century theologians relating deeply to twenty-first-century poets.[7] Some of these areas or key thoughts animate Ford's theological reading of the canto Thirty-Twos. Ford concludes his chapter with a 'cadenza' consisting of four as-yet-unpublished sonnets by Micheal O'Siadhail, a poet with whom Ford has engaged intensively.[8] Towards the conclusion of our 'Vertical Readings' project, these four sonnets provide, then, a dialogue between a contemporary poet and Dante. In the main body of the chapter, Ford provides a theological meditation on 'facing', sound, and the imagery of the Transfiguration of Jesus that runs, as he shows, through the three canto Thirty-Twos. As in Boitani's reading, Ford emphasises Dante's daring figural representation of Beatrice; here, Beatrice takes Christ's place in passages that recall the drama of the Transfiguration. In the section 'Grace and Surprises', Ford explores some broader theological points raised by Dante's poem that are especially pertinent to contemporary theology: first, the relationship between human freedom, God's freedom and grace, and secondly, the theological importance of surprise, daring and diversity. For Ford, Dante's audacious appropriation of his predecessors and contemporaries might model a 'comparatively daring improvisation today' in the area of inter-religious dialogue.

Rowan Williams's chapter presents a vertical reading of the final cantos of each canticle and is the only reading to account for four cantos, the Thirty-Threes and Thirty-Four. Williams traces a trajectory from the frozen stasis at Hell's centre, through the flowing grace of the Earthly Paradise to the intellectual movement of the Empyrean, from the betrayal of language itself (Satan and Judas silencing each other), through confessional truth-telling, to a wordless intensity as God impresses on the human mind that which memory cannot fully retain, let alone language adequately communicate. Dante's forgetfulness and 'baby-talk' nonetheless testify, Williams suggests, to the reality of the truth forgotten. Picking up on various strands of

---

7   See David F. Ford, 'Dante as Inspiration for Twenty-First-Century Theology', in *Dante's 'Commedia': Theology as Poetry*, pp. 318–28.

8   *Ibid.*, pp. 327–28.

discussion in this volume on the strains of the inconceivable and ineffable, Williams joins with Ford in reflecting on the significance of the face and human inter-relationship (or its failure) in the closures of each canticle. The human face in the final vision of God, Williams argues, renders all faces worthy of contemplation and all voices (even those encountered in Hell) worthy of being heard.

23. Our Bodies, Our Selves: Crucified, Famished, and Nourished

Peter S. Hawkins

When I first learned about the Cambridge Vertical Reading project, I felt a sense both of recognition and trepidation. First, the recognition. In 1980, the American *Dante Studies* published my initial foray into literary criticism, 'Virtuosity and Virtue: Poetic Self-Recognition in the *Commedia*'.[1] In it I looked at cantos xxiv–xxvi in all three *cantiche* as forming a programme of reflection on poetry- and poet-making. I focused on the canto Twenty-Sixes and traced what seemed to me a poem-long move from Ulysses, to Guido Guinizzelli and Arnaut Daniel, to Adam. In my fervour I believed I had found a pilgrim's progress of sorts — a growth in understanding of what it means *sub specie aeternitatis* to be a maker of language. Not everyone at *Dante Studies* agreed. One dyspeptic reader found the argument 'preposterous', a 'Procrustean bed'; the journal editor, however, was more tolerant of the essay, which I now see (thanks to this Cambridge series) as a vertical reading *avant la lettre*. At the time I wrote it, however, I had no idea that I was up to anything theoretical; I was simply following a hunch, dazzled as I was (and am) by the *Commedia*'s coherence.

Rereading the essay thirty-five years later, it strikes me as overly schematic in its predictable march onward and upward from Hell to Heaven, from virtuosity to virtue. Nonetheless, the poet's evolving meditation on language in this trio of cantos remains compelling to me.

---

1 Peter S. Hawkins, 'Virtuosity and Virtue: Poetic Self-Reflection in the *Commedia*', *Dante Studies, with the Annual Report of the Dante Society*, 98 (1980), 1–18.

    http://dx.doi.org/10.11647/OBP.0119.02

When decades later I put together *Dante's Testaments*, I only included 'Poetic Self-Recognition in the *Commedia*' in my bibliography.[2] Nonetheless, looking backward, I take it as a sign, so to speak, that vertical reading need not involve a trespass. Indeed, it may give us clues as to how Dante, like Adam, 'used and shaped' (*Par.*, xxvi. 114) his linguistic material so that his impossibly complex poem could, like something organic, *grow* from dark wood to heavenly rose.

In his *Conversation about Dante*, Osip Mandelstam famously likened the *Commedia* to a body governed by the 'incessant craving for the creation of form'; for him it was a work less plotted and pieced than 'guided by instinct'. To conceive how Dante might have imagined 'this form of thirteen thousand facets, so monstrous in its exactitude', Mandelstam asks his readers to compare the poet to a colony of bees, all of them endowed with a 'brilliant isometric instinct [...] constantly keeping their eye on the whole': 'Their cooperation expands and grows more complicated as they participate in the process of forming the combs, by means of which space virtually emerges out of itself'.[3] Verticality, therefore, may very well take us into the mind of the maker to reveal the deep structure of the hive as well as the honey packing its combs; it may keep in sight the burgeoning organic form of the whole amid the 'monstrous exactitude' of the parts.

And yet (here comes my trepidation), there is always the threat in Dante studies of what my doubtful reviewer called the 'Procrustean bed', finding not what is there but what you are determined to make appear. The vertical reading enterprise, with its expectation of as yet undetected patterns within the poem — enigma codes to be cracked — can fall into this trap. Easily so, given that so much in the *Commedia* is, in fact, carefully ordered (like the Creator's handiwork the poet was imitating) in 'measure, weight, and number' (Wisdom 11:21). We all know the pleasure, nay the *jouissance* of this text. We routinely enjoy observing (as I will here) the *Commedia*'s symmetries, its significant rhyme schemes and recurring privileged words, its continuous revisiting of the poet's past works as well as earlier moments in the poem, its intertextual networks — what Mandelstam called its currents, flows and metamorphoses.[4] The *Commedia* has been likened to

---

2   Peter S. Hawkins, *Dante's Testaments: Essays in Scriptural Imagination* (Stanford, CA: Stanford University Press, 1999), p. 352.

3   Osip Mandelstam, 'Conversation about Dante', trans. by Jane Gray Harris and Constance Link, in *The Poets' Dante: Twentieth-Century Reflections*, ed. by Peter S. Hawkins and Rachel Jacoff (New York: Farrar, Straus and Giroux, 2001), pp. 40–93, 54–55.

4   Mandelstam, in *The Poets' Dante*, p. 54.

an echo chamber, a hall of mirrors. Nonetheless, there are open windows in the hall of mirrors, and a life-giving breeze that blows through it. The poem is not airtight. There are provocative inconsistencies, subversions of order, exceptions to rules, precise measurements that play with exactitude. And none of these moments may necessarily fall into a numbered sequence.

Commentators have always found reasons why this or that in the poem should be precisely so, but Dante himself works under no such burden of explanation. He shifts gears when he wants to, repeatedly catches us off guard, stages moments of wonder within the text when we are forced to exclaim with Ser Brunetto Latini, 'Qual maraviglia!' (*Inf.*, xv. 24) or ask with the poet himself, 'Chi crederebbe?' (*Par.*, xx. 67).[5] We mount to Paradise along a well-marked path, to be sure, but climb nonetheless 'by the stairway of surprise'.[6]

In my vertical reading of the canto Twenty-Threes, therefore, I want to give both predictability *and* surprise their due. As a case in point, recall the extraordinarily complex simile that ends *Paradiso* x, given such beautiful readings by John Freccero and Christian Moevs.[7] A luminous ring of circling theologians is likened first to maidens dancing in a round, and then to monastics rising at the dawn office to the call of a mechanical clock. Its inner works — whirling wheels, springs, and balances — perform as needed, with precision. Yet, as we learn in the simile, the mechanical 'works' utterly transcend the coils of rhythm and number; they call to erotic love as well as to prayer. So too the poem. It is evidently constructed of coordinated parts but is also much more than an assemblage. Mandelstam likens it to a body that 'emerges out of itself' into organic form. Its orderly tick-tock resounds with *dolcezza*, even as

---

5 All citations of the *Commedia*, unless otherwise noted, are from Allen Mandelbaum (Berkeley, CA: University of California Press, 1980–1984).

6 The suggestive phrase 'stairway of surprise' comes from Ralph Waldo Emerson, 'Merlin', in *Poems by Ralph Waldo Emerson* (Boston, MA: Phillips, Sampson & Co., 1846):
    'Pass in, pass in', the angels say,
    'Into the upper doors,
    Nor count compartments of the floors,
    But mount to paradise
    By the stairway of surprise'.

7 John Freccero, 'The Dance of the Stars. *Paradiso* X', in *Dante, The Poetics of Conversion*, ed. by Rachel Jacoff (Cambridge, MA: Harvard University Press, 1986), pp. 221–44; Christian Moevs, 'Miraculous Syllogisms: Clocks, Faith and Reason in *Paradiso* 10 and 24', *Dante Studies, with the Annual Report of the Dante Society*, 117 (1999), 59–84.

> l'una parte e l'altra tira e urge,
> tin tin sonando con sì dolce nota
> che il ben disposto spirto d'amor turge.
> (*Par.*, x. 142–44, Durling and Martinez)

> [one part pulls and the other pushes sounding *tin tin* with so sweet a
> note that a well-disposed spirit swells with love.]

The rhyme scheme of these verses makes the corporality of the timepiece
unmistakably erotic: *surge, urge, turge.* There is such delectable telling of
time in eternity 'dove gioir s'insempra' (l. 148), where the unending drive
of desire 'rejoicing forevers itself' among the blessed.

My title, 'Our Bodies, Our Selves' is not meant to suggest that each of
the canto Twenty-Threes is particularly 'about' the body, but rather that
physicality *per se* — the pilgrim's 'vera carne', the figurations of the shades,
and the Word made flesh — are not only a recurring interest but even a
preoccupation in these parallel texts. I have no idea if Dante planned it this
way *ab initio* in some imagined blueprint of his poetic afterlife. I only know
that upon reading these cantos vertically — after more than thirty years
of treating them as totally independent of one another — I have found a
remarkable sequence at play: bodies crucified, bodies wasting away, and
bodies richly nourished.

'Our Bodies, Our Selves' also suggests the different worlds of discourse I
draw upon as a critic. One world is sacred, theological, and liturgical — in
this instance drawn not from Dante's Latin Mass but from my own Anglican
imaginary. I am referring to a sentence that first appears in the Communion
Service of Thomas Cranmer's 1549 *Book of Common Prayer*, which reads,
'And here we offer and present unto thee, O Lord, ourselves, our souls
and bodies, to be a reasonable, holy and lively sacrifice unto thee'.[8] This
unity of soul and flesh together constituting 'ourselves' — a 'lively' unity
guaranteed by the resurrection of the body and the life of the world to
come (to recall the Apostles' Creed) — is Christian doctrinal commonplace;
it is also imaginative bedrock for Dante. Indeed, we learn of it throughout
the *Commedia*: in Hell from Virgil (*Inf.*, vi. 94–99) and Pier della Vigna
(*Inf.*, xiii. 94–118); in Purgatory from Statius (*Purg.*, xxv. 31–108) — who
supplements the infernal accounts with his 'eternal view' ('veduta etterna',
l. 31) — and finally from Solomon in the Heaven of the Sun, who speaks

---

8 'The Holy Eucharist', p. 336 in *The (Online) Book of Common Prayer*, http://www.bcponline.
   org/HE/he1.html

of the deep longing of the blessed both for their own dead bodies and for those of their beloveds:

> [...] per le mamme,
> per li padre, e per li altri che fuor cari
> anzi che fosser sempiterne fiamme. (*Par.*, xiv. 64–66)

> [for their mamas, for their fathers, and for others who were dear before they became eternal flames.]

The *embodied* soul, in other words, is the only way that Dante can imagine ourselves. But if my title links me to theological tradition, it also evokes the secular time and place of someone who intellectually came of age in the 1970s. I am referring in particular to feminist and queer reading practices that influence what I have come to notice in any text. *Our Bodies, Our Selves*, is the title of a formative publication in 1973 that grew out of the Boston women's movement and then quickly became required reading for American women who wanted to take charge of their own health and pleasure — to reclaim their bodies and selves. Although the book itself had no direct impact on me, feminist ways of thinking and reading did, primarily through their emphasis not only on the presence (or absence) of women in any given text, but more generally on the representation of human physicality. I do not think it a coincidence that so many medievalists who have stressed the body in their scholarship — Rachel Jacoff (whose study of the body in the *Commedia* is also titled, 'Our Bodies, Ourselves'), Caroline Bynum, Nancy Vickers, Margaret Miles, Heather Webb, Christiana Purdy Moudarres — are women.[9]

---

9 Rachel Jacoff, 'Our Bodies, Our Selves: The Body in the *Commedia*', in *Sparks and Seeds. Medieval Literature and its Afterlife: Essays in Honor of John Freccero*, ed. by Dana Stewart and Alison Cornish, Binghamton Medieval and Early Modern Studies, 2 (Turnhout: Brepols, 2000), pp. 119–38; Caroline Walker Bynum, *The Resurrection of the Body in Western Christianity, 1200–1336* (New York: Columbia University Press, 1995); Margaret R. Miles, *Carnal Knowing: Female Nakedness and Religious Meaning in the Christian West* (Boston, MA: Beacon, 1989); Heather Webb, *The Medieval Heart* (New Haven, CT: Yale University Press, 2010). To this roster I would add the commentary of Robert Durling and Ronald Martinez; Gary Cestaro, *Dante and the Grammar of the Nursing Body* (Notre Dame, IN: University of Notre Dame Press, 2003); Manuele Gragnolati, in both *Experiencing the Afterlife: Soul and Body in Dante and Medieval Culture* (Notre Dame, IN: University of Notre Dame Press, 2005) and *Amor che move: linguaggio del corpo e forma del desiderio in Dante, Pasolini e Morante* (Milan: Il Saggiatore, 2013); and *Dante and the Human Body*, ed. by John C. Barnes and Jennifer Petrie (Dublin: Four Courts Press, 2007), esp. Vittorio Montemaggi, '"La Rosa che il verbo divino carne si fece": Human Bodies and Truth in the Poetic Narrative of the *Commedia*', pp. 159–94.

This interest in the literary representation of the body has sensitized me to the presence of what I might otherwise have missed in the canto Twenty-Threes. Let me start with the pilgrim, who is unique in the afterlife by virtue of being in his flesh, 'questa vera carne' (*Purg.*, xxiii. 123); or, as he tells the astonished hypocrites, 'son col corpo ch'i ho sempre avuto' [I am here with the body I have always had] (*Inf.*, xxiii. 96). Because of his living flesh Dante's hair curls up when he is terrified (*Inf.*, xxiii. 19–20); his throat throbs when he speaks (*Inf.*, xxiii. 88); his solidity 'veils the sun' (*Purg.*, xxiii. 114); and his gait is slow or quick depending on the company he keeps.

The shades he encounters have their aerial bodies variously disposed. The arch-hypocrites are nailed to the ground, writhing, their beards ruffled with their agonized sighs (*Inf.*, xxiii. 112–13). Among the penitent gluttons we note taut skin dried out with scabs, faces barely more than skulls, and eye sockets that seem like rings that have lost their gemstones: 'chi nel viso de li uomini legge *omo* / ben avria quivi conosciuta l'emme' [those who read *omo* on the human face would have recognized the *M* there clearly] (*Purg.*, xxiii. 32–33). In addition to the bodies we observe in *bolgia* or terrace there are those we hear about, either from the poet or from the shades. In *Purgatorio* xxiii, for instance, there is Mary, a starving mother in ancient Jerusalem, who turned cannibal and who 'nel figlio diè di becco' [plunged her beak into her son] (ll. 28–30); there is a bloodied Christ on the cross who cries out '*Eli*' in paradoxical joy (l. 75); and there are 'le sfacciate donne fiorentine / l'andar mostrando con le poppe il petto [the brazen ladies of Florence [who] flaunt their nipples with their breasts] (ll. 101–02, Hollander), about whom Forese Donati vents his misogynistic spleen.

Also present off-stage, so to speak, is Forese's faithful widow Nella, celebrated lovingly in *Purgatorio* xxiii but the object of derision in the *tenzone* Dante once exchanged with his erstwhile friend.[10] In the first of those six sonnets Forese's 'malfatata / moglie' [poor, ill-fated wife] (l. 1) is conjured as unflatteringly as possible. She is wracked by a cough, gripped by cold ('infredatta'; l. 5), frozen in bed because of her husband's sexual inattention. In his poetic response Forese gave back as good as he received. Now in Purgatory Dante confesses to his old friend the heavy memory of 'qual fosti meco e qual io teco fui' [what you have been with me and I with you] (l. 116).

---

10 For Dante's dispute with Forese, see 'Dispute with Forese Donati — I', in *Dante: Lyric Poems: New Translation*, trans. by Joseph Tusiani, http://www.italianstudies.org/poetry/cn13.htm

Bodies are largely invisible in *Paradiso* xxiii with the exception of Dante and Beatrice, the one in his *vera carne*, the other encountered in her resurrection body. Otherwise luminosity is all. Christ's risen and ascended flesh, his 'lucente Sustanza' (l. 32), is a sun too bright for Dante to behold (ll. 32–33). Mary, also assumed bodily into Heaven and later identified as having 'la faccia che a Cristo / più si somiglia' [the face that most resembles Christ] (*Par.*, xxxii. 85–86), can be glimpsed (*Par.*, xxiii. 91) but not quite seen (ll. 118–19). She can be made present, however, by repeated naming: twice by title, 'Donna del ciel' [Lady of Heaven] (l. 106) and 'Regina coeli' [Queen of Heaven] (l. 128); three times as 'Maria' [Mary] (ll. 111, 126, 137) — 'the name', the poet says, 'I ever invoke / both morning and evening' ('Il nome [...] ch'io sempre invoco / e mane e sera'; ll. 88–89) — and by resort to multiple traditional metaphors: she is a 'rosa' [rose] (l. 73), a 'bel fior' [lovely flower] (l. 88), a 'viva stella' [living star] (l. 92), 'il bel zaffiro / del quale il Ciel più chiaro s'inzaffira' [the beautiful sapphire with which the brightest Heaven is ensapphired] (ll. 101–02), and a 'coronata fiamma' [crowned flame] (l. 119).

Although we never see the bodily forms of the blessed who fill the ranks of the Church Triumphant in *Paradiso* xxiii, we are nonetheless asked to imagine them alternately as male 'armies' ('schiere', l. 19; 'turbe', l. 82) and 'good plowmen' ('buone bobolce', 132); as a 'bel giardino / che sotto i raggi di Cristo s'infiora' [lovely garden blooming under the rays of Christ] (ll. 71–72) and as 'gigli / al cui odor si prese il buon cammino' [lilies whose perfume won people to the good path] (ll. 74–75); and, most touchingly, as infants satisfied at the breast (ll. 121–26). Last but not least, there is an unnamed angel who descends to the Fixed Stars as a flame, but who, in the poet's kaleidoscope of metaphor, becomes a ring that seems first a crown (l. 95), then a revolving garland (l. 96), and finally a circulating melody (l. 109). As a figure of 'angelico amore' (l. 103), his acts of fervid devotion to the Virgin evoke the Marian liturgical celebrations that no doubt inform Dante's composition of the scene: first the Annunciation, when "'l verbo divino / carne si fece' [the Word of God became flesh] (ll. 73–74), then the Assumption, and finally Mary's Coronation in Heaven at the hands of 'l'alto Filio / di Dio e di Maria' [the high Son of God and Mary] (ll. 136–37).

Amid this explosion of metaphor — in a realm where materiality is vividly imagined but almost entirely absent — it is important to recognize the specifically *maternal* relationship that brackets *Paradiso* xxiii and gives it its distinctive emotional quality. The canto opens with Beatrice likened to a mother bird perched on her nest after a nightlong vigil over her brood (ll. 1–12).[11] She is up just before daybreak, ready to feed the 'longed for faces' of her beloved fledglings 'as she awaits with warm affection, / steadfastly watching for the dawn to break' ('con ardente affetto il sole aspetta, / fiso guardando pur che l'alba nasca', ll. 8–9). With the word *alba* in play, critics have referenced the literary dawn song, a genre that typically laments the moment when lovers are forced to leave their illicit bedroom 'nest' at daybreak.[12] Here, however, the erotic register becomes filial and maternal, regret turns into joy, and the morning light — John Donne's detested 'busie old foole, unruly Sunne'[13] — is eagerly awaited and even longed for (ll. 7–9).

From this maternal beginning the canto moves toward a vision of Mary as mother and nurse. Just when the Blessed Virgin rises to the Empyrean following closely upon the ascension of her Son, the blessed, who are totally enamoured of her, are likened collectively to an infant, a 'fantolino' envisioned at the precise moment *after* he has nursed his fill. We have license to imagine cheeks messy with milk, eyes fluttering closed and him only a hair's breadth away from sleep — a child who raises his arms in wordless love to the *mamma* who has just given suck:

> E come fantolin che 'nver ' la mamma
> tende le braccia, poi che 'l latte prese,
> per l'animo che 'nfin di fuor s'infiamma;
>   ciascun di quei candori in sù si stese
> con la sua cima, sì che l'alto affetto
> ch'elli avieno a Maria mi fu palese. (*Par.*, xxiii. 121–26)

[And like an infant who, when it has taken its milk, extends its arms out to its mother, its feeling kindling into outward flame, each of those blessed splendours stretched its peak upward, so that the deep affection each possessed for Mary was made plain to me.]

---

11 See Rachel Jacoff, '*Paradiso* 23: Circular Melody', in *California Lectura Dantis: 'Paradiso'*, ed. by Allen Mandelbaum, Anthony Oldcorn, and Charles Ross (Berkeley, CA: University of California Press, forthcoming): 'The canto reveals the poet to be making one of his fundamental moves: he "maternalizes" Beatrice to neutralize the erotic dimension of his love for her, and then eroticizes the maternal to restore the affective component so important to the poem's texture. Beatrice is like the attentive nurturing mother bird, but the bird is described in language which retains the lexicon of stilnovistic love lyric'.

12 In their commentary on *Paradiso* xxiii. 1–15, Durling and Martinez refer to a sacred version of the *alba*. See also their notes on *Par.*, ix. 9.37–42.

13 John Donne, 'The Sunne Rising', in *Metaphysical Lyrics & Poems of the Seventeenth Century, Donne to Butler*, ed. by Herbert J. C. Grierson (Oxford: Clarendon, 1921); Bartleby.com, http://www.bartleby.com/105/3.html

La mamma... s'infiamma: *Paradiso* xxiii is all about the 'kindling' of kind, as mother love bursts into flame, an infant in arms is nurtured at the breast, and deep mutuality brightens the Heaven. The effect is spectacular; it is also what one might expect from a poet whose journey to Paradise is constructed around female mediation, a full circle that begins in the Empyrean at the behest of 'tre donne benedette' (*Inf.*, ii. 124) and also ends there with the intercession of the 'Vergine madre' (*Par.*, xxxiii. 1).

In this canto, therefore, the poet gives us a foretaste of Paradise as a realm of blissful maternal nurture and female abundance ('ubertà', l. 130). It celebrates not only Beatrice and Mary, but also (in the poet's lengthy address to the reader, in ll. 49–69) Polyhymnia and her sisters (ll. 55–57), the Muses who are his literary wet nurses. Unlike the composite coliseum and rose of the actual City of God (*Paradiso* xxx–xxxii), the image-rich preview of the Empyrean we witness here is a celestial nursery — a 'kindergarten' made possible by the fruit of Mary's *ventre*, 'ventre / che fu albergo del nostro disiro' [womb that sheltered our desire] (ll. 104–05). This is Dante's version of Augustine's region of unending plenty ('regionem ubertatis indeficientis', *Confessions* 9.10).[14] Or, better yet, it is the Heaven that the seventeenth-century poet Richard Crashaw characterized as 'Milk all the way'.[15]

To climb down the ladder of verticality from this richly female space to the depths of *Inferno* xxiii is to descend from the blessed singing the *Regina coeli* to smart-talking thirteenth-century Frati Gaudenti — hypocrites weighed down by gilded leaden habits, who walk in ponderous procession over the supine forms of ancient Hebrew religious hierarchy. It is a return to the world of men that is also an infernal travesty of the Church Triumphant, the 'collegio / de l'ipocriti tristi' [college of the sad hypocrites] (ll. 91–92). No more roses, lilies, and infantile bliss! Instead, as *Inferno* xxiii opens up, we move between the hardscrabble realms of barratry and hypocrisy. Pilgrim and guide frantically flee the pursuit of the winged Malebranche, the two sliding down the fifth *bolgia*'s embankment in a striking reenactment of

---

14 *St. Augustine's Confessions*, trans. by William Watts, Loeb Classical Library, 2 vols (Cambridge, MA: Harvard University Press, 1970), vol. 2, pp. 48–49. In an earlier passage Augustine imagines the eternal life of a recently deceased friend as a kind of eternal nursing: 'Now lays he his ear no longer unto my mouth; but lays his spiritual mouth unto thy fountain, and drinketh as much of wisdom as he is able to contain, proportional to his thirst: now without end happy' (p. 13). Cf. the unhappy nursing infants, envious of one another's hold on the breast, in *Conf.* 1. 7 (pp. 20–23).

15 Richard Crashaw, 'To the Infant Martyrs', Poetry Foundation, http://www. poetryfoundation.org/poem/181069#poem

their embrace and scary descent on the back of Geryon (*Inf.*, xvii. 81–96). But now we are presented not with two grown males securely seated on a divinely-controlled monster, but (at least as seen through the lens of simile) with Virgil as a panicked mother and Dante as a child ('figlio', ll. 40, 49) holding tight to the parental breast.

The simile is lengthy, a double comparison that stretches to a full five tercets. It is also, in the first instance, intensely dramatic: a house in flames at night, a startled mother forgetful of her *déshabillé*, a rescued child she loves more than herself. The alacrity of the mother's care, her great haste in the face of danger, is what sets up the likeness to Virgil's speedy vigilance. But with the shift from simile to narrative, melodrama quickly becomes comedy as the briefly imagined *madre* turns back into the pilgrim's *maestro*. The scene is disarmingly antic: the *altissimo poeta* of antiquity is indecorously on the run, sliding down the *bolgia*'s embankment as if careening down a millrace, with the thirty-five-year-old pilgrim held in his arms, borne on his chest, 'come suo figlio, non come compagno' [just like a son, and not like a companion] (l. 51).

In *Purgatorio* xxiii the pilgrim refers to Virgil as 'più che padre' (l. 4). And for good reason: over the course of the second canticle he is seen more and more as a mother than as a father, most explicitly when Statius, without knowing that he stands in the presence of 'Virgilio dolcissimo patre' (*Purg.*, xxx. 50), credits the Latin master's great epic poem as the source of his own poetic inspiration. Virgil's celebration of that 'giusto / figliuol d'Anchise che venne di Troia / poi che 'l superbo Ilïon fu combusto' [just son of Anchises who came from Troy when proud Ilion was destroyed by fire] (*Inf.*, i. 73–75), was, he says, the divine flame from which he gathered his own embers and sparks: 'de l'*Eneïda* dico, la qual mamma / fummi, e fummi nutrice, poetando' [Of the *Aeneid* I mean, which was my mama and was my nurse in writing poetry] (*Purg.*, xxi. 97–98, Durling and Martinez).

At the beginning of the poem the pilgrim offers a similar encomium when, upon meeting the one who would be his *guida, duca, signore, saggio*, he praises Virgil as the honour and light of other poets:

> 'Tu se' lo mio maestro e 'l mio autore,
> tu se' solo colui da cu' io tolsi
> lo bello stilo che m'ha fatto onore'. (*Inf.* i. 85–87)

[You are my master and my author, you alone are he from whom I have taken the pleasing style that has won me honour] (Durling and Martinez).

Although Dante and Statius are separated by millennia, the venerable Roman *pater* played the role of *mamma* and *nutrice*, mother and nurse, for both of them. And not only in *poetando*: Virgil also nurtured the spiritual conversions that launched them on their respective journeys to God. For Statius, reading the *Fourth Eclogue* in the light of the Gospel in effect rolled away the stone ('coperchio', *Purg.*, xxi. 94–95) that had long concealed his apprehension of the good; for Dante, Virgil the shade (at the bidding of Mary, Lucy, and Beatrice) led him out of the dark wood, setting him on the 'vera via' that brings him to the Empyrean. That itinerary is in fact recalled in *Purgatorio* xxiii. 124–29.

There are many micro-observations one could make about the correspondences among the canto Twenty-Threes. There are, for instance, references to Jerusalem in each set (*Inf.*, xxiii. 115–23; *Purg.*, xxiii. 28–30, 73–75; *Par.*, xxiii. 133–34: 'lo essilio / di Babillòn'). There is also a foregrounding of the human breast in quite different contexts: the 'petto' (*Inf.*, xxiii. 50) of Virgil on the run, the salaciously displayed 'poppe' (*Purg.*, xxiii. 102) of Florentine women, and the *Maria lactans* of *Paradiso* xxiii, whose spiritual nursing inspires the deep affection ('l'alto affeto', l. 125) of the blessed.

In addition to these minute connections, there is a larger feature shared by all three cantos, a dramatic moment when the pilgrim looks into the eyes of another and is stopped in his tracks by wonder. The most elaborate of these is the last in the sequence. It takes place in *Paradiso* xxiii, when Beatrice, after previously withholding her gaze in the Heaven of Saturn — and withholding her smile in particular — now bids Dante see her 'face to face':

> 'Apri li occhi e riguarda qual son io;
> tu hai vedute cose, che possente
> se' fatto a sostener lo riso mio'. (*Par.*, xxiii. 43–48)

> [Open your eyes and see what I now am; the things you witnessed will have made you strong enough to bear the power of my smile.]

It is impossible at this point not to recall the refusal of Beatrice to be seen directly in *Purgatorio* xxx, and then the very hesitant, gradual way in which she unveils herself over the course of the following canto. First she gave the pilgrim her eyes, then the 'second beauty' of her mouth — which prompts the poet to give his readers what amounts to the first ineffability *topos* of the *Paradiso*:

> 'O isplendor di viva luce etterna:
> chi palido si fece sotto l'ombra
> sì di Parnaso, o bevve in sua cisterna,
>   che non paresse aver la mente ingombra,
> tentando a render te qual tu paresti
> là dove armonizzando il ciel t'adombra,
>   quando ne l'aere aperto ti solvesti?' (*Purg.*, xxxi. 139–45)

[O splendor of living light eternal, who has ever grown so pale under Parnassus' shade or drunk so deep of its well that he would not seem to have a mind disabled, trying to render you as you appeared there, Heaven with its harmonies overhanging you, when in the open air you disclosed yourself?] (Singleton).

In *Paradiso* xxiii, by contrast, there is nothing gradual about Beatrice's self-revelation, no need for wooing by her attendant virtues; indeed, she could not be more direct: 'Apri li occhi e riguarda qual son io' [Open your eyes and see what I now am] (l. 46). Yet, rather than describe the increased splendour of her face, eyes, mouth, and smile, the poet struggles in vain to recall the memory. In an address to the reader that stretches for seven *terzine*, he confesses what he once saw 'face to face': her visage aflame ('suo viso ardesse', l. 22), the joy ('letizia', l. 23) flashing in her eyes, her holy smile ('santo riso', l. 59). Despite the effort of memory and art, however, not even a thousandth part of the truth ('al millesmo del vero', l. 58) can be told:

> e così, figurando il paradiso,
> convien saltar lo sacrato poema,
> come chi trova suo cammin riciso. (*Par.*, xxiii. 61–63)

[And thus, in representing Paradise, the sacred poem has to leap across, as does a man who finds his path cut off.]

If the poet's inability to represent Beatrice marks a representational failure, it is nonetheless one extravagantly rich in literary reward. It enables him to review his career as a love poet starting from his launch in the *Vita nuova* 21.4, when he first registered the ineffability of Beatrice's smile;[16] then it brings him to the present moment of his writing as he leaps across a visionary

---

16 *VN.* XXI. 4: 'Quel ch'ella par quando un poco sorride, / non si può dicer né tenere a mente, / sì è novo miracolo e gentile' [When she a little smiles, her aspect then / No tongue can tell, no memory can hold, / So rare and strange a miracle is she.] (*Dante, Vita nuova*, trans. by, Barbara Reynolds (Harmondsworth: Penguin Books, 1969), p. 61).

chasm with whatever words he can muster.[17] The term 'cammino riciso' [path cut off] (l. 63) takes us back to the very beginning of the poem — 'Nel mezzo del cammin' — and provides a metaphor not only for the pilgrim's journey but also for the literary path of the *Commedia* itself. So, too, the comparison of the poet to a navigator and the *Commedia* to a 'picciola barca' (*Purg.*, xxiii. 67–69) recalls the openings of both *Purgatorio* i (ll. 1–3) and *Paradiso* ii (ll. 1–18).

Yet not everything is retrospective as the passage also looks forward. Two cantos hence, in *Paradiso* xxv, Dante will once again refer to his work as a sacred poem, but will do so in still more ambitious terms. His *Commedia* is a 'poema sacro' to which both Heaven and earth have set a hand (ll. 1–2): God is his co-author. We are reminded there as well that the trembling of his mortal shoulder under the burden of his theme, confided in *Paradiso* xxiii 64–66, has indeed taken its toll on his person. No longer a lamb in the Florentine sheepfold, he acknowledges that he is grizzled and worn (l. 6), barred from the city where he would be a shepherd of the flock. Perhaps in part because of what he has earned through suffering, he no longer scruples to reserve the title of 'poeta' exclusively for the poets of antiquity. He openly claims it for himself — 'ritornerò poeta' (l. 8) — even if receiving the laurel crown at the font of his baptism remains only in the future conditional tense, 'Se mai continga' [if it ever should come to pass] (l. 1).

Finally, although the splendour of Beatrice's holy smile and face in the Heaven of Fixed Stars defy description, her ineffable *riso* and *aspetto* nonetheless prepare us for the poet's plight in the Empyrean: 'A l'alta fantasia qui mancò possa' [Here my high imagining failed of power] (*Par.*, xxxiii. 142). His initial incapacity in the face of Beatrice becomes his failure before the face of Christ, 'la nostra effige' (l. 130). In either case, however, his poetic defeat is not only 'fairly honorable' but fully resonant. It 'says' more than he can say.

To descend the vertical ladder from this paradisiacal height to *Purgatorio* xxiii entails a falling off in splendour and implication. Nonetheless, on the sixth terrace there is another carefully established 'face to face' moment and yet another cause for wonder. The scene is initially set up by liturgical chanting as the penitent gluttons sing an appropriate phrase from Psalm 50

---

17 See Teodolinda Barolini, 'The Sacred Poem is Forced to Jump', in *The Undivine Comedy: Detheologizing Dante* (Princeton, NJ: Princeton University Press, 1992), pp. 218–56 (esp. pp. 226–29).

(51). That psalm's incipit, '*Miserere*', was the pilgrim's first spoken word in the poem (*Inf.*, i. 65). Here, the gluttons choose another verse, '*Labïa mëa, Domine*', that specifically calls attention to what lips, mouth, and tongue are meant to do in lieu of consumption: 'O Lord, open thou my lips; and my mouth shall show forth thy praise' (Psalms 50 [51]: 15). Immediately, Dante and Virgil are overtaken by a crowd of souls who look upon them with wonder ('ci ammirava', l. 20). The pilgrim is no less astonished by their extreme 'leanness and sad scurf' (l. 39). Soon one stare begets another:

> ed ecco del profondo de la testa
> volse a me li occhi un'ombra e guardò fiso;
> poi gridò forte: 'Qual grazia m'è questa?'
>   Mai non l'avrei riconosciuto al viso;
> ma ne la voca sua mi fu palese
> ciò che l'aspetto in sè avea conquiso.
>   Questa favilla tutta mi raccese
> mia conoscenza a la cangiata labbia,
> e ravvisai la faccia di Forese. (*Purg.*, xxiii. 40–48)

> [when — there! — a shade, his eyes deep in his head, turned toward me, staring steadily; and then he cried aloud: 'What grace is granted me!' I never would have recognized him by his face; and yet his voice made plain to me what his appearance had obliterated. This spark rekindled in me everything I knew about those altered features; thus, I realized it was Forese's face.]

'Ravvisai la faccia di Forese': Dante's recognition of an old friend's 'viso' and 'faccia' has less to do with what he sees than with the unique sound of what he hears: 'la voce sua mi fu palese'. There follows an encounter as warm as those shared earlier in Purgatory with two other Florentine *compagni*, Casella (*Purgatorio* ii) and Belacqua (*Purgatorio* iv). Dante learns about how Purgatory 'works': how someone like Forese, deceased for only five years (l. 78), could rise so high on the mountain because of his wife Nella's intercessory prayer (ll. 76–90); how aerial bodies through hunger and thirst can 'resanctify' themselves ('si rifà santa', l. 60); and how the gluttons' starvation is also the source of their comfort and joy (ll. 61–75).

Purgatorio xxiii concludes with Dante telling Forese about the one who has been *his* comfort and joy thus far, the companion who led him down through the infernal 'deep night of those truly dead' ('profonda note [...] d'i veri morti', ll. 121–22) and up the purgatorial mountain that straightens all 'whom the world twisted' ('che 'l mondo fece torti', l. 126). Paradise will be the end of his long journey, but when the pilgrim reaches that goal it will no longer be in the company of Virgil: 'quivi convenien che sanza lui rimagna' [there I must remain without him] (l. 129).

This painful departure takes place in *Purgatorio* xxx, but has been foretold from the very beginning of the poem, and by none other than Virgil. Because he did not know God, was even a 'rebel to his law' (*legge*), the Emperor who reigns on high bars his entrance to Heaven's gate:

> 'In tutte parti impera e quivi regge;
> quivi è la sua città e l'alto seggio:
> oh felice colui cui' ivi elegge!' (*Inf.*, i. 124–29)

> [In every place he commands, and there he rules (*regge*); there is his city and high throne: O happy the one he chooses (*elegge*) to be there!] (Durling and Martinez).

Dante's personal shepherd is kept from the company of the elect.

Another such moment of painful recognition takes place earlier within our vertical span, in *Inferno* xxiii, after Dante and the hypocrites have exchanged mutual wonder over their respective bodies — the pilgrim's living flesh, the shades' cheeks distilled by grief, their bodies grotesquely impaled upon the ground. The poet then turns our attention to Virgil. Like Dante, he has learned that the naked soul 'crucifisso in terra con tre pali' [crucified on the ground by three stakes] (l. 111) is Caiaphas, the high priest who provided the Sanhedrin's warrant for handing over Jesus to his Roman crucifixion: 'che convenia / pore un uom per lo popolo a' martiri' [it was prudent to let one man — and not one nation — suffer] (ll. 115–17). These words are a close translation of John 11:50 in the Vulgate: '*expedit nobis ut unus moriatur pro populo et non tota gens pereat*'. Prudence here is a cover for expediency, however: it is meant to get Jesus, who has just raised Lazarus to the people's acclaim, out of the way. Recollected in the sixth *bolgia*, the verses bring us into the world of the New Testament, and to the saying that in effect sets the Passion of Christ in motion.

At first sight of Caiaphas, Dante's attention is caught ('l'occhio mi corse', l. 110) even *before* the high priest is identified: simply seeing him crucified on the ground is enough. But we are told that Virgil stands transfixed only *after* the Friars' three-terzina identification. What follows is a 'freeze frame' that intensifies the theme of amazement. For the one and only time in Hell,

Virgilio is spellbound by what he sees. Yet rather than bring us inside his thoughts, the poet chooses simply to show him mid-marvel:

> Allor vid' io maravigliar Virgilio
> sovra colui ch'era disteso in croce
> tanto vilmente ne l'etterno essilio. (*Inf.*, xxiii. 124–26)

> [Then I saw Virgil stand amazed above that one who lay stretched out upon a cross so squalidly in his eternal exile.]

Because so much is left unsaid, Dante in effect gives us license to 'flesh out' the scene: to imagine Virgil stooping to behold the distended form of Caiaphas 'in croce'; to imagine his astonished face registering shock before the one who appears 'tanto vilmente' beneath his gaze. This intense absorption in the damned, often reproved when indulged in by the pilgrim, stands in contrast to Virgil's deportment elsewhere in the *Inferno*. We cannot help but take notice. What does his wonder mean?

Commentators have their theories. As a Roman, whose death in 19 BCE made him a near contemporary with Caiaphas, both Virgil and the high priest would have been no strangers to the horrors of crucifixion. Virgil would not, however, have seen this particular cast of characters — or this punishment — during his earlier descent through Hell (referenced in *Inferno* ix). Nor as a pagan could he ever imagine that the opprobrium of the cross in all its 'vileness' might ever be understood as an instrument of salvation. The transformation of agony into something like pleasure is precisely what Forese alludes to in *Purgatorio* xxiii when he and the other penitents interpret Christ's cry of dereliction — *'Eloi, eloi, lema sabbachthani'* (Matthew 27:46, Mark 15:34) — as a joyful utterance ('Christo lieto a dire *"Eli"'*, l. 74). There is no solace in *this* sight, however — no paradoxical amazement.

As we are so often reminded in the *Commedia*, between Virgil and Christian reality there is 'a great gulf fixed'. How poignant, then, that Dante should bring Caiaphas and Virgil together in a gaze. One shade who knew Christ in the flesh and rejected him, the other who lived only decades before the Word was made flesh, 'nel tempo de li dèi falsi e bugiardi' [in the time of the false and lying gods] (*Inf.*, i. 72), and therefore was too late for the age of grace.[18]

---

18 See my longer discussion of this moment in *Dante's Testaments*, pp. 114–19.

Virgil's amazement here is perhaps meant to remain a mystery, but I wonder if his fascination with Caiaphas may have as much to do with what he has *overheard* as with what he sees before him on the ground. I am thinking of the Friar's incrimination of the high priest when he quotes the notorious words addressed to the Sanhedrin's 'concilio' [council] (l. 122): 'un uom per lo popolo a' martiri' [one man — and not one nation — suffer] (l. 117). In this close translation of John 11:50 there is an uncanny echo of a line towards the end of *Aeneid* 5, when Aeneas and his men are approaching the shore of Italy. The hero's fearful mother, Venus, intercedes with Neptune for Trojan safe passage; her prayer is granted, but only with Neptune's proviso. Someone must die so that the Trojan remnant can live: '*unum pro multis dabitur caput*' [one life must be given for many] (5. 815).

What do we make of this intertextual link between Gospel and epic? Is it that Virgil hears his own words in those of the high priest and is amazed, perhaps horrified, at their superficial congruence? I am not suggesting any equivalence between Caiaphas' stratagem and the call for human sacrifice that Virgil puts into the mouth of Neptune, nor any commonality between a '*nescius*' Trojan like the helmsman Palinurus (as unknowing as Virgil's other fated victims) and Christ, who made himself a sacrifice, who suffered his death as a martyr ('un uom [...] a' martiri', to quote Caiaphas), and not only for his own nation, but 'to gather together in one the children of God, that were dispersed' (as John 11:52 goes on to assert). Rather, I wonder if, given Virgil's startling fixation, together with the resonance of these two texts, we are meant to find in the high priest's *etterno essilio* a grotesque, pitiless image of the ancient poet's own exile. For all their differences, they have some words in common.

Although the damned all live in a state of exile, Virgil's *essilio* is the one we are forced to keep in mind, in part because he refers to it again and again. In *Inferno* i he tells Dante that he is banished forever from the heavenly 'regna' (l. 124); on the brink of Limbo he explains the rationale for his exile (*Inf.*, iv. 31–42); and then in the second canticle he returns to it several times when speaking with Cato (*Purg.*, i. 76–78), the pilgrim (iii. 37–45), Sordello (vii. 7–8), and Statius (xxi. 16–18). In this latter exchange, Statius initially mistakes Virgil and Dante as fellow penitents when he extends them the *Dominus vobiscum*, 'O frati miei, Dio vi dea pace!' [O my brothers, God give you peace] (l. 13). To this, *Virgilio* (l. 14) replies appropriately — in whatever form such a reply might take! ('*et cum spiritu tuo?*') — before he sets the record straight: 'Nel beato concilio / ti ponga in pace la verace corte / che me rilega ne'etterno essilio' [May the true *court* which binds me in eternal *exile* bring you in peace to the assembly of the blest though it binds me to eternal exile] (ll. 16–18).[19]

Virgilio, concilio, essilio: in a slightly different order we first heard these same rhyme words in *Inferno* xxiii, when Dante presented Virgil's amazement over Caiaphas: *concilio, Virgilio, essilio*. But this second instance is not the final rhyming. We hear these words once more resounding across the vertical universe of the poem at the conclusion of *Paradiso* xxiii. There is, however, one telling substitution to note there. The passage in question marks a transition in the eighth Heaven between mothers and fathers, breast and brain, garden nursery and university examination hall. St Peter, holding the keys to the kingdom, appears on the horizon of the canto's final line ready to begin a three-canto interrogation of the pilgrim on the theological virtues. Just before that shift in scene, the poet reflects on what he has encountered in the Heaven of the Fixed Stars. With what may be an allusion to the reversal of fortune celebrated in Psalm 125 (126) — 'They that sow in tears shall reap with joy' (5) — he contrasts the eternal bounty of Heaven, its milky *ubertà*, with the struggles of the blessed while on earth. Speaking of Paradise, he says: 'Quivi si vive e gode del Tesoro / che s'acquistò piangendo ne lo essilio / di Babillòn [...] sotto l'alto Filio / di dio e Maria [...] e con l'antico e col novo concilio' [Here do they live, delighting in the treasure they earned with tears in Babylonian *exile* [...] under the high Son of God and of Mary [...] together with the ancient and the new / *councils*' (ll. 133–38). In this summary, the *essilio* of Babylon is juxtaposed with Heaven's bicameral *concilio*. The verbal repetition is almost exact. Missing from the familiar rhyme scheme, however, is the name we have come to treasure, *Virgilio*. Taking its place in the rhyme now — in Paradise — is Christ, the '*Filio* di Dio e di Maria'. Before doing my vertical reading, I had missed the fact of this substitution — a new name in place of the old — as well as the bitter-sweetness of the absent presence.

Two exilic fates haunt the *Commedia*: Virgil's from the City of God, known from the outset, and Dante's from the commune of Florence, slowly revealed over the course of the poem. The first is eternal and absolute, reiterated even in the eleventh-hour of *Paradiso* xxxiii, where a final Virgilian allusion strikes a tragic note by focusing on the experience of loss — 'si perdea la sentenza di Sibilla' (l. 66). In this closing moment we are asked

---

19 I am grateful to Joy Lawrence Clark for her insights on the 'essilio' rhyme scheme in 'Dante's Virgil: A Poet's Type of Exile' (doctoral thesis, Boston University, 2006).

to experience once again the plangent repetition of *Purgatorio* xxx's Virgilio, Virgilio, Virgilio, albeit this time without Beatrice's reproof. The sheer loss of Virgil, however, is not to be lost on us.

By contrast, the whole effort of the *Commedia* is meant to transform the disaster of Dante's temporal exile into a spiritual exodus, a release from Babylonian captivity into that heavenly Promised Land 'onde Cristo è romano' [where Christ is a Roman] (*Purg.*, xxxii. 102). What finally marks the difference between the lost *madre-padre*, on the one hand, and the 'found' *fantolino-figlio*, on the other, is none other than Christ, the figure whose 'triumph' ('trïunfa', l. 136) and 'victory' ('vittoria', l. 137) bring *Paradiso* xxiii to a celebratory close. Like the *poema sacro* itself, the 'Filio di Dio e di Maria' joins together Heaven and earth, eternity and time. Because of him, there is no exile from the 'councils old and new' that the pilgrim will see in the Empyrean, but that Virgil will not.

One of the surprises of this investigation is the fact that Christ's physical presence is so subtly woven through the canto Twenty-Threes. In one passage or another we take in the full course of his life's story, from his conception in the Virgin's womb, to his Passion and death on the cross, to his Ascension to the highest sphere. Following this itinerary, we focus on his body and perceive him — and it — according to different perspectives: perversely, through the crucifixions depicted in *Inferno* xxiii; paradoxically, in the recollection of the bloodied joy uttered in his cry '*Elì*' in *Purgatorio* xxiii; salvifically, in Beatrice's celebration of him as 'la Sapïenza e la Possanza / ch'aprì le strade tra 'l Cielo e la terra' [the Wisdom and the Power that / opened the pathways between Heaven and earth] (*Par.*, xxiii. 37–39). With the canto Twenty-Threes read vertically, therefore, it would almost seem as if Dante had intended us to see that Christ's Incarnation cuts across the *Commedia*. In the poet's disembodied afterlife, flesh is all. His body, ourselves.

24. True Desire, True Being, and Truly Being a Poet

Janet Soskice

'To be called a name is one of the first forms of linguistic injury that one learns. But not all name-calling is injurious. Being called a name is also one of the conditions by which a subject is constituted in language…'[1]

The New Testament writers were Jewish followers of Jesus who read their received scriptures, what Christians came to call the Old Testament, in light of the conviction that Jesus was the promised Messiah. Early Christian writings, including the texts of scripture, are symphonies of *eisegesis* — of 'reading meanings in' — finding Jesus in the Psalms, the promises of Isaiah, and even conversing with Moses from the burning bush. But this way of reading is in continuity of form, if not substance, with Jewish reading practices: the later prophets had reworked the earlier ones; second Isaiah had transformed first Isaiah. These writings are 'saturated' texts, layered with meanings for the communities who received and read them as scripture.

The biblical books of Jews and Christians, unlike the Qu'ran, have always been understood to be historical deposits written at different times and places. Even after the fixing of canons, Rabbinic and Christian readers happily conflated texts in their commentaries and sermons. Liturgy and the glossed medieval bibles brought readers and worshippers into a universe of received interpretation. Although we should not necessarily

---

1 Judith Butler, *Excitable Speech: A Politics of the Performance* (New York and London: Routledge, 1997), p. 2.

    http://dx.doi.org/10.11647/OBP.0119.03

regret the Renaissance and Reformation turn to *sola scriptura* and the unglossed text as we have it in modern printed Bibles, nonetheless there was a community of mind in older ways of text-making and guided reading. Dante himself is not only the recipient of layered readings (layered not only in Bibles but in liturgy, architecture and art) but happily layered his own authorities — pagan, literary, scriptural and theological — creating his own poetic midrash and, in a sense, inviting us to do likewise, as we do in this project of *Vertical Readings in Dante's 'Comedy'*.

In the canto Twenty-Fours we move from thieves and gluttons to apostles but find ourselves, I suggest, in the company of poets and reflecting on the obligations of poetic truth throughout. In *Inferno* xxiv Virgil and Dante are still in the eighth circle of the fraudsters, who include the corrupters of public office and those guilty of the vices that infest political and economic negotiations — flattery, hypocrisy, simony, sooth-saying. This brew of calculated self-interest may seem to us to involve wrongdoing of lesser severity or even to be 'just the way the world works', but Dante Alighieri was painfully aware of the ways in which these vices erode the common good and civic life — Dante and Virgil, after all, have glided into the eighth circle on the back of a monster with an honest man's face and the tail of a scorpion.[2]

The eighth circle has ten 'pockets' (the 'Malebolge') of deceivers. As *Inferno* xxiii opens, Dante and Virgil have only just narrowly escaped the devils of the fifth pocket (*Inferno* xxii and xxiii) by an *opera buffa* expedient in which Virgil clutches Dante to his stomach and 'sledges' down the slope with him. In the sixth pocket (*Inferno* xxiii), they find themselves amongst the slow moving hypocrites — defeated, weeping souls who move with creaking difficulty, weighed down by parodic Benedictine robes of lead. The hypocrites are startled by the signs of vitality they see in Dante — the pulse at his throat a sign not only of his bodiliness but of his present fear. Dante and Virgil pass the crucified Caiaphas, the prototype, from the trial of Jesus, of one willing to sacrifice the innocent for political expedience. Thus they make their way to the seventh pocket of the thieves and to our canto, *Inferno* xxiv.

Tone and tempo change from the opening verses which provide a Virgilian description of the softening of Virgil's troubled countenance. This, at first cold as a late winter morning, is described in an extended simile as lifting like the movements of a peasant who, at first seeing morning

---

2   This essay will refer to the textual Dante as 'Dante', as does Beatrice and find different means of referring to the authorial Dante.

frost grumbles and delays but, finding some hope and under pressure of time, grabs his goad, goes out and prods his lambs to pasture (*Inferno* xxiv. 1–15). The weightless Virgil now proceeds to shepherd his flock of one with vigour, variously hauling and pushing Dante up the steep face from ledge to ledge until they reach the top, where the exhausted Dante flops, his lungs 'milked of breath' ('la lena m'era del polmon sì munta', *Inf.*, xxiv. 4–45).[3] Virgil now issues a stern rebuke:

> 'Omai convien che tu così ti spoltre',
> disse 'l maestro, 'ché seggendo in piuma
> in fama non si vien, né sotto coltre;
>   sanza la qual chi sua vita consuma,
> cotal vestigio in terra di sé lascia
> qual fummo in aere e in acqua la schiuma.
>   E però leva sù; vinci l'ambascia
> con l'animo che vince ogne battaglia,
> se col suo grave corpo non s'accascia'. (*Inf.*, xxiv. 46–54)

['Now you must needs', my teacher said, 'shake off your wonted indolence. No fame is won beneath the quilt or sunk in feather cushions. Whoever, fameless, wastes his life away, leaves of himself no greater mark on earth than smoke in air or froth upon the wave. So upwards! On! And vanquish laboured breath! In any battle mind power will prevail, unless the weight of body loads it down'.]

Why speak so harshly to the exhausted Dante? Is it because of what they have just escaped? Charges of corruption in public office, however much he contested them, must have been in Dante Alighieri's mind as he devised the eighth circle. He had been convicted of being a 'barrator', fined and banished.[4] In the poem only Virgil's athletic sledging facilitates their escape from the demon guardians of the barrators. Ronald Martinez and Robert Durling suggest there may be an historical basis for this — perhaps Dante in his exile was nearly seized and tortured by enemies? Yet on an existential and literary level we can also see the exhausted and nearly defeated Dante as being saved, in cantos xxiii and xxiv, by poetry. It is on the breast of a poet that he sledges to safety and it is Virgil who pushes him up, ledge by ledge, to the cusp of the next pocket. The softening of Virgil's face gives a foretaste of redemption to come, and hints at the first

---

3 All translations, unless otherwise specified, are from Robin Kirkpatrick's three volume translation of the *Commedia*. I am also indebted to his notes throughout.

4 'Autobiography in Cantos 21–23', in Durling and Martinez, I, pp. 567–68.

cantos of *Inferno* where Dante glimpses the sunlit heights that it will take much travail to reach.

If poetry is indeed what saves Dante here, what danger had he been in? What temptation had he been under? Not barratry, to my mind, but very likely *acedia*, a medieval sin somewhere between sloth and despair. Surely our author, barred from office and exiled from his city, must have despaired and even followed the strategy of the depressed — staying in bed all day under a quilt with cushions over one's head? If so, Virgil's bracing admonition at the beginning of *Inferno* xxiv is that Dante not hide under the pillows, not accept exile as defeat or cloak himself in hypocrisy (a leaden weight) in order to secure pardon back in Florence, but rather move upwards and on. Virgil tells him 'you've longer ladders to climb' ('più lunga scala convien che si saglia', *Inf.*, xxiv. 55) and insists that 'in any battle mind power will prevail, unless the weight of body loads it down' ('l'animo che vince ogne battaglia, / se col suo grave corpo non s'accascia', *Inf.*, xxiv. 53–54). Dante rebounds with a fiat: 'Let's go […] I'm all strength and dash' ('Va, ch'i' son forte e ardito', *Inf.*, xxiv. 60).

From his new vantage point, the reinvigorated Dante looks down into the *bolgia* of the thieves, and even asks for a closer look. There are snakes everywhere — exotic and multifarious — from Libya, Ethiopia, the Red Sea and beyond, and all transposed from Ovid's *Metamorphoses*. It is a parody of Eden, with each Adam tormented by his or her own bespoke viper. There seems to have been no end to the different ways one might be guilty of theft, even before the age of internet fraud and insider trading on the stock market. Snakes bind the sinners' hands behind their backs, and send tails and necks between their buttocks in a savage simulacrum of coitus. Dante sees one dart forward and bite a sinner at the nape — a standard animal way to dispatch prey. Then, faster than you could scribble 'I' and 'O', the letters that in Italian compose the first person singular, the sinner ignites, becomes ashes and is recomposed, 'becoming instantly the self it was' ('la polver si raccolse per sé stessa', *Inf.*, xxiv. 105). This is one of the saddest phrases in the *Inferno*, and perhaps its motto. These heaps of ashes are not returning to the Edenic dust recalled in the liturgy of Ash Wednesday ('to dust you shall return'), dust which hopes to be raised incorruptible in the Resurrection. This is a collapse into dust that will happen again and again, which will not resurrect but simply reassemble the same self-deceiving, thieving wretch as before. Advocates of cryogenics take note! If you are brought back from a frozen state, you will still… be you.

Unusually for the *Inferno*, one of the denizens recomposed in this way names himself, and that twice over, declaring himself to be 'Vanni Fucci', known as 'Beast'. Dante knows Vanni to have been a violent man of war, a sobriquet of which Fucci might be proud as he is, apparently still, unendingly proud of his brutal life. Vanni is 'pissed off' ('mi duol', *Inf.*, xxiv. 133) to be found in the pocket of thieves for stealing sacred vessels from the sanctuary and 'grassing' someone up for it — an indolent crime since these vessels customarily lay unprotected. This crime returns us to the Edenic theme evoked by the snakes. Theft is a sin of Eden, associated with the serpent's hypocritical coaching. The apple, like the silver vessels, was low-lying fruit. The first couple take something which is not theirs to take and release a tide of successive sins into the world. This includes, in Adam's as in Vanni Fucci case, 'grassing' on people: 'it was Eve who made me do it'. Eve blames the snake. This shifting of blame is, then, the first human discord recorded in the Book of Genesis.

Theft is lazy — a way of getting something without having to work for it — a clandestine hit on the stock market. Theft is a crime against neighbour and, for Adam and Eve in Eden, evidence of a lack of faith that God will provide for all they need. The violent speech from Vanni that ends the canto marks a contrast with the canto's sweet, pastoral opening and presages the crude 'finger' Vanni gives to God, which opens the following canto: 'Togli Dio, ch'a te le squadro!' [Take that! I'm aiming, God, at you!] (*Inf.*, xxv. 3).

Purgatorio xxiv

We've come thus far without any mention of desire. This is because I believe Dante Alighieri to be enough of a Thomist to have doubted that *true* desire was to be found in the souls in *Inferno*. There are dashings and couplings and self-absorbed moanings, but true desire is divinely graced and, as such, we should not expect it in Hell. There are however two clear instances of desire in *Inferno* xxiv, though significantly neither in the permanent denizen. There is desire in the softening of Virgil's frozen face, his turning to prod the weary Dante, and there is the corresponding desire of Dante's fiat: 'Va, ch'i' son forte e ardito' [Let's go [...] I'm all strength and dash] (*Inf.*, xxiv. 60).

Desire is a Christian good, at least in the Augustinian and Thomistic synthesis which informs the *Commedia*. All theologians of the early church believed, as Augustine memorably recorded, that *our hearts are restless until they rest in thee* and so, too, did Dante. This desiring love for God was the solid conviction of medieval theologians who figure in the *Commedia*: Bernard of Clairvaux, Bonaventure and Aquinas. To be a Christian is to be *in via*, to be a pilgrim travelling to God. They understood love of God to be a desiring love and, in this sense, an erotic love, as had many of the Rabbis. The *Song of Songs*, possibly in origin an Egyptian love poem which somehow made it into the canons of Jewish and Christian scripture, was the text most commented on by the rabbis with Christian theologians following their lead. Bernard of Clairvaux preached over eighty sermons to his brethren on this tiny book, full of expressions of longing and desire and, in the Christian *idiom*, transformed from love of woman and man to love of God.[5]

These writers thought love to be divine and at the same time a universal and natural thing. It is not surprising that in the *Commedia* Virgil provides both the strongest and most theological expressions of natural, desiring love, nor that he does so in *Purgatorio* xvii:

> Lo naturale è sempre sanza errore,
> ma l'altro puote errar per malo obietto
> o per troppo o per poco di vigore.
>   Mentre ch'elli è nel primo ben diretto,
> e ne' secondi sé stesso misura,
> esser non può cagion di mal diletto;
>   ma quando al mal si torce, o con più cura,
> o con men che non dèe corre nel bene,
> contra 'l Fattore adovra sua fattura.
>   Quinci comprender puoi ch'esser convene
> amor sementa in voi d'ogne virtute
> e d'ogne operazion che merta pene. (*Purg.*, xvii. 94–105)

[The natural love can never go astray. The other, though, may err when wrongly aimed, or else through too much vigour or the lack. Where mind-love sets itself on primal good and keeps, in secondaries, a due control, it cannot be the cause of false delight. But when it wrongly twists towards the ill, or runs towards the good foo fast or slow, what's made then works against its maker's plan. Hence of necessity, you'll understand that love must be the seed of all good powers, as, too, of penalties your deeds deserve.]

---

5   It is not always clear which 'voice' in the *Song* is male or female, beloved or lover.

Dante quite naturally credits to Virgil a 'natural theology' in which the world is made for the Good and all things move towards this source of life.[6]

Here we may point to a Christian influence which would not be within the historical Virgil's gift — the doctrine of *creatio ex nihilo*. This was not a concept taken over from Plato or Aristotle but one derived, albeit with Platonic influences, by Jews and Christians from their scriptures. On such an understanding 'all that is' has its being from God who freely creates everything, including space and time. *Creatio ex nihilo* is at the heart of Aquinas's final great work, the *Summa Theologiae* which, like the *Commedia*, is a cosmic narrative in which all things come from God and find their fulfilment in flowing back to God.

It is this God who made all and who moves all who is Love (I John 4:8). Dante Alighieri also believed, or so Kenelm Foster argued in 'Dante and Eros', 'that all human desires *are* radically one'. So did Augustine believe this and, building upon him, Aquinas, and so here does Virgil. It is not a uniquely Christian conviction. There are Platonic and Aristotelian variants including a famous twentieth-century one in the philosophy of Iris Murdoch, and especially her *Sovereignty of the Good*. We are made by Primal Good (in Virgil's term) and long for the Primal Good. All our desiring actions are inflections of this life force within us which is part of our animal — or better, our *creaturely* nature — the force which through the green fuse drives the flower. All things desire the Good, although reasoning creatures like human beings, with complex and circuitous lives, can mistake lesser, shabby and second-rate substitutes for this good.

It is for mistaking the Good and for misdirected desire that the gluttons are now undergoing purgation in *Purgatorio* xxiv. Dante and Virgil have been traversing the terrace of gluttony, Purgatory's sixth terrace, since canto xxi, which seems an extraordinary amount of coverage for what many today would regard as a minor peccadillo. Today we think gluttony is an offence against health and waistline rather than against God. Also surprising is the presence of so many poets in this part of *Purgatorio*. Dante and Virgil meet early on and are accompanied by the Latin poet, Statius, whom Dante-author has made Christian for his purposes. In *Purgatorio* xxiii Dante has come across his old friend and poetic sparring partner, Forese, and the two repent of the callous vulgarity of their *tenzone*, a poetic dialogue in which they traded insults for amusement — or, one might even

---

6   Note that this is not at all the 'natural theology' of the eighteenth century which becomes elements of proofs for the existence of God.

say, for the hell of it — including references to Forese's sexual relations with his wife, Nella, whose prayers now speed his travels through Purgatory. But what does poetry have to do with gluttony?

Of the three *cantiche*, it is *Purgatorio* that is the pre-eminent poem of desiring love. The souls in *Purgatorio*, certain of their salvation, generally move along briskly. As *Purgatorio* xxiv opens, Virgil, Dante, Statius and Forese are striding forward and talking apace: 'sì come nave pinta da buon vento' [like ships driven by a favouring wind] (*Purg.*, xxiv. 3), all in sharp contrast, that is, to the leaden movement of the hypocrites of *Inferno* xxiii and the hectic agitation of the thieves of *Inferno* xxiv. Here we have a Pope who ate too many Bolsena eels and men who drank as though unable to stop. This gluttony makes them more like the thieves in *Inferno* xxiv than first appears. They have sought satisfaction in what cannot satisfy. The desiring itself is not wrong, and nor are Bolsena eels and Vernaccia wine. But gorging 'oltra misura' [past all norms] (*Purg.*, xxiii. 65) shows a disordered life whose wretched exemplar is Lucifer in the deepest pit of *Inferno*, insatiably and forever chewing on the flesh of traitors.

How might gluttony relate to the transgression of Eden? In Genesis, Adam and Eve are somehow concerned that they will not have 'enough', that they will not get everything they need (as the serpent suggests), and so they steal the apple. The glutton eats beyond hunger and even enjoyment driven by an emptiness that can never be filled by food stuffed into a body no longer hungry or thirsty. In an analogous way, then, scurrilous and indecent literary jousting is a kind of gluttony. It is toying with or trivializing what is fundamentally good, a piddling away (or worse) of the poet's gift. This bears on the fact that in *Purgatorio* xxiv (as in the preceding canto) Dante brings before the reader the question of the poet's calling and of the nature of true poetry. This need not be Christian, for otherwise Virgil and possibly Statius would be excluded, but it must be oriented to the Good which, for Dante, is God.

Given the *Commedia*'s particular attention to naming (recall, for example, Dante's own longing for the Baptistry of St John in Florence where he was named), it is significant that Forese tells Dante that the souls they meet can now be named. Indeed, Dante says, they 'were happy to be named' ('del nomar parean tutti contenti', *Purg.*, xxiv. 26). Vanity and self-importance stripped away, they are becoming their true selves: 'sì munta / nostra sembianza via per la dieta' [milked dry, by fasting, of the way that once we seemed] (*Purg.*, xxiv. 17–18).

The discussion with Forese prepares the way for Dante's encounter with Bonagiunta — a respected composer of vernacular love poetry.[7] If Forese enabled Dante to acknowledge what went wrong in his poetry, the encounter with Bonagiunta gives a glimpse into what, or when, Dante thinks it went right. In what seems a self-aggrandizing passage, our poet has Bonagiunta marvel that he should behold a poet whose love writings excel his own:

> 'Ma dì s'i' veggio qui colui che fòre
> trasse le nove rime, cominciando:
> "Donne ch'avete intelletto d'amore"'? (*Purg.*, xxiv. 49–51)

> ['But tell me: do I see the man who drew those new rhymes forth, whose opening line ran so: "Ladies, who have intelligence of love...?"']

Note that the text *does not name* Dante who, thus far in the *Commedia*, has not been called by name and will be so only once in the entire poem — when he is upbraided by Beatrice in *Purgatorio* xxx. Dante, unlike the souls he meets here in canto xxiv, is not yet fit to be named and is instead identified with what Saul Kripke calls a 'rigid designation' — a description which, if it has a referent, can identify only one individual — 'the man who drew the new rhymes forth'. By touching on the *Vita nuova*, Dante Alighieri calls up what he regarded as a decisive turn in his poetry.[8] In his reply to Bonagiunta, we learn that this transition from tinny expertise to a poetics of love and praise was spiritual as well as literary, or perhaps literary because spiritual:

> 'I' mi son un che, quando
> Amor mi spira, noto, e a quel modo
> ch'e' ditta dentro vo significando'. (*Purg.*, xxiv. 52–54)

> ['I am just one who, when Love breathes in me, takes note and then goes on showing the meaning that's ordained within'.]

Robin Kirkpatrick notes that the very form of the work marks this transition: 'The give-and-take of the conversation with Bonagiunta emphasizes how far Dante has progressed beyond the univocal, self-regarding lyrics that even he was inclined to write while he still remained within the lyric tradition.

---

7   Kirkpatrick, *Purgatorio*, notes, 439.
8   Durling and Martinez, II, p. 413.

In the *Commedia* he creates a drama of competing voice. Meaning is to be established and recorded through dialogue with others'.[9] Dante speaks of his poetry as 'redeemed'. The Love that now breathes in Dante ('Amor mi spira') is the Love through which the world was made, described in Genesis as a divine breath hovering over the waters and as the breath blown by God into the nostrils of the first human to make the creature of dust a living being. Bonagiunta observes that this is the creative power behind which Dante's winged pens fly, transcribing what the Divine *dittator* says, something Bonagiunta's own poetry never attained (*Purg.*, xxiv. 58–59).

Meanwhile all around him the souls are quickening their pace. Forese strikes ahead leaving Virgil, Statius and Dante making their way to a laden fruit tree. Souls have paused below it to reach and cry inarticulately, like little children ('quasi bramosi fantolini', *Purg.*, xxiv. 108). 'Fantolini' — the inarticulacy is tied to this child-like status. Dante uses the work 'fante' to designate the speaking subject, and here we have a diminutive. It is worth noting that Augustine makes play with the Latin *infans* (deriving etymologically from being unable to speak) when telling of his own conversion in the Milan garden, a conversion that rendered him temporarily unable to speak.[10] This is not the inarticulacy of infancy but of souls born again who can sense and scent what they long for, can glimpse but not yet reach.

The three poets proceed in silence until encountered by an angelic voice. With what must be an allusion to the conversion of St Paul on the road to Damascus, Dante shies in terror like an untamed animal. He cannot see and becomes, like Paul in Acts 9, dependent on his friends to lead him. These are in Dante's case his fellow poets. He senses wind like a breeze of May, 'annunziatrice de li albori' [first messenger of whitening dawn] (*Purg.*, xxiv. 145), and feels his brow touched by the feathers of a wing as the penultimate mark is removed from his brow. Purged, it would seem, of misdirected ambition, he is able to hear the words from the Beatitudes, which have underscored pilgrim life on the whole of the terrace of gluttony: 'Blessed are those who hunger and thirst for uprightness / justice; for they shall have their fill' (Matthew 5:6). More than that, as a sign of his maturing faith, he is bold enough to cast these in his own words:

---

9 Kirkpatrick, *Commentary* on *Purgatorio* xxiv, p. 441–42.
10 For an account of this incident in the *Confessions* see Soskice, Janet, 'Monica's Tears', *New Blackfriars* 83. 980 (October 2002), 448–58.

'Beati cui alluma
tanto di grazia, che l'amor del gusto
nel petto lor troppo disir non fuma,
esurïendo sempre quanto è giusto!' (*Purg.*, xxiv. 151–54)

['The truly blessed are lit with so much grace that in their hearts a lot of food fumes forth no false desire, esurient always for the good and true!']

Paradiso xxiv

Paradiso xxiv finds us in the midst of the Heaven of the Fixed Stars, a celestial location which is the setting for *Paradiso* xxii–xxvii. Vittorio Montemaggi has pointed out that these cantos are 'the only time in the *Commedia* in which Dante explicitly presents himself as doing something like academic work in theology' and this is done by means of Dante's interrogation by three apostles, Peter, James and John on the three 'theological' virtues of faith, hope and charity.[11]

Dante continues his layering of biblical motifs and themes. No one can be accused of eisegesis in finding here themes of eating and drinking which have already emerged in our discussion of *Inferno* xxiv and *Purgatorio* xxiv. Eating and drinking is precisely where *Paradiso* xxiv begins, with Beatrice addressing guests at the celestial banquet:

O sodalizio eletto a la gran cena
del benedetto Agnello, il qual vi ciba
sì, che la vostra voglia è sempre piena. (*Par.*, xxiv. 1–3)

[You chosen confrères of the Blessèd Lamb who feeds you at his solemn feast so well that you are full in all you wish and will.]

One might suppose that the desire which suffused *Purgatorio* would now drop out of the picture in Heaven for if, following Augustine, our 'hearts are restless' in this life then presumably they will rest when they 'rest in thee' in Heaven. But not so in the *Paradiso*. This is not merely because the souls Dante meets have yet to be reunited with their bodies — something

---

11 Vittorio Montemaggi, *Reading Dante's Commedia as Theology: Divinity Realized in Human Encounter* (Oxford: Oxford University Press, 2016), p. 90. The whole of Montemaggi's chapter here, 'Truth and Theological Virtue', is worth reading for wonderful insights on faith, truth and theology in these cantos and throughout the *Commedia*.

they very much desire. Dante's blessed souls are still desirous in a manner akin to the eschatology of Gregory of Nyssa for whom desire will be ever present even in the next life not, as in this life, by virtue of lack but because of the unending splendour and beauty of God. Beatrice is accordingly full of desiring love and, introducing Dante to this heavenly host, speaks of his immense ardour ('l'affezione immensa', *Par.*, xxiv. 7). It is interesting that she does not identify Dante by name (as she has in her accusatory encounter in the *Purgatorio*), but by ostensive reference — 'this man here'. She tells the blessed souls that the same springs of grace from which they forever drink, now refresh his thought.

The guests at the celestial banquet are so filled with love that it is natural to them, in the Augustinian rubric, 'to love and do what you will'. It is not that they have ceased to desire — not at all — they are alive, spinning and golden with it, like so many fiery comets. Now, however, their 'wish and will' is rightly ordered to love, the love that is the cause and ground of all that is. Paradise, of course, is not a spiritual realm to be contrasted with a material one. It too is part of God's creation and the blessed souls participate in the joy of created life which will only be enhanced when, after the final judgement, they are reunited with their resurrected bodies.

The souls are whirling in a dance of measured delight, in an intricately balanced mechanism — a perfection of order in which the right ordering of the one goes up to make the harmony of all. Beatrice asks that Dante's evident zeal be tested, and then:

> Di quella ch'io notai di più carezza
> vid' ïo uscire un foco sì felice,
> che nullo vi lascio di più chiarezza (*Par.*, xxiv. 19–21)

> [From one I'd marked of dearer worth, I saw a fire flare out with so much joy that none now left behind it was so clear.]

This is St Peter, holder of the keys to Heaven, who circles around Beatrice three times (a point to which I will return) and at her instigation quizzes Dante on his faith.

We should pause on the wonderful irony, of which Dante Alighieri would be aware, that it should be Peter, who is the rock on which the Church is founded, who holds the keys to Heaven and who now tests Dante on his faith. In the Gospel narratives Peter is devoted, rash and persistently gets things wrong: as Jesus explains he must suffer and die, Peter corrects him: 'this will never happen to you!' (Matthew 16); witnessing the Transfiguration, Peter proposes lingering to embellish the occasion with three booths for Moses, Elijah and Jesus, thus misunderstanding the necessity of proceeding to Jerusalem and the cross (Matthew 17); in the ignominious walking on water incident, of which Beatrice lightly reminds him: 'per la qual tu su per lo mare andavi' [by which you came to walk across the sea] (*Par.*, xxiv. 39), Peter is directly accused by Jesus of lacking faith (Matthew 14). And yet, in *Paradiso* xxiv, Peter is clearest of the bright souls.

Dante Alighieri captures Peter's flawed perfection wonderfully. Now a kind of blazing comet, he comes forward to test Dante, circling Beatrice three times, a movement he will complete at the end of the canto. Three is a salient number for St Peter because on the night of Jesus's arrest and before the cock crowed Peter betrayed his master, as Jesus had predicted, three times: 'Jesus said to him, "Truly I tell you, this very night, before the cock crows, you will deny me three times"' (Matthew 26:75). In *Paradiso* xxiv the forgiven, faithful Peter performs the threefold sign of his betrayal and yet — just as the risen Christ bears the wounds of his crucifixion — Peter's circling of Beatrice is no longer a source of pain, but a sign of glory. This blessed fire is Peter post-Pentecost, filled with the Holy Spirit, the tongues of fire which descended on the followers of Jesus and enabled them to speak intelligibly to all peoples: 'Poscia fermato, il foco Benedetto / a la mia donna dirizzò lo spiro' [Then, when that blessèd fire had come to rest, / it breathed directly to my lady there in words of fire] (*Par.*, xxiv. 31–32). The Italian here is Latinized to accentuate the connection between breath, spirit, speech and inspiration that we have seen in Dante's exchanges with the poets in *Purgatorio* xxiv. Although there are no poets apart from Dante (and maybe Beatrice) in *Paradiso* xxiv, there are other writers who write with 'verace stilo' [truthful pen] (*Par.*, xxiv. 61). It may turn out that to be a poet is to be such a one for, as much as *Paradiso* xxiv concerns Dante's faith, it is also concerned with *graced writing and speaking*.

St Peter questions Dante about his faith, the first and foundational of the three theological virtues. Since these virtues are not attainments, Dante cannot claim to have earned what has come as a gift. He can, nonetheless, build on it, present it, as Aquinas insists one should, as bedizened reason. A reasoned account is what Dante attempts. He begins his account of faith by praying for God's aid, as was normal in medieval theological writing:

'La Grazia che mi dà ch'io mi confessi',
comincia' io, 'da l'alto primipilo,
faccia li miei concetti bene espressi'.
   E seguitai: 'Come 'l verace stilo
ne scrisse, padre, del tuo caro frate
che mise teco Roma nel buon filo,
   fede è sustanza di cose sperate
e argomento de le non parventi;
e questa pare a me sua quiditate'. (*Par.*, xxiv. 58–66)

['Let grace, which grants that I confess my faith to you, the noblest of
centurions, make', I began, 'my thoughts be well expressed'. And next:
'As written by the truthful pen, Father, of your dear brother, Paul, who
set, with you, great Rome upon its rightful track: "Faith is substantial to
the things we hope, the evidence of things we do not see". And such, in
essence, I believe it is'.]

Dante's language here is scholastic and sounds technical (speaking for
instance of faith's quiddity — *quiditate*), and carries echoes of Aquinas's *De
Veritate* and *Summa Theologiae*, yet the fulcrum of Dante's account of faith is
profoundly scriptural. It is scripture to which Dante turns, specifically the
Epistle to the Hebrews. Decisive is his direct citation of Hebrews 11:1: 'Faith
is substantial to the things we hope, the evidence of things not seen', a text
which had of long-standing been taken as the biblical definition of 'faith'
(*Par.*, xxiv. 64–65), and a key text for Thomas Aquinas in his treatment of the
virtue of faith.[12] It should not be thought, however, that resort to scripture
is in contrast with being 'scholastic'. Perhaps nothing is more 'scholastic'
in Dante's theology than his constant recourse to scripture — Thomas
Aquinas was after all, by profession, *Magister in Sacra Pagina*, his further
writings intended to illuminate the reading of scripture.

   The author of the Epistle to the Hebrews unfolds the meaning of faith
by a series of incidences in the lives of the biblical forerunners in faith.
To a beleaguered early Jewish Christian church, the author of Hebrews
holds forth a list of the faithful who have gone before, this great 'cloud of
witnesses' (Hebrews 12:1):

By faith Abel's sacrifice was found more acceptable than Cain's.
By faith, though it was without precedent, Noah built an ark.

---

12 Aquinas, *Summa Theologiae*, IIaIIae, q. 1, a. 4.

By faith Abraham left his homeland and old religion to follow the LORD.
By faith Sarah, though well past child-bearing age, bore Isaac, the son of promise.
By faith her husband, Abraham, took that same son, the son through whom his posterity was promised, and at God's request, prepared to slaughter him, until a ram trapped in a thicket was given instead.
It was by faith that Moses' parents hid him in a basket of rushes and by faith that the adult Moses refused to be known as the son of Pharaoh's daughter and sided instead with the enslaved Israelites. It was by faith that the Israelites crossed the Red Sea, pursued by Egyptian chariots.
It was by faith that the prostitute Rahab welcomed spies and was not killed in the taking of Jericho.

The author of the Epistle to the Hebrews gives us a list of the things *hoped for*, and realities as yet *unseen*. Not all are success stories in worldly terms. Noah floated to dry land but Abel, also on the list, was slain. Abram (later renamed 'Abraham') left his native land without any certainty of the future. The Israelites fled the abundance of Egypt into a lifeless desert. Moses never saw the promised land. Hebrews 11 continues by noting that many of the faithful were pilloried, imprisoned, flogged and killed. They were homeless, ill-treated and reduced to dressing in sheepskins:

All of these died in faith without having received the promises, but from a distance they saw and greeted them. They confessed that they were strangers and foreigners on the earth, for people who speak in this way make it clear that they are seeking a homeland. If they had been thinking of the land that they had left behind, they would have had opportunity to return. But as it is, they desire a better country, that is, a heavenly one. Therefore God is not ashamed to be called their God; indeed, he has prepared a city for them. (Hebrews 11:14–16)

This chapter of Hebrews is, in short, a *cri de coeur* for exiles and pilgrims, for those who have lost one homeland and must seek, by faith, another. No wonder Dante can insist to St Peter that his own coin will pass assay! But has he got it in his purse?

Although faith as a theological virtue is profoundly rational, it is not just the possession of a set of propositional convictions about God. Faith is faith 'in' God. To have faith is to trust in God, to be orientated to God and that is why faith is foundational to hope and love, as Peter confirms in a further question:

> [...] 'Questa cara gioia
> sopra la quale ogne virtù si fonda,
> onde ti venne?' (*Par.*, xxiv. 89–91)

> [That precious gem of joy in which all other virtues find their
> ground — whence does that come to you?]

Dante replies that it is the gift of the Holy Spirit, flowing from the texts of scripture, Old Testament and New. St Peter asks him on what basis he can trust these, to which Dante replies:

> La prova che 'l ver mi dischiude,
> son l'opere seguite, a che natura
> non scalda ferro mai né batte incude. (*Par.*, xxiv. 100–02)

> [The proof, for me, that unlocks truth is found in deeds that followed
> from that faith. Nature can't heat or hammer steel like that.]

Several verses later Dante refers to these 'deeds that follow from faith' as 'miracoli' [miracles] (*Par.*, xxiv. 107). Durling and Martinez suggest that Dante Alighieri is here referring to 'the miracles it (the Bible) narrates, obviously regarding them as historical fact'.[13] I struggle with this interpretation especially if, as the remark suggests, they are thinking of 'miracles' as referring to the miracles of Jesus, which appear to be violations of the laws of nature. Dante's text nowhere suggests the miracles of Jesus are the 'miracles' under discussion here. Instead, 'Se 'l mondo si rivolse al cristianesimo [...] sanza miracoli' [Suppose the world had turned to Christian faith without these miracles] (*Par.*, xxiv. 106) appears to refer back directly, in my view, to lines 100–02.

These are the miracles performed, not by Jesus, but by the faithful hammered to steel by their faith in God. The key text here is precisely that which Dante has already quoted, Hebrews 11, which chronicles these acts of faith — Rahab housing the spies of the Israelites, Moses choosing to identify with his enslaved forebears and not Pharaoh's daughter, Abel offering a lamb. These are not miracles like walking on water. The pioneers of faith in the Book of Hebrews perform wonderous things because, in the midst of adversity, they trust in their God:

---

13 Durling and Martinez, III, p. 495.

And what more should I say? For time would fail me to tell of Gideon, Barak, Samson, Jephthah, of David and Samuel and the prophets — who through faith conquered kingdoms, administered justice, obtained promises, shut the mouths of lions, quenched raging fire, escaped the edge of the sword, won strength out of weakness, became mighty in war, put foreign armies to flight. Women received their dead by resurrection. (Hebrews 11:32.34)

Dante no doubt did believe in the miracles of Jesus but it is much more potent and pertinent to his case (as well as making better sense of the text) if we take the 'deeds that followed from that faith' as deeds of the faithful like those praised in the Epistle to the Hebrews, deeds performed by girls, widows, a prostitute, weak people made strong like St Peter and Dante himself. His clinching argument, taken from Christian antiquity, is the historical fact that a group of poor, uneducated Galilean provincials, as were Peter and the Apostles, founded a faith that took the world by storm. Dante seemed to have found this kind of faith at his moment of near despair, the moment he thought to pull the coverlet and pillows over his head and give up on lost fortune, lost reputation, lost city. At this moment, guided by Virgil but directed to God, he found the faith to go on, despite a future unseen.

Having justified his faith, Dante is now asked by Peter to confess it. It might appear odd that Dante, now in the realm of certainty, should be asked to make a further confession.[14] This is an overly 'epistemological' way to look at it. Faith is not the opposite of uncertainty. The biblical demons and Satan himself are certain of the reality of God but have no faith. Confession of faith is not just a matter of contradicting doubt but, from antiquity, a form of praise. Most Christians and all Catholic Christians confess their faith in reciting the Creed. At a baptism, those in the congregation are asked to join in the public confession of faith that the postulant for baptism must make. This Christian confession is doxological — personal but not private — and, tellingly, Dante is assisted by Beatrice in coming to speech. He now makes what, as Montemaggi observes, is both a 'richly traditional and a strikingly original profession of faith':[15]

---

14 Durling and Martinez seem to find it paradoxical that Dante pilgrim is asked to confess his faith since his whole journey has expressed it and, having just seen Christ, Mary and now St Peter, is in the realm of certainty. See Durling and Martinez, III, p. 490.

15 Montemaggi, p. 107.

> [...] Io credo in uno Dio
> solo ed etterno, che tutto 'l ciel move,
> non moto, con amore e con disio. (*Par.*, xxiv. 130–32)

> [I believe in one true God, sole and eternal who, Himself not moved, moves all the spheres by love and with desire.]

This confession is based on proofs taken from physics and metaphysics and comes to him as the waters of revelation from Moses and the prophets, the writers of Gospels and Psalms and, from the writings of St Peter himself: 'per voi che scriveste / poi che l'ardente Spirto vi fè almi' [the words you wrote when once the ardent Spirit raised you high] (*Par.*, xxiv. 137–38).[16] Dante now underscores his own participation in this celestial order. Our pilgrim is here the template for the faithful Christian on earth, and even now bears flashes of the celestial glory that already illumine the guests at the heavenly banquet. St Peter circles Dante three more times and the canto ends.

Many have noted that it is difficult, if not impossible, to separate Dante author and Dante pilgrim in much of the first person confessional poetry of *Paradiso* xxiv. Can we presume that Dante's stated faith is that of the historical Dante? There is a similar challenge in Augustine's *Confessions* and a similar consideration to make. If Augustine in writing his *Confessions* and Alighieri in composing *Paradiso* xxiv are not being honest here they are not simply being dishonest with their readers but dishonest to their God. We are left with radical alternatives. Maybe Dante Alighieri was not really a Christian but just using shared cultural motifs to further his poetic ambitions? A radical variant of this would be to affirm that Dante does not risk damnation for this artful deception since he knows there is no God anyway (I have heard such arguments made about Augustine's *Confessions*.) I find the first suggestion wholly implausible for Dante, or even for a man of his time. In the canto Twenty-Fours, as I have tried to trace them, Dante seems to me to give an account of being snatched from the brink of either death or despair by hope. In *Inferno* xxiv he glimpses the goodness of the

---

16 Durling retains the plural and translates *Paradiso* xxiv. 136–38 as 'through Moses, through prophets, and through psalms, through the Gospel and through all of you, who wrote when the burning Spirit made you nourishers'. The translation 'nourishers' fits well with the feasting and feeding themes which open this canto, and which (in their longing) are anticipated by the souls in *Purgatorio* xxiv.

created order in Virgil's face softening like the promise of spring. Virgil, that is 'Poetry', in the same canto carries Dante forward when he is heavy with despair, hinting at salvation by poetry — the one thing never lost to Dante, the author, is his poetic gift. *Purgatorio* xxiv interrogates this gift and Dante's earlier misuse of it with Forese. In *Purgatorio* xxx, the sole instance in the entire poem where Dante is called by name, Beatrice not only names him but accuses him of squandering his talents. *Purgatorio* xxiv delineates his turn to a true, or truthful poetry which is a poetry of love, inspired and fed by the waters of the tree of life. Here Beatrice herself speaks as a 'Word' of God.[17] *Paradiso* xxiv finds Dante praising God by confessing his faith amongst those who are themselves breathers of fire, tongues of God. It is the fulfilment of his life as a Christian and as a poet.

Although Dante is not named in the passages which chronicle the Heaven of the Fixed Stars (*Paradiso* xxii–xxvii), these cantos contain one of the more telling instances of self-denomination in the whole work, and it is tied directly to his confession of his baptismal faith. These are the only cantos where Dante names himself as 'Poet' and one of the few places where Dante, both character and poet, refers to the completed work we know as the *Commedia*:

> Se mai continga che 'l poema sacro
> al quale ha posto mano e cielo e terra,
> [...]
> vinca la crudeltà che fuor mi serra
> del bello ovile ov' io dormi' agnello,
> [...]
> con altra voce omai, con altro vello
> ritornerò poeta, e in sul fonte
> del mio battesmo prenderò 'l cappello.
> però che ne la fede, che fa conte
> l'anime a Dio, quivi intra' io, e poi
> Pietro per lei sì mi girò la fronte.

[If ever it should happen that this sacred work, to which both Earth and Heaven have set their hands, [...] might overcome the cruelty that locks

---

17 On this, see Kevin Grove, 'Becoming True in the *Purgatorio*: Dante on Forgetting, Remembering, and Learning to Speak' in *Dante, Mercy, and the Beauty of the Human Person*, ed. by Leonard J. DeLorenzo and Vittorio Montemaggi (Eugene, OR: Cascade Books, 2017), pp. 45-64.

me out from where I slept, a lamb in that fine fold, [...] with altered fleece, with altered voice, I shall return as poet, taking, at my fount of baptism, the laurel for my crown. For I first entered there within the faith that makes us known, in soul, to God, and then, for that same faith, St Peter ringed my brow.] (*Par.*, xxv. 1–12)

In this return, if not to Florence and the Baptistry of St John where he first entered the faith, then to the heavenly home of all exiles and pilgrims, the 'true Dante' and the 'true poet' will be one.[18]

---

18 I am grateful to Vittorio Montemaggi for pointing out that it is only in these cantos that Dante accords himself the name 'poet'.

25. Changes

George Ferzoco

Over the centuries, much scholarship on Dante's *Commedia* has taken the form of the *lectura Dantis*, in which one digs as deeply as one can into the depths of the poem's text. The project of Cambridge's vertical readings, on the other hand, is reminiscent not of the deep shafts dug by miners but rather of long narrow trenches, of the sort gently excavated by archaeologists. The trenches we are digging in our enterprise follow not a physical structure but a numerical one. Someone like Dante, whose faith in names and numbers as revelatory interpretive keys is so blatant, surely intended readers to observe these numbers and to meditate on their appearances: what there is that leaps to the eyes, and what might lie slightly below the surface. This particular trench follows the straight line that is the number twenty-five; it is dug knowing that in the medieval mental universe of Italy, there existed a sort of cultural synesthesia. Unlike physical symptoms of synesthesia that can associate a number with a precise colour, its medieval cultural equivalent is the association of a number with a precise concept. Although this trench barely scrapes the surface, one should allow the number twenty-five to trace its path and lead the reader, first in a literal narrative and then to the text's allegory and beyond.

A Literal Synopsis of the Canto Twenty-Fives

Inferno xxv shows Vanni Fucci at his memorable best, blaspheming God and getting attacked by serpents; the sight of this leads the poet to vent his disgust with Pistoia. Returning to the action, Vanni leaves the scene, covered with snakes, pursued by a centaur-like creature identified by

http://dx.doi.org/10.11647/OBP.0119.04

Virgil as Cacus, who paid for his crimes by being bludgeoned to death by Hercules. Three thieves then appear, startling Dante and Virgil. They do not notice the pair, however, and speak to each other. The poet addresses his readers, saying they cannot be blamed for not believing what he is about to narrate, since he himself can barely accept what happened. Two of the thieves, Agnello and Cianfa, strangely share their bodies in a new form. With tremendous speed, two other thieves arrive, one in human form, the other reptilian. The poet warns in no uncertain terms that he is going to do something beyond the capacities of other great poets, and proceeds to describe Buoso and Francesco actually exchanging their own natures. Apologising for being unable to register the continual changing, the poet identifies another thief, Puccio Sciancato, and notes that of all the thieves seen here, this is the only one whose nature did not change at all.

Purgatorio xxv finds Dante and Virgil ascending the terrace of gluttony steadily and rapidly in the mid afternoon; with them is their new companion Statius. Dante wants to say something yet gets nervous, so Virgil needs to encourage him to say what is on his mind. Dante blurts out his problem: if the shades on this terrace do not need food or drink, how is it that they clearly are losing weight? Virgil provides two brief replies; both seem to the reader, and probably to the discussants, insufficient, so Virgil invites Statius to provide an answer. Statius says he will do so only because Virgil asked him, and says immediately that he can answer the question successfully. Blood becomes perfected by being digested in four parts of the body, lastly the heart; from there, in the man, it descends to the genitals, and from *there* it joins with the perfect blood in the woman, which rests in her genital area. His blood is 'active', her blood is 'passive'. The active blood is instrumental in creating a new animating soul in the new being in the woman's womb. The embryo develops, and when its brain reaches a certain point, God infuses into it a rational soul. This rational soul unites with the animal soul that already was present, such that the two become one single being.

What happens when this being, this person, dies? The soul leaves the body. It carries both states of the original two souls; the animal or physical one goes silent, while the rational one makes up for that by becoming even more active than it had been while the person was alive in the body. The soul is judged: if it is condemned for eternity, it goes to the bank of the river Acheron; if it is deemed to be worthy of Heaven, it finds itself next to the Tiber. The soul discovers its fate only when arriving at the appropriate river.

The soul acquires a new body, one that consists largely of air. This new body stays with the old soul, which informs it of how the old body used to be and used to operate. Its senses work as did the old body's, and with this body of air it becomes a new form of being: a shade. Statius's explanation ends exactly when the ascent is completed. The pilgrims' path runs right next to a fire, and they must go one after the other, as Virgil warns his ward to take care not to fall. The souls here sing the hymn *Summae Deus clementiae* [God of the greatest mercy] (*Purg.*, xxv. 121). The pilgrim looks at these singers intently but knows he must look down from time to time to ensure his feet are treading safely. The souls call out the examples of chastity that are Mary and Diana, as well as historical examples of chaste spouses.

In *Paradiso* xxv the reader reaches the Heaven of the Fixed Stars, and confronts the poet's reflections on what he hopes will happen to him in the future. Declaring that the poem is the product of both Heaven and earth, and of years of effort, he wishes to return to his native Florence, from where he has been so savagely excluded. He departed as an exile; he wishes to return as a poet, a poet who will be honoured with the laurel crown, bestowed upon him in the Baptistry. The poet, who is there with Beatrice and St Peter, is joined by a new light; this is St James the Great. The two apostles join in the manner of paired doves, and exude such light as to blind Dante. Beatrice invites James, who wrote of God's generosity, to speak to them about hope, the virtue he embodied from the time of his discipleship. James tells Dante to look up and to reassure himself, since all things in Heaven reach a most ready or ripe state. The pilgrim does as requested, and is able now to see again. James says he wants Dante to strengthen hope not only in himself but also in those who read the poem; to that end, he poses three questions concerning hope: 'dì quel ch' ell' è, dì come se n'infiora / la mente tua, e dì onde a te venne' [tell what it is, tell how your mind blossoms with it, and tell whence it came to you] (*Par.*, xxv. 46–47).

Beatrice interrupts, answering the second question for the pilgrim, saying in essence that no living Christian has greater hope than Dante. She then lets the pilgrim answer the other two questions. He defines hope, and says he got hope from the psalmist and from James himself. James likes this answer; glowing more brilliantly, he asks a fourth question: 'What does hope promise you?', to which Dante answers 'This is found in Scripture' (*Par.*, xxv. 79–96). With this, the pilgrim's examination is complete. Angels sing 'Sperent in te' [May they trust in you] (xxv. 98), just when a new figure arrives. Beatrice explains that this is St John. Dante strains his eyes, trying to discern the contours of the saint's body, but John chastises him, telling him his body is not there. Like tired rowers who stop in unison, the three apostles' dance ends abruptly, and Dante turns to look for Beatrice but cannot do so, since he is now, once more, blind.

The Incipits of the Twenty-Fives

Now, this literal synopsis of the Twenty-Fives is at once short and long. It is short because there are many details that have been omitted. It is long for the simple fact that these three cantos are incredibly detailed and complicated. Many have drawn attention to at least one of these three cantos as being worthy of the closest scrutiny.[1] Nonetheless, one finds thematic continuity within them, and it is my intention here to note this but also to draw upon the tradition of Cambridge Dante studies in examining our cantos with an eye to theology, to spirituality, and particularly to religious cultural outlook and practice. My contention is that Dante intended the Twenty-Fives to be particularly noteworthy, and that there are explicit signs of this in his writings; moreover, these signs are indicative of the cultural milieu of his readers.

   Starting at the beginning, one can profit from looking at the openings of each of Dante's one hundred cantos. Except for the ends of each canto's first and third lines, and of the antepenultimate and final lines of each canto, Dante's terza rima has three rhymes for each sound in concatenated fashion — ABA, BCB, CDC, DED, and so on — throughout the entire poem. At the start and end of each canto, however, there are only two rhymes. Of the hundreds of rhymes used by Dante throughout the poem, only a couple of dozen or so are used once. And of these, only a handful are used solely at the start of cantos. Of these rarest of rhymes, three different ones are chosen by Dante to start the Twenty-Fives:

---

1   An entire book of essays has been devoted to themes raised by the twenty-fifth canto of
     Paradiso: Se mai continga... Exile, Politics and Theology in Dante, ed. by Claire Honess and
     Matthew Treherne (Ravenna: Longo editore, 2013). In a recent *lectura Dantis* of *Purgatorio*
     xxv, Dennis Costa's first sentence was 'I somehow can't believe that I offered, actually
     offered, to present to you this evening the most difficult, the most opaque canto of the
     entire *Commedia*'. See http://frontrow.bc.edu/program/costa/. In relation to *Inferno* xxv,
     the poet himself draws attention to the peculiarity of the canto, stating that Vanni Fucci's
     pride was the most extreme of anyone encountered in the pilgrim's infernal journey: 'Per
     tutt' i cerchi de lo 'nferno scuri / non vidi spirto in Dio tanto superbo' [Through all the
     dark circles of Hell I saw no spirit so proud against God] (*Inf.*, xxv. 13–14).

Inferno xxv. 1–3: '-adro'

> Al fine de le sue parole il ladro
> le mani alzò con amendue le fiche,
> gridando: 'Togli, Dio, ch'a te le squadro!'

> [At the end of his words the thief raised his hands with both the figs,
> crying: 'Take them, God, I'm aiming at you!']

The rhyme '-adro' appears only once in the entire poem, and it appears here,
at the beginning of the canto, only twice rather than the usual three times.

Purgatorio xxv. 1–3: '-orpio'

> Ora era onde 'l salir non volea storpio;
> chè 'l sole avea il cerchio di merigge
> lasciato al Tauro e la notte a lo Scorpio.

> [It was an hour when our climbing brooked no lameness, for the sun had
> left the meridian circle to the Bull and night to the Scorpion.]

The rhyme '-orpio' similarly appears only once in the entire poem, and it
appears here, at the beginning of the canto, only twice.

Paradiso xxv. 1–3: '-acro'

> Se mai continga che 'l poema sacro
> al quale ha posto mano e cielo e terra,
> sì che m'ha fatto per molti anni macro

> [If it ever happen that the sacred poem, to which both Heaven and earth
> have set their hand, so that for many years it has made me lean]

Unlike '-adro' and '-orpio', the rhyme '-acro' does not appear only once;
however it appears but twice in the entire *Commedia*: once here, and the
other time also at the beginning of a canto, *Purgatorio* xxxi, re-using the
word 'sacro' in reference to the river Lethe.[2]

---

2   'O tu che se' di là dal fiume sacro', / volgendo suo parlare a me per punta, / che pur per
taglio m'era paruto acro' ['O you who are beyond the sacred river', turning toward me
the point of her speech, whose mere edge had seemed sharp to me] (*Purg.*, xxxi. 1–3).

No other trio of identically numbered cantos begins with rhymes that are used so rarely as we find here with the Twenty-Fives. The reader may take this break in Dante's usual phonetic and poetic strategy to signal other changes. Given the literal summary of the cantos provided above, one may already sense that the number of these changes is large in comparison to the rarity of these initial rhymes.

Changes in the Twenty-Fives

From the very moment one starts reading *Inferno* xxv, it is clear that things are amiss, even by the standards of Hell and of the cantica. Dante's usual strategy in the *Inferno* is to finish a canto when a character completes his or her movements through a given sphere of Hell. In the case of canto twenty-four, one witnesses the punishment meted out to a damned soul — in this case, a thief — as well as that individual's dramatic prophecy. But canto twenty-five of *Inferno* makes its topsy-turvy character evident from its first words: we have here a canto beginning not with an *In principio* but with the words *Al fine* [At the end], and this marks the end of one series of words, directed to the pilgrim, only to replace it with another series of words, forming an invective aimed at God.

> Al fine de le sue parole il ladro
> le mani alzò con amendue le fiche,
> gridando: 'Togli, Dio, ch'a te le squadro!' (*Inf.*, xxxv. 1–5)

> [At the end of his words the thief raised his hands with both the figs, crying: 'Take them, God, I'm aiming at you!']

The words *le sue parole* metamorphose into an expression of physicality, *le mani alzò*, and that physicality metamorphoses from the literal, and natural, *le mani*, to another body part represented figuratively — and, thereby, with an artificially imposed physical gender — by the *fica*. Moreover, whereas the female body has only one such part, the sinner here has created two of them. The days of the Roman culture, with the omnipresence of phalluses at city gates and house entrances, even as doorbells, are gone; Dante is following the nascent medieval practice of using the symbols of genitalia for negative, hostile purposes.[3] Indeed, a defensive tower in Pistoia, Vanni's

---

3   See George Ferzoco, *Il murale di Massa Marittima. The Massa Marittima Mural*, 2nd edn (Florence: Consiglio Regionale della Toscana, 2005).

home city, presented carved representations of two hands in the form of the *fiche*, pointed directly at the enemy, Florence.[4] (Even the very form of the *fiche* is subject to the changing interpretations of readers: some would have them in the form of the *corna*, others making a circle with the thumb and index finger, but most in placing the tip of the thumb between the bent index and middle fingers.[5])

More than one sin is evident here — not just theft, but pride and blasphemy too, and a perverse twisting of lust; the neat demarcations of Dante's infernal architecture give the appearance of falling apart. This link to Pistoia, through Vanni Fucci, can be tied to bad blood — not simply of a feuding or criminal sort, but genetically, as the reference in line 12, 'il seme tuo', makes clear: the inhabitants of Pistoia descend from the soldiers of Catiline, known for their ferocity.[6]

There begins a sort of *danse macabre*, led by the damned and by serpents. Attention must be drawn, albeit most briefly, to a couple of elements here; they involve something the pilgrim does, and something the poet says. For the former: in lines 44–45, quite exceptionally, there is a change in the leadership of this travelling duo, as the pilgrim takes over the lead from his guide, by giving Virgil an order to keep quiet. He does so not in words but in deed: 'io, acciò che 'l duca stesse attento, mi puosi 'l dito su dal mento al naso' [I, so that my leader should pay attention, stretched my finger from chin to nose] (*Inf.*, xxv. 44–45). In the realm of sign language, literally Dante is telling Virgil to keep quiet; but figuratively, he is drawing attention to another guide, another poet. By deliberately pointing to his *naso* he invokes Publius Ovidius Naso, or Ovid.[7] Dante is thereby saying that we are entering a terrain that is Ovidian, and that he knows at least as much about this as does his guide, Virgil.

---

4   Alberto Agresti, *Dante e Vanni Fucci. Nota letta all' Accademia Pontaniana nella tornata del 24 aprile 1892* (Naples: Tipografia della Regia Università, 1892), p. 7.

5   Re the *corna*, see Vittorio Gassman's interpretation in his recitation of the canto: https:// youtu.be/L6bKBACp0Uo; for the circular gesture, see Ignazio Baldelli, 'Le "fiche" di Vanni Fucci', *Giornale storico della letteratura italiana* 174 (1997) 1–38; and for the thumb between the fingers, see Andrea Mazzucchi, 'Le "fiche" di Vanni Fucci (Inf. XXV 1–3). Il contributo dell'iconografia a una disputa recente', *Rivista di studi danteschi* 1 (2001), 302–15. Mazzucchi's argument agrees with the representation in the mid-fourteenth-century manuscript Oxford, Bodleian Library, Holkham misc. 48, p. 38.

6   Giampaolo Francesconi, 'Infamare per dominare. La costruzione retorica fiorentina del conflitto politico a Pistoia', in *Lotta politica nell'Italia medievale. Giornata di studi, Roma, 16 febbraio 2010*, ed. by Isa Lori Sanfilippo (Rome: Istituto storico italiano per il Medio Evo, 2010), pp. 95–106 (p. 102).

7   For similar observations, see Madison U. Sowell, 'Dante's Nose and Publius Ovidius Naso: A Gloss on *Inferno* 25.45', *Quaderni d'italianistica* 10 (1989), 157–71.

For the latter (something the poet says): from being an equal to Lucan and Ovid when visiting Limbo in Canto 4, Dante now becomes their superior, as he announces:

> Taccia Lucano omai, là dov' e' tocca
> del misero Sabello e di Nasidio,
> e attenda a udir quel ch'or si scocca.
>   Taccia di Cadmo e d'Aretusa Ovidio,
> ché se quello in serpente e quella in fonte
> converte poetando, io non lo 'nvidio (*Inf.*, xxv. 94–99)

> [Let Lucan now be silent, where he touches on miserable Sabellus and Nasidius, and let him listen to what the bow now looses. About Cadmus or Arethusa let Ovid be silent, for if in his poetry he converts him into a serpent and her into a fountain, I do not envy him.]

What we begin to see here is the way our Christian poet presents the alternating natures of the creations of these two classical poets, creations that he himself will better with a literary portrayal of metamorphosis that, as shall be seen, transcends even the talent and imagination of those with whom he shared company while visiting Limbo. Soon after Dante's challenge to Lucan and Ovid, we see the transmutation of Buoso and Francesco, whose very natures are changed from one to the other. Notice also the beautiful pun that Dante could not pass up: in referring to Lucan's literary work, he mentions the figure of Nasidius — in Italian, that is *Nasidio*, a word that looks suspiciously close to *Naso Dio*, or 'Ovid God', a sign of the poetic god that Dante is about to meet face to face, and to overtake.

The shifts of the shapes of the damned in this episode of Hell are well studied, but the very story of the acquisition of the relic that drew Vanni Fucci to Hell involves an unusual example of shifting matter. Around 1140, the bishop of Pistoia sent his deacon to Compostela in order to request a relic of St James. The Galician bishop, accustomed to such requests, did as he had done before: he reached into the urn containing St James's relics, and without looking grabbed hold of some hair to pass along to the visiting deacon. Onlookers were amazed to see that there was more than just hair, for attached to it was part of the base of the saint's skull, thus making the relic much more impressive and potent. This was taken back to Pistoia where an ornate chapel was dedicated on 25 July 1145, in the year that witnessed the start of the Second Crusade in which Dante's ancestor Cacciaguida was to fight and die.[8]

The presence of this relic caused Pistoia to become one of the Italian peninsula's leading pilgrimage sites, and certainly the greatest one dedicated to St James. As Pistoia is close to the Via Francigena, the primary north-south pilgrimage route leading to Rome, many pilgrims could make safe and convenient detours to Pistoia, bringing more renown and more money to the city. These factors permitted the creation of a staggeringly impressive reliquary in Pistoia's cathedral; work on this began in 1287, and it was here, about 1295, that Vanni Fucci and his henchmen committed their most dastardly crime: the theft not only of sacred vessels and art, but of relics, too.[9]

Rather like the pilgrim, in moving quickly to *Purgatorio* xxv, one finds Virgil using a metaphor in encouraging his charge to speak: 'Scocca l'arco del dir, ch 'nfino al ferro hai tratto' [Loose the bow of speech, which you have drawn to the very iron] (*Purg.*, xxv. 17–18). The metaphor appears to be classical, but in fact it resounds in a contemporary Christian context, as the great Dominican theologian Hugh of St Cher instructed his charges that 'First the bow is bent in study, then the arrow is released in preaching': a balance between learning and the active life is necessary.[10]

We are now about to get a great deal of learning from Statius, who presents a detailed explanation — presented in a form one could consider an oral treatise, or perhaps a university exercise such as a disputed question or a *quodlibet* — regarding the formation of the human body and of its afterlife version. This explanation is given not by Virgil, nor by a person known for his scientific knowledge, but by a poet dead for over a millennium. Why should Statius have such knowledge, and in such detail? This marks a mysterious shift in the narrative thrust of the entire cantica,

---

8   Diana Webb, 'St James in Tuscany: The Opera di San Jacopo of Pistoia and Pilgrimage to Compostela', *Journal of Ecclesiastical History* 50 (1998), 207–34.

9   The relic was of such importance that on 22 November 1145, Pope Eugenius III sent a letter to Bishop Atto of Pistoia, granting an indulgence to those visiting the altar containing the relics of James; see *Patrologia Latina* 180, col. 1063. Even the chanting of the liturgical hours needed to be altered here, due to the noise made by the crush of pilgrims for the feast of the saint; see Benjamin Brand, 'The Vigils of Medieval Tuscany', *Plainsong and Medieval Text* 17 (2008) 23–54 (p. 38).

10 M. Michèle Mulcahey, *'First the Bow is Bent in Study...'. Dominican Education before 1350* (Toronto: Pontifical Institute of Mediaeval Studies, 1998).

emphasising that the closer one gets to the realm of the heavenly, the less obviously useful is Virgil's presence. Everything to be learned here has to do with Christian perfection, and with that education comes, almost by osmosis, an understanding of how the true soul, the Christian one, moves through the various phases of nascence, life and afterlife with its changing bodies. Statius's discourse — at 78 lines (31–108) his longest by far, and one of the longest of the entire *Commedia* — is timed to end just as the terrace of the lustful is reached. In this manner, the poet shows not only that humans are unities of body and soul, but that because of this it is necessary to keep both parts healthy and holy.

At this point of the narrative, the pattern of noting the exemplars of chastity starts typically, with penitents singing an appropriate hymn, the *Summae Deus clementiae*, regarding the desire to be purged of lust, and calling upon Mary and a classical model of chastity (Diana). In starting to sing again, they evoke the names of chaste spouses, and precisely here, at the top of the terraces of Purgatory, the pattern changes: no names are given. Cynics might be quick to say that there are no such things as chaste spouses, but such a response would in this regard be out of keeping with the trends of medieval spirituality, which permitted and in some cases glorified people who lived in matrimony without intercourse. St Cecilia and her husband Valerian mark the *locus classicus* for this;[11] more recently, in the thirteenth century, Marie d'Oignies was but one woman with an international reputation for holiness who lived chastely with her husband.[12]

But living chastely within marriage was not an easy thing, perhaps not so much because of the passions of people but because of the strict and often (to us) inadvertently hilarious regulations that priests were told to use with their flock. Penitentials — guide books on how to judge sin and to allocate appropriate penance — were a minefield for all concerned. To illustrate this point, James Brundage created in 1987 a flow chart indicating when it would be licit for people to engage in sexual intercourse;[13] according to these guidelines, almost every person having sex would sin at some point,

---

11 Carolyn Muessig, 'Paradigms of Sanctity for Medieval Women', in *Models of Holiness in Medieval Sermons. Proceedings of the International Symposium (Kalamazoo, 4–7 May 1995)*, ed. by Beverly Mayne Kienzle (Louvain-la-Neuve: Fédération International des Instituts d'Études Médiévales, 1996), pp. 85–102.

12 Jennifer N. Brown, 'The Chaste Erotics of Marie d'Oignies and Jacques de Vitry', *Journal of the History of Sexuality* 19 (2010), 74–93.

13 James A. Brundage, *Law, Sex, and Christian Society in Medieval Europe* (Chicago, IL: University of Chicago Press, 1987), p. 162

and upon confession would need to do penance. But as Dyan Elliott has demonstrated, chaste couples could and did exist, and could and did serve as models for others.[14]

Entering the realm of the fixed stars, one finds a link between hagiographical history and St James, when he is referred to by Beatrice as a 'barone'. Here we see the direct influence of a book that was widely disseminated, and seen by many to be a literary model for a range of works, including the *Paradiso*. This is the part of the Codex Calixtinus often referred to as the *Historia Turpini*, which tells of how St James convinced Charlemagne to clear Iberia of the infidel. The *Historia* narrates how Charlemagne, exhausted from fighting, observed a massive body of stars in the sky, moving from the north and then across to the west, and then how St James appeared to him as a most handsome nobleman and beseeched him to restore religious order to Galicia and the rest of the peninsula. Here, Dante is clearly using the model of James as baron, and setting him among those same fixed stars that enthralled Charlemagne (although ironically, the *Historia*'s fixed stars change position and direction).[15]

In proceeding to examine Dante, James's questions seem to lack the diamond-edged precision that we saw in Statius's speech on the development of the body. This is because here the educative model is, interestingly, reflective not of the scholastic milieu but rather of the mendicant one, where student friars would be examined by a provincial minister in matters of faith in order to ensure the candidate could take up the office of preacher. As Neslihan Şenocak and Ian Wei — both of them experts in mendicant and university education — have noted, we do not know anything about pass rates, but one gets the impression that the less gifted would have been weeded out before any such examinations.[16] One witnesses, in the precision and readiness of Dante's answers, an expertise in the subject matter that far outstrips that of his former master Virgil when he was, so to speak, examined by the pilgrim back in *Purgatorio* xxv.

---

14 Dyan Elliott, *Spiritual Marriage. Sexual Abstinence in Medieval Wedlock* (Princeton, NJ: Princeton University Press, 1993).

15 See *The Chronicle of Pseudo-Turpin. Book IV of The Liber Sancti Jacobi (Codex Calixtinus)*, ed. and trans. by Kevin R. Poole (New York: Italica Press, 2014), pp. 7–9.

16 Both these scholars have kindly communicated this with me privately. Among their relevant publications are Neslihan Şenocak, *The Poor and the Perfect. The Rise of Learning in the Franciscan Order, 1209–1310* (Ithaca, NY: Cornell University Press, 2012), and Ian Wei, *Intellectual Culture in Medieval Paris. Theologians and the University, c.1100–1320* (Cambridge: Cambridge University Press, 2012).

Interest in the epistle of James changed radically around the time that Dante lived. For centuries the only notable commentary had been by Bede, although a short letter from Augustine discussed one verse regarding the role of work in salvation.[17] In the thirteenth century, it was once again Hugh of St Cher who seems to have been the writer of a new commentary on James, and it was he who followed the trends established by Pope Innocent III and St Anthony of Padua earlier in the century by identifying the three apostles most emblematic of the three greatest virtues: Peter of faith, James of hope, and John of charity.[18] It may well be that it was Dante's education at the Dominican *studium* at Santa Maria Novella that familiarised Dante with this trinity of apostles and their allocated virtues. Far from being fixed for centuries, Dante's religious reality was one that had changed from previous times. We see that many sermons based on the theme of the Epistle of James (1. 17) were delivered throughout Europe in the later Middle Ages, as this reading featured in the liturgy for the fourth Sunday after Easter, commonly known as Cantate Sunday: 'Omne datum optimum et omne donum perfectum desursum est descendens a Patre luminum apud quem non est transmutatio nec vicissitudinis obumbratio' [Every best gift, and every perfect gift, is from above, coming down from the Father of lights, with whom there is no change nor shadow of alteration].[19] Given the content of this verse, and the singing that pervades Dante's Paradise, we see a good match between content and character here, one that may not have been possible even fifty years before Dante wrote the *Commedia*.

The examples touched upon here — and many others present in these cantos — make clear the extent to which change is in the air in all three of the Twenty-Fives. This brings us back to our beginning, and to the notion that the very number twenty-five may be considered a significant symbol for change, for renewal, for remembering, so that one may act in an invigorated and improved manner.

---

17 On this theme in Augustine and its relation to Dante, see Debora Marletta, 'Aspects of Dante's Theology of Redemption. Eden, the Fall, and Christ in Dante with respect to Augustine' (doctoral thesis, University College London, 2011), p. 187.

18 Mulchahey, *'First the Bow is Bent in Study…'*, p. 203.

19 Johann-Baptist Schneyer, *Repertorium der lateinischen Sermones des Mittelalters für die Zeit von 1150–1350*, 11 vols, Beiträge zur Philosophie und Theologie des Mittelalters. Texte und Untersuchungen, 43 (Münster: Aschendorff, 1969–1990), vol. 9, p. 534.

Dante and the Number Twenty-Five

In the terms of Dante's cultural framework, the number twenty-five can be seen as an important one objectively and, for Dante, subjectively. Objectively, the number twenty-five can be linked to the passage of time, to the celebration of liturgical feasts, to salvific and terrestrial history, and even to a particularly relevant part of popular culture.[20]

Why the passage of time? Because in Florence, like in so many other places, the calendar year began on 25 March. The Roman calendar equated this date with the vernal equinox, but for medieval Europeans this date relied on a liturgical view of salvific history: given that Mary conceived on 25 March, the Saviour was able to enter the world as flesh, and thus the Feast of the Annunciation was observed on this same day. New life for humankind led to a new calendar year to mark the passage of time.

It is obvious, of course, but nine months later Jesus was born on 25 December (the date on which the Roman calendar marked the winter solistice). The two-hundred and seventy-five days between these two dates can be seen to be eleven times twenty-five days, but much more importantly the imprint of this numeral twenty-five led to its liturgical observance in other months of the year, and probably in another calendar-related time period, the fifteen-year period known as the indiction. Depending on where one lived, indictions, so essential for the dating of legal or diplomatic agreements, began either on 25 December or 24 September (not simply very nearly the twenty-fifth day of the month, but also the Roman calendar's autumnal equinox).

A strong argument can be made for the feasts of the twenty-fifth day to be among the most important of any day in the liturgical calendar. Here are just some of the major feasts of the universal church that fall on the twenty-fifth day:

- 25 March: the Annunciation

- 25 April: St Mark

- 25 May: St Bede, Gregory VII

---

20 Among the works relevant to the discussion of dates and feasts that follow are: John Harper, *The Forms and Orders of Western Liturgy from the Tenth to the Eighteenth Century* (Oxford: Oxford University Press, 1991); and *Computus and its Cultural Context in the Latin West, AD 300–1200: Proceedings of the 1st International Conference on the Science of Computus in Ireland and Europe, Galway, 14–16 July, 2006* (Turnhout: Brepols, 2010).

- 25 August: Louis the King; St Genesius (Genesius is regarded as the patron saint of those who work in the theatrical arts, and these seem to include lawyers and barristers)
- 25 November: St Catherine of Alexandria
- 25 December: Christmas
- 25 January: the conversion of St Paul

This is but a partial list of the more universally famous saints. There are other very important local saints with feasts on the twenty-fifth; these were the patron saints of Florence, Zenobius and Miniatus, whose feasts were on 25 May and 25 October respectively.

Like the indiction that could begin on 24 September, there were two major saints' feasts celebrated very near to the twenty-fifth. One is the 26 September feast of Sts Cosmas and Damian, who would soon become so important as patrons of the Medici family, and the other is the hugely significant feast of St John the Baptist held on 24 June; six months apart from Christmas and the Roman calendar's summer solstice, this feast was often considered throughout Western Christendom as a sort of mid-year festival, both liturgical and lay. For the purposes of this focussed liturgical calendar, one other feast — not a minor one — must not be forgotten. It is the feast of St James, the star attraction of *Paradiso* xxv, celebrated in the month of July and, not surprisingly, on the twenty-fifth day.

Finally, a further feast must be considered here, not simply for the sake of completeness but also to help us understand another aspect of the importance of the twenty-fifth day of the month. St Dismas was celebrated on 25 March. Overshadowed by the feast of the Annunciation, poor Dismas would rarely if ever get a look into liturgical festivities, but his feast is hugely symbolic. Tradition has it that St Dismas was the name of the good thief on the Cross next to Jesus. According to Scripture, Jesus promised Dismas that he would be in Heaven that day. The feast of Dismas is celebrated on 25 March because it was customarily considered that this was the actual date of the Crucifixion.[21]

---

21 I therefore find it very difficult to believe that Dante intended his comedic journey to begin on any day other than Friday 25 March 1300 — the symbolic value of this date would surely trump the more likely one, in terms of calendrical measurement, which is Friday 8 April 1300.

What else can be said about the twenty-fifth day of a month? It is also the day that Adam was created, on 25 March. Some held that this was the date on which Abraham sought to obey the order to sacrifice his son, Isaac, the subject of James's Epistle 2. 21–23:

> Abraham pater noster nonne ex operibus iustificatus est offerens Isaac filium suum super altare? Vides quoniam fides copperabatur operibus illius et ex operibus fides consummata est? Et suppleta est scriptura dicens credidit Abraham Deo et reputatum est illi ad iustitiam et amicus Dei appellatus est.

> [Was not Abraham our father justified by works, offering up Isaac his son upon the altar? Seest thou, that faith did co-operate with his works; and by works faith was made perfect? And the scripture was fulfilled, saying: Abraham believed God, and it was reputed to him to justice, and he was called the friend of God.]

These very lines, this very event, is implicit in *Paradiso* xxv. 88–90, when Dante answers James's fourth and final question regarding what promise hope holds to him: He says, 'Le nove e le Scritture antiche / pongon lo segno, ed esso lo mi addita, / de l'anime che Dio s'ha fatte amiche'. [The new Scriptures and the old set forth the target for the souls whom God has made his friends, and that fact points it out to me.]

To finish with the date of 25 March, there is an event that is obviously anti-scriptural but drawn by the weight of all the other important events of this day: there were some in medieval Europe who held that the Last Judgement would take place on this date. The religious calendar for the twenty-fifth is most imposing, but Dante is also reflecting an aspect of Florentine popular culture in his interest in the twenty-fifth day of March, because traditionally Florentines would eat bread that was made on 25 March in order to become fertile.

These are what could be termed objective reasons for Dante to take twenty-five seriously, but there are others that, although not shared by the entire populace, would be held to be of vital importance by our poet. In Book 4 of the *Convivio* (xxiv. 4), Dante discusses the divisions of the human life cycle. He says:

> Avemo dunque che la gioventute nel quarantacinquesimo anno si compie. E sì come l'adolescenzia è in venticinque anni che precede, montando, a la gioventute, così lo discendere, cioè la senettute, è [in] altrettanto tempo che succede a la gioventute; e così si termina la senettute nel settantesimo anno.

[Maturity is completed in the forty-fifth year. Just as adolescence lasts for the first twenty-five years, ascending toward maturity, so the descent, that is, old age, lasts for the same number of years following maturity; and so old age concludes in the seventieth year.]

Dante's division is one that is not unusual for his century, but it does differ from those of previous times in the Christian West. For earlier monks and clerics, life was more or less a steady continuum, and any age was a good age to convert and live well. Dante would not deny this, but he emphasises that there is a peak in human existence, and that peak runs from the twenty-fifth to the forty-fifth years of one's life.

Now, it is obvious that Dante sets the *Comedy* in the thirty-fifth year of his life, the apex of the arc, down from which he can look, Janus-like, to the past and to his future. But in the crafted autobiography of Dante's earlier years, the *Vita Nova*, we find something I believe to be significant:

> Io dico che, secondo l'usanza d'Arabia, l'anima sua nobilissima si partìo ne la prima ora del nono giorno del mese; e secondo l'usanza di Siria, ella si partìo nel nono mese de l'anno, però che lo primo mese è ivi Tisirin primo, lo quale a noi è Ottobre; e secondo l'usanza nostra, ella si partìo in quello anno de la nostra indizione, cioè de li anni Domini, in cui lo perfetto numero nove volte era compiuto in quello centinaio nel quale in questo mondo ella fue posta, ed ella fue de li cristiani del terzodecimo centinaio. (*VN.*, XXIX. 6)

> [I say, then, that according to the division of time in Italy, her most noble spirit departed from among us in the first hour of the ninth day of the month; and according to the division of time in Syria, in the ninth month of the year: seeing that Tisirin, which with us is October, is there the first month. Also she was taken from among us in that year of our reckoning (to wit, of the years of our Lord) in which the perfect number was nine times multiplied within that century wherein she was born into the world: which is to say, the thirteenth century of Christians.]

If Beatrice died on 8 June 1290, and if scholars are correct in believing Dante to have been born in late May 1265, then this makes him barely twenty-five years old at the moment of the death of his beloved. Dante's passage to manhood, to maturity, is linked inextricably to the most important moment of his artistic, if not emotional, life. In the midst of life is death, and we see this perfectly demonstrated with these dates. Dante's mature life, wherever it may have led him, changed the moment he became a man.

Moreover, that age of twenty-five coincides with the highly symbolic age at which, according to Numbers 8. 24, Levites could begin to be priests, and at which the Council in Trullo (held in Constantinople, 691–692) decreed that one could take religious orders; it is also the age at which one fully acquired legal rights in Roman law.[22]

As a result of this possible coincidence, it may be considered whether Dante's dark night of the soul might be reflected numerically. That dark night, as represented in his *Comedy*, would be the journey to and through Hell. If one were to count the divisions of the *Inferno* in which Dante met the souls of that cantica's human inhabitants — starting from the beginning of his journey, where he meets Virgil in the dark wood, to the bottom where he sees Judas, Brutus and Cassius before escaping to Purgatory — one finds twenty-five of them: one per year of his *iter* to maturity.[23]

Paradiso xxv ends with Dante's blindness that accompanies the sudden halt of the dance of the three apostles, who stop like tired rowers in unison. The first great rowers of antiquity were the Argonauts who are recalled, in an extremely precise manner, almost at the very end of the *Commedia*. In *Paradiso* xxxiii. 94–96, we read, after Dante sees everything in the universe all together at once: 'Un punto solo m'è maggior letargo / che venticinque secoli a la 'mpresa / che fé Nettuno ammirar l'ombra d'Argo'. [One point alone is greater forgetfulness to me than twenty-five centuries to the enterprise that made Neptune marvel at the shadow of the Argo.] In other words, because of the incapacity of his memory, Dante has forgotten more of what he perceived in that fleeting instant, in which he saw all things in unity, than what all of humanity has forgotten since the enterprise of the Argo, twenty-five hundred years ago.

---

22 'Haec est lex Levitarum: a viginti quinque annis et supra ingredientur ut ministrent in tabernaculo foederi'. [This is the law of the Levites: from twenty-five years old and upwards, they shall go in to minister in the tabernacle of the covenant.] See also *The Council in Trullo Revisited*, ed. by G. Nedungatt and M. Featherstone (Rome: Pontificio Istituto Orientale, 1995), pp. 87–88, and Emiel Eybel, 'Young Priests in Early Christianity', *Jahrbuch für Antike und Christentum*. Supplementary volume 22 (1995), 102–20. Regarding late medieval Florence, see Ilaria Taddei, 'La notion d'âge dans la Florence des XIVe et XVe siècles', *Mélanges de l'Ecole française de Rome. Moyen-Age* 118 (2006), 149–59.

23 The pilgrim meets human souls in the following areas of the *Inferno*: 1) dark wood; 2) the neutrals; 3) Limbo; 4) the lustful; 5) gluttons; 6) the avaricious and the prodigals; 7) the angry and the sullen; 8) heretics; 9) the violent against others; 10) the violent against one's self; 11) the violent against God; 12) panders and seducers; 13) flatterers; 14) simoniacs; 15) diviners; 16) barrators; 17) hypocrites; 18) thieves; 19) false counsellors; 20) schismatics; 21) counterfeiters; 22) fraudulent against relatives; 23) fraudulent against party or homeland; 24) fraudulent against guests; 25) fraudulent against rightful lords.

Everything in the flow of *Paradiso* xxxiii's narrative stops here, just like the apostles who stopped so suddenly. There is a sudden shift to the present tense. The rhythm breaks completely, and this helps us to understand completely the next line, 'Così la mente mia, tutta sospesa' [Thus my mind, entirely lifted up]. The Argonauts enter onto the domain of Neptune, just as a living man, Dante, enters into the realm of the blessed. The Christianization of antique myth, of classical religion, is completed right here. We recall John Scott's observation that in line 7 of *Paradiso* xxv, Dante hopes to return with 'altro vello' [with another fleece]; he can only accomplish this by changing Jason's fleece into that of Dante's civic patron.[24]

This Christianization of antique myth is completed by reference to the number twenty-five. Surely Dante did not absolutely need to use this number, or any number, here. Perhaps this number twenty-five would have been a throw-away detail anywhere it appeared in the *Comedy*. I highlight it for a number of reasons. One is that twenty-five is not a number used often in the *Comedy*; in fact, its appearance in *Paradiso*'s final canto marks its only explicit reference. If Dante were desperate to use this number in relation to the Argo, he could have used it to describe the number of the pairs of oarsmen, the same men who would have stopped from exhaustion just as the three saints in *Paradiso* xxv paused: twenty-five. He could have made a point of mentioning that Ovid's *Metamorphoses* consist precisely of 250 tales, or that poor Lucan met his death at the horribly young age of twenty-five. Instead, he uses it to amplify the ultimate change, from a classical to a Christian universe, and for Dante, this number twenty-five seems to be one he associates strongly with change.

In these cantos deeply packed with action, with science, and with theology, many changes are clearly seen. We move from the *fiche* of Hell to the uterus of Purgatory to the anticipation of the glorified body in Paradise, and from the hellish bodies of the thieves to the emaciated ones of Purgatory to the spiritual ones of Heaven. We move from mythology to science to theology, and from the hellish bad blood of Pistoia to the perfect blood that gives earthly life to the spilled blood that brings eternal life to James, the first apostle to be martyred. From darkness we move to fire to

---

24 On this transformation from classical to Christian writing, see Michelangelo Picone, 'Dante argonauta. La ricezione dei miti ovidiani nella *Commedia*', in *Ovidius redivivus. Von Ovid zu Dante*, ed. by M. Picone and B. Zimmermann (Stuttgart: M&P Verlag für Wissenschaft und Forschung, 1994), pp. 173–202. See also John A. Scott, *Understanding Dante* (Notre Dame, IN: University of Notre Dame Press, 2004), p. 296.

blinding light. In Hell we witness the monstrous body; in Purgatory the human body is explained before the fate of the blessed body is exposed in Paradise. Sex in *Inferno* is actual and violent; in *Purgatorio* it is described in its natural manner, and chastity is presented as an ideal; and in *Paradiso* the chaste apostles hold centre stage. We see how monstrous metamorphoses in Hell transform into a poetic union of wine and sun when discussing the human soul in Purgatory, and from then to consideration of how the perfection of the soul affects the fate of its partner, the body. We moreover see that St James is present in the Pistoia of sinner Vanni Fucci as a relic, and in Heaven as himself.

In short, the number twenty-five is not limited to infernal shifts or purgatorial progression but to the perfection of the Christian, where the embodiment of the three theological virtues meet and shock and blind him, a blinding that proves temporary and whose cure, like that of Saul, keeps the pilgrim on the road.

26. The Poetics of Trespassing

Elena Lombardi

On a first reading, one textual detail links the three canto Twenty-Sixes: the image of flames. In *Inferno* xxvi, the fraudulent counsellors are placed inside tongues of fire, and among them Virgil and Dante meet the two-pronged flame engulfing Ulysses and Diomedes. The speech that follows, retelling Ulysses's journey in the southern hemisphere, is considered one of the high points of the poem (and of world literature). In *Purgatorio* xxvi, the purging souls of the lustful lovers are surrounded by flames. Homosexual and heterosexual ranks meet and exchange embraces and kisses, shouting out examples of their erotic excesses. Here Dante encounters the soul of Guido Guinizzelli, the 'padre' [father] (*Purg.*, xxvi. 97) of the sweet new style ('dolce stil novo') previously celebrated in *Purgatorio* xxiv. 49–63 (especially line 57), as well as the Occitan poet Arnaut Daniel (*Purg.*, xxvi. 136–48). *Paradiso* xxvi brings to completion the so-called 'cycle of exams': Dante is tested on the last theological virtue, *caritas*, or divine love, by the Apostle John, and meets the soul of the first human being, Adam, with whom he discusses language and original sin, among other things. The blessed souls appear as flames in this canto as well.

These three cantos act like magnets within the *Comedy* — they attract multiple readings and diverse textual alliances, and they have drawn uninterrupted critical attention since the early commentaries. Indeed, the canto of Ulysses is one of the pillars of the *Comedy*, as the Greek hero stands as an exciting and threatening alter ego of Dante, and his flight beyond Hercules' pillars is an image of Dante's daring intellectual and poetic enterprise. With one unforgettable line, 'dei remi facemmo ali al folle volo' [of our oars we made wings for the mad flight] (*Inf.*, xxvi. 125), Dante makes

   http://dx.doi.org/10.11647/OBP.0119.05

Ulysses a creature of flight and folly, establishing a thread of navigation, flight, and madness that crosses the entire poem.

Echoes of the canto Twenty-Sixes resound throughout the poem at several levels. For instance, in the discourse on charity, Dante inserts the image of 'il mare dell'amor torto' [the sea of twisted love] (*Par.*, xxvi. 62), from which the love for God has saved the traveller by putting him on the shore of the right love:[1]

> ché l'essere del mondo e l'esser mio
> la morte ch'el sostenne perch' io viva,
> e quel che spera ogne fedel com' io,
>   con la predetta conoscenza viva,
> tratto m'hanno del mar de l'amor torto,
> e del diritto m'han posto a la riva. (*Par.*, xxvi. 58–63)

> [for the existence of the world and my existence, the death that he underwent that I might live, and what each believer hopes for, as I do, along with the aforesaid lively knowledge, have drawn me from the sea of twisted love and placed me on the shore of right love.]

In the expression 'mare dell'amor torto' readers encounter one of the great ciphers of the *Comedy*, which encapsulates and weaves complex and crucial discourses within the poem. With it, Dante brings them back to the beginning of his poem, just after a 'diritta via' [straight way] (*Inf.*, i. 3) is lost, to find him represented as a sailor that has just survived shipwreck, with the same rhyme 'riva' / 'viva' establishing a clear link between the passages:

> E come quei che con lena affannata,
> uscito fuor del pelago a la riva,
> si volge a l'acqua perigliosa e guata,
>   così l'animo mio, ch'ancor fuggiva,
> si volse a retro a rimirar lo passo
> che non lasciò già mai persona viva. (*Inf.*, i. 22–27)

> [And like one with laboring breath, come forth out of the deep onto the shore, who turns back to the perilous water and stares: so my spirit, still fleeing, turned back to gaze again at the pass that has never yet left anyone alive.]

---

1   For this image, and for *Paradiso* xxvi, see Elena Lombardi, 'Identità lirica e piacere linguistico: una lettura di *Paradiso* xxvi', forthcoming in *Studi danteschi*.

Readers are almost automatically redirected to Ulysses, who has navigated the sea of twisted love because of his excessive desire for knowledge, and to the beginning of *Purgatorio* and the non-mad flights of both the poet, his talent lifting the sails and leaving behind the 'mar sì crudele' [sea so cruel] (*Purg.*, i. 3), and the traveller, who witnesses the angel's anti-Ulyssean navigation-cum-flight (*Purg.*, ii. 31–36). From there, readers are led to the great discourse on just and twisted loves and on desire at the centre of *Purgatorio* (cantos xvi–xix), which ends, not by chance, with a Siren, full of pleasure ('di piacer [...] piena', *Purg.*, xix. 21), who twists sailors (and Ulysses himself, according to her) away from their journey. This is the same misleading and illusive pleasure that Beatrice criticizes in Eden, when accusing her lover of having forsaken her memory for the attraction of temporal and deceptive delights (*Purg.*, xxx. 131: 'imagini di ben [...] false' [false images of good]; and xxxi. 34–35: 'le presenti cose / col falso lor piacer' [present things with their false pleasure]), delights that have very complex and compelling links with Dante's own lyrical and philosophical past. The image of the sea then brings the readers to the beginning of Paradise, where natural desire helps all creatures to navigate 'lo gran mar de l'essere' [the great sea of being] (*Par.*, i. 113), but can also set the creatures off course when that desire is 'torto da falso piacere' [twisted by false pleasure] (i. 135). That very sea is, according to Piccarda Donati in *Paradiso* iii, the image of God: 'ell' è quel mare al qual tutto si move / ciò ch'ella crïa o che natura face' [he is that sea to which all moves that his will creates or Nature makes'] (*Par.*, iii. 86–87). In sum, the image of the twisted and right seas of love in *Paradiso* xxvi evokes a complex and structural discourse on natural desire, and its relation to reason, will, the senses, divine and human love, and poetry.

Moreover, each canto is deeply embedded in its own surroundings. In particular, *Inferno* xxvi is fastened to the following canto xxvii by both the image of navigation (employed literally by Ulysses and metaphorically by Guido da Montefeltro) and by a linguistic puzzle that involves grammatical languages (Latin and Greek) and the Lombard dialect. *Purgatorio* xxiv–xxvi, known as the 'cantos of the poets', constitute a rather compact cluster where Dante conceptualizes the novelty of his 'sweet new style' with the help of two predecessors (Bonagiunta da Lucca in canto xxiv and Guido Guinizzelli in canto xxvi) and through a very interesting excursus on embryology (canto xxv). Finally, *Paradiso* xxiv–xxvi, known as the 'cantos of exams', are very similar in structure and pattern: the examinations that Dante is required to pass on the three theological virtues in order to ascend to the highest (and only) section of Paradise, display a regular format.

Some crucial alliances, however, can be established solely within the three canto Twenty-Sixes.[2] In them, we see the merging of two great fault lines of the *Comedy*: the discourse of poetry (poetic ambition and poetic authority) merges and clashes with that of desire (erotic and intellectual alike). Such themes are threaded by the equally crucial discourse on language. The expression 'fault lines' is employed consciously: these are the elements that 'make and break' the *Comedy* — language, desire, and poetic authority constitute the *Comedy*'s strength and vulnerability. All such themes are also tied to the question of transgression, which in these very cantos is embodied and consolidated by the figure of a tri-headed alias for the poet-traveller, Ulysses — Adam — Dante, a metamorphic and unstable figure that attracts and deflects Dante's challenge to established genres, established languages, and to the very representation of the divine.

My reading of the cantos focuses on the themes of language, desire and trespassing, and of the three-headed alias, but, to begin on a somewhat light note and to do justice to how excited and daunted one feels when reading these three cantos, it is worth taking a quick look at another superficial *trait d'union* between them: the somewhat over-excited reaction of the traveller upon meeting the three great souls, which measures not only the magnitude of the three characters, but also the authorial excitement in writing or re-writing them. When hearing that Ulysses and Diomedes are trapped in the double burning tongue, Dante behaves in a rather childish manner:

> 'S'ei posson dentro da quelle faville
> parlar', diss' io, 'maestro, assai ten priego
> e ripriego, che 'l priego vaglia mille,
>   che non mi facci de l'attender niego
> fin che la fiamma cornuta qua vegna;
> vedi che del disio ver' lei mi piego!' (*Inf.*, xxvi. 64–69)

> ['If they can speak within those flames', I said, 'master, much do I beg you, and beg again that each prayer may be worth a thousand, that you not refuse to wait until the horned flame comes here: see that I bend toward it with desire!']

2 For previous vertical readings of the canto Twenty-Sixes, see Peter Hawkins, 'Virtuosity and Virtue: Poetic Self-Reflection in the Commedia', *Dante Studies* 98 (1980), 1–18; Franco Fido, 'Writing Like God — or Better? Symmetries in Dante's 26th and 27th Cantos of the *Commedia*', *Italica* 53 (1986), 250–64; Sebastiano Valerio, 'Lingua, retorica e poetica nel canto XXVI del *Paradiso*', *L'Alighieri* 44 (2003), 83–104.

Upon hearing that he has been speaking to the soul of his dear precursor Guido Guinizzelli, Dante stages himself within a fairly remote simile from Statius' *Thebaid* (v. 710–24), half-comparing himself to the sons of Hypsipyle saving their mother by throwing themselves in the middle of the guards who are escorting her to capital punishment.

> Quali ne la tristizia di Ligurgo
> si fer due figli a riveder la madre,
> tal mi fec' io, ma non a tanto insurgo,
> quand' io odo nomar sé stesso il padre
> mio e de li altri miei miglior che mai
> rime d'amore usar dolci e leggiadre. (*Purg.*, xxvi. 94–99)

> [Such as in Lycurgus' grief the two sons became, seeing their mother again: so did I become — though I do not rise so high — when I hear our father name himself, the father of me and of the others, my betters, who ever used sweet and graceful rhymes of love.]

Finally, again from the *Thebaid* (vi. 854–59, with an antecedent in *Aeneid* iv. 442–49) comes the slightly odd simile with which Dante describes his desire to meet Adam, that of a tree stretched by strong winds. Very much like with Ulysses, here the traveller 'bends in desire' toward Adam:

> Come la fronda che flette la cima
> nel transito del vento, e poi si leva
> per la propria virtù che la soblima,
> fec' io in tanto in quant' ella diceva,
> stupendo, e poi mi rifece sicuro
> un disio di parlare ond' ïo ardeva. (*Par.*, xxvi. 85–90)

> [Like a branch that bends its summit at the passing of the wind and then lifts itself again, its own strength driving it upward: so did I as she spoke, marveling, and then I gained confidence again from a desire to speak that burned within me.]

To Dante's elastic desire, Adam responds with the equally odd image of the restless animal under cover (ll. 97–102), which has sparked much discussion about whether it represents a war-horse or a cat.[3] Such stretchings

---

3 *Par.*, xxvi. 97–102: 'Talvolta un animal coverto broglia, / sì che l'affetto convien che si paia / per lo seguir che face a lui la 'nvoglia; / e similmente l'anima primaia / mi facea trasparer per la coverta / quant' ella a compiacermi venìa gaia' [Sometimes a hidden

and bendings and burnings illustrate the quintessential narrative of the *Commedia*: an ardent desire for bursting into language, for telling new stories, or retelling them anew, and for trespassing into poetry.

Language

Insofar as language is concerned, the canto Twenty-Sixes provide a wonderful microcosm of Dante's non-conventional, ever-flexible, poetry-obsessed linguistic thought.[4] In order to reconstruct such a complex scenario, it is helpful to begin with the end, with Adam's famous observations on the mutability of language. While in his *De vulgari eloquentia* Dante had claimed that Hebrew was the original sacred language co-created with Adam, which had been the universal language until Babel, and the language of grace until the diaspora (*DVE.* I. iv–vii), in *Paradiso* xxvi he features Adam as not only the user, but also the maker of his language, having him mention 'l'idioma ch'io usai e che io fei' [the language that I spoke and that I devised] (l. 114). Adam explains that while the faculty of speech is a work of nature, language, since its inception, has been a mutable system:

> La lingua ch'io parlai fu tutta spenta
> innanzi che a l'ovra inconsummabile
> fosse la gente di Nembròt attenta:
> ché nullo effetto mai razïonabile,
> per lo piacere uman che rinnovella
> seguendo il cielo, sempre fu durabile.
> Opera naturale è ch'uom favella;
> ma così o così, natura lascia
> poi fare a voi secondo che v'abbella. (*Par.*, xxvi. 124–32)

> [The language that I spoke was all extinct before Nimrod's people became intent on the unfinishable work, for no rational effect, because of human preference, which changes following the heavens, has ever been enduring. It is a natural operation that man speaks, but whether in this way or that, Nature allows you to do as it may please you.]

---

animal stirs in such a way that its affect appears as its covering follows it; similarly the first-made soul made me see through its wrapping how gaily it came to please me]. A quick browse of the commentaries to these lines from the Dartmouth Dante Project, http://dante.dartmouth.edu/search.php, gives a sense of the controversies that this image has sparked: see in particular Hollander and Fosca *ad locum*.

4   On Dante's linguistics and Adam's language see Elena Lombardi, *The Syntax of Desire. Language and Love in Augustine, the Modistae, Dante* (Toronto: University of Toronto Press, 2007), pp. 121–60.

Adam denies any degree of stability even to Hebrew, pointing out that the language he used was already extinct prior to Babel. Even the name of God, the 'sign of all signs', was subjected to the fluctuations of time. It first was *I* and only then *El*, whilst in the *De vulgari eloquentia* (I. iv. 4) he had argued that the first word ever pronounced by Adam was the name of God, *El*.

> Pria ch'i' scendessi a l'infernale ambascia,
> *I* s'appellava in terra il sommo bene
> onde vien la letizia che mi fascia;
>   e *El* si chiamò poi: e ciò convene,
> ché l'uso dei mortali è come fronda
> in ramo, che sen va e altra vene. (*Par.*, xxvi. 133–38)

[Before I descended to the oppression of Hell, the highest Good, whence comes the gladness that envelopes me, was called *I* on earth and later was called *El*. And that is necessary, for the usage of mortals is like a leaf on the branch, which departs and another comes.]

The explanations for the two names of God are diverse and convincing: while *El* is traditionally understood as the most typical of the Hebrew names for God, *I* can be interpreted as a simple letter, a number, a shortened form for *Ia*.[5] More significantly, this is, as Zygmunt Barański observes, 'a perfect synthetic example of the instability of human linguistic creation'.[6] The two other canto Twenty-Sixes precisely dramatize such fickleness, diversity and humanity of language, but also its creativity and poetic nature.

As mentioned earlier, in *Inferno* xxvi, Dante creates a veritable riddle with regards to language, beginning with the lines in which Virgil bids the eager pilgrim to hold his tongue and let him do the speaking because 'the Greeks' might disdain his speech, positing an inextricable question of language and style:[7]

> Lascia parlare a me, ch'i' ho concetto
> ciò che tu vuoi; ch'ei sarebbero schivi,
> perch'e' fuor greci, forse del tuo detto. (*Inf.*, xxvi. 73–75)

---

5 For the different names of God, see Gino Casagrande, "I s'appellava in terra il sommo bene" (*Par.*, XXVI. 134)', *Aevum* 50 (1976), 249–73.

6 Zygmunt Barański, 'Dante's Biblical Linguistics', *Lectura Dantis* 5 (1989), 105–43 (p. 126).

7 For the riddle of language in *Inferno* xxvi and xxvii, see Elena Lombardi, 'Plurilingualism *sub specie aeternitatis*. Language/s in Dante's *Commedia*', in *Dante's Plurilingualism. Authority, Vulgarization, Subjectivity*, ed. by M. Gragnolati, S. Fortuna and J. Trabant (Oxford: Legenda, 2010), pp. 133–47.

[Let me speak, for I have conceived what you wish; for perhaps they would shun, because they were Greeks, your words.]

In the *captatio benevolentiae* that follows (ll. 79–84), Virgil appears to address the heroes with the formalities of the 'alta tragedìa' [high tragedy] (*Inf.,* xx. 113), using the 'parola ornata' [ornamented speech] (*Inf.,* ii. 67) that traditionally belonged to the 'grammatical' languages, Latin and Greek. In the *De vulgari eloquentia* (I. i. 3 and I. ix 11) such languages are posited as the antidote to the unruliness and degradation of the vernacular. However, at the beginning of the next canto, Virgil's supposedly lofty and ornate *licentia* — 'la licenza del dolce poeta' [the permission of my sweet poet] (*Inf.,* xxvii. 3) — is overheard as spoken in dialect by Guido da Montefeltro, who reduces the presumably highly ornate ending of his speech to a quite basic, popular, and comic language.

> 'O tu a cu' io drizzo
> la voce e che parlavi mo' lombardo,
> dicendo "Istra ten va, più non t'adizzo"'. (*Inf.,* xxvii. 19–21)

['O you to whom I direct my voice and who were just now speaking Lombard, saying: "*Istra* you may go, I incite you no further"'.]

Moreover, in *Inferno* xxvi and xxvii, Dante also dramatizes the torturous nature of utterance, underlining what Leo Spitzer calls 'the self-mutilating, sadistic power of speech'[8] with Ulysses's painful expression through the tongue of fire (xxvi. 85–89) and the comparison of Guido's language to a torture machine (xxvii. 7–15). The puzzle of language in *Inferno* xxvi and xxvii, and the reference to the pain of utterance, represent the grotesque inscription of the fickleness of human language. In this truly post-babelic realm, high style and ruled language clash with comic style and Lombard dialect to create a parodic and disconcerting effect on the reader. Paradigmatically, in the pouch of evil counsellors who used their speech for sinful purposes, there is no difference between the 'ornamented language' of the classics and humble dialect: they both turn grotesque, as well as painful.

Purgatorio xxvi is the only place in the *Comedy* where a substantial excerpt of a foreign language is recorded, and it has the same puzzling

---

8   Leo Spitzer, 'Speech and Language in *Inferno* XIII', in *Representative Essays* (Stanford, CA: Stanford University Press, 1988), pp. 143–71 (p. 155).

effect on the reader as the riddle of *Inferno* xxvi. Dante pays homage to one of his poetic masters, Arnaut Daniel, from whom he had 'borrowed' and transported into Italian the complex sestina strophe, and to whom, and whose language, he now lends his terzina. As opposed to the diverging extremes of high ruled language and dialect, here Dante offers his readers an extract in Occitan, the foreign variant of the very 'illustrious vernacular' that the *De vulgari eloquentia* seeks as an alternative to both Latin and dialect. The linguistic shock of a long passage in Occitan is devised, in my view, precisely to flag up the role of the vernacular in its quintessential poetic form. Moreover, as opposed to Ulysses's torturous and fatigued speech, Arnaut speaks freely and liberally:

> El cominciò liberamente a dire:
> '*Tan m'abellis vostre cortes deman,*
> *qu'ieu no me puesc ni voill a vos cobrire.*
> *Ieu sui Arnaut, que plor e vau cantan;*
> *consiros vei la passada folor,*
> *e vei jausen lo joi qu'esper, denan.*
> *Ara vos prec, per aquella valor*
> *que vos guida al som de l'escalina,*
> *sovenha vos a temps de ma dolor!'.*
> Poi s'ascose nel foco che li affina. (*Purg.*, xxvi. 139–48)

[He began freely to say: '*So pleasing to me is your courteous request, that I cannot nor will not hide myself from you. I am Arnaut, who weep and go singing; with chagrin I view my past folly, and rejoicing I see ahead the joy I hope for. Now I beg you, by the Power that guides you to the summit of the stairway, remember my suffering at the appropriate time!'* Then he hid himself in the fire that refines them.]

Quite aptly we find here a beautiful thread that joins *Paradiso* xxvi and *Purgatorio* xxvi. To describe the role of human pleasure in language, Adam uses a Provençal word — 'v'abbella' (*Par.*, xxvi. 132) — which recurs in the *Comedy* only in Arnaut's speech, where he expresses his joy at meeting Dante as '*Tan m'abellis vostre cortes deman*' (*Purg.*, xxvi. 140).

As in *Inferno* xxvi, Arnaut's speech is a matter of the inversion of both language and style. As a poet, the 'historical' Arnaut exercised the so-called *trobar clus* (a formally difficult and complex poetics) whereas Dante rewrites him in a much lighter form, technically called *trobar leu*. Moreover, in Arnaut's excerpt we find many keywords of courtly poetry that are somehow re-semanticized in a Christian and purging mode, as shown, for instance, by the last word 'affina' (l. 148), technically the courtly word for the art of poetry (the tuning and perfecting of the song) here turned into the operation of the purgatorial fire. With this excerpt, Dante shows the adaptability of the poetic vernacular and points out that this language not only beautifully and elegantly expresses the matter of love, but is indeed able to convey the spiritual discourse as finely.

Arnaut's experience of language is one of craftsmanship. Like Adam, Arnaut is the forger of his language, indeed a 'miglior fabbro del parlar materno' [a better fashioner of his mother tongue] (*Purg.*, xxvi., 117). However, while Adam is a motherless man — 'vir sine matre, vir sine lacte' [the man who never had a mother nor drank her milk] (*DVE*. I. vi. 1) — Arnaut shapes his mother tongue. This brings into focus a crucial aspect of Dante's linguistics: the feminine and maternal aspect of the vernacular, the language that, with the exception of Adam, all human beings learn 'without any formal instruction, by imitating our nurses' ('sine omni regola, nutricem imitantes', *DVE*. I. i. 2).[9]

Thus, Adam's statement on the mutability of all languages, which is central to the poetics of the *Commedia*, is illustrated from the vantage point of the canto Twenty-Sixes on the one hand by the demolition of ruled and authoritative languages (when Virgil's lofty speech is assimilated by Guido's dialect) and, on the other, by the elevation of the poetic use of the 'maternal' vernacular (Arnaut's excerpt) to a very relevant spiritual status.

Desire and Trespassing

Crucially, the three canto Twenty-Sixes are about desire.[10] Ulysses is the image for the desire for knowledge and experience — that which is established at the beginning of the *Convivio* as the very aim of the human being: 'Sì come dice lo Filosofo nel principio della Prima Filosofia, tutti li uomini naturalmente desiderano di sapere' [As the Philosopher says at the beginning of the *Metaphysics*, all men naturally desire to possess knowledge]

---

9   On this aspect, see Gary Cestaro, *Dante and the Grammar of the Nursing Body* (Notre Dame, IN: University of Notre Dame Press, 2003), and Sara Fortuna and Manuele Gragnolati, '"Attaccando al suo capezzolo le mie labbra ingorde": corpo, linguaggio e soggettività da Dante ad *Aracoeli* di Elsa Morante', *Nuova corrente* 55 (2008), 85–123.

10 For the theme of desire in Dante's work, see Elena Lombardi, *The Wings of the Doves: Love and Desire in Dante and Medieval Culture* (Montreal: McGill-Queen's University Press, 2012).

(*Conv.*, I. i. 1). Such a natural impulse transforms Ulysses's circular journey, his *nostos* towards Ithaca, where other, more familiar desires would attract him, into a mad linear tangent toward the unknown:

> 'Quando
> mi diparti' da Circe, che sottrasse
> me più d'un anno là presso a Gaeta,
> prima che sì Enëa la nomasse,
>   né dolcezza di figlio, né la pieta
> del vecchio padre, né 'l debito amore
> lo qual dovea Penelopè far lieta,
>   vincer potero dentro a me l'ardore
> ch'i' ebbi a divenir del mondo esperto
> e de li vizi umani e del valore'. (*Inf.*, xxvi. 90–99)

[When I departed from Circe, who held me back more than a year there near Gaeta, before Aeneas gave it that name, neither the sweetness of a son, nor compassion for my old father, nor the love owed to Penelope, which should have made her glad, could conquer within me the ardour that I had to gain experience of the world and of human vices and worth.]

The keyword of these lines is the word 'ardore', the burning desire that compels the Greek hero to forego all other dutiful loves (to son, father, wife, homeland) and impels him relentlessly on his quest for the experience of human worth and vices. It is important to stress that this burning desire is part of Ulysses's story, not of his 'sin': the turning away from localized desires toward a more important, higher aim is precisely how Dante understood the way in which the Christian must desire God, for instance in the fourth book of the *Convivio* and in the central cantos of the *Purgatorio*. With Ulysses, however, Dante inscribes in Hell an idolatrous desire for knowledge and experience, one that makes itself God, as he had already done with Francesca and erotic desire in the fifth canto of *Inferno*.

The terrace of lust evokes the theme of erotic desire, and its population of poets invokes the specific declension of erotic desire that is lyric poetry, as the sublimation and extension of desire in language. The way in which Dante stages the relation between lust and love poetry is very polarized, quite the opposite to what he had done in the episode of Francesca in *Inferno* v, where the two were presented as dangerously similar. While Arnaut Daniel transfers with apparent ease his refined courtly language to spiritual matters, the other poet, Guido Guinizzelli, defines (heterosexual) lust quite brutally, with the example of Pasiphae's coupling with the bull.[11]

> Nostro peccato fu ermafrodito
> Ma poiché non servammo umana legge,
> Seguendo come bestie l'appetito
>   In obbrobrio di noi, per noi si legge,
> Quando partinci, il nome di colei
> Che s'imbestiò ne le 'mbestiate schegge. (*Purg.*, xxvi. 82–87)

[Our sin was hermaphrodite; but because we did not keep human law, following our appetite like beasts, in our own reproach we read out, when we part, the name of her who made herself a beast within the beast-shaped planks.]

By choosing to illustrate heterosexual excess through bestiality, Dante evokes one of the subspecies of lust, species crossing, which, according to Aquinas, is by far the worst form of lust, because it goes beyond the bounds of humanity.[12] Thus, by having Guido Guinizzelli quote the example of Pasiphae, Dante seems to draw the reader's attention to the ultimate similarity *sub specie aeternitatis* of two extreme happenings of what in *Inferno* v he discusses ambiguously as 'love': on the material/bodily side, the extreme sexual choice of 'species crossing', on the intellectual/spiritual side, the extreme expansion of courtly poetry.

The discussion of charity in *Paradiso* xxvi verges again on the role of love and desire in the soul's dealing with the divine, a desire that is at once rational and passionate. Dante discusses divine love first 'per filosofici argomenti' [by philosophical arguments] (l. 25), explaining it rationally as the necessary desire for the highest and most perfect good, and supporting his speech with evidence from philosophical and scriptural authorities (*Par.*, xxvi. 25–45). Yet, when the apostle asks him to verify his belief in a rather more passionate way, a new mystical lexicon, powerfully erotic, erupts into his speech. In the discourse on love of *Paradiso* xxvi, we find reflections of the other canto Twenty-Sixes. In the philosophical syllogism

---

11 For the definition of lust in the terrace of the lustful, see Elena Lombardi, '"Che libido fe' licito in sua legge". Lust and Law, Reason and Passion in Dante', in *Dantean Dialogues. Engaging with the Legacy of Amilcare Iannucci*, ed. by M. Kilgour and E. Lombardi (Toronto: University of Toronto Press, 2013), pp. 125–54.

12 Thomas Aquinas, *Summa Theologiae*, IIaIIae, q. 154, aa. 11–12.

about the greatest good, there is an echo of Ulysses' fixation with the idea of a higher good that must be pursued by overcoming all other goods, and in the quite blunt mystical language, a trace of the instinctual passion of the lustful.

The passionate desire for God is described with two images, the 'pulling of the heart' and the 'biting of the heart'.

> 'Ma dì ancor se tu senti altre corde
> tirarti verso lui, sì che tu suone
> con quanti denti questo amor ti morde'.
> [...]
> Però ricominciai: 'Tutti quei morsi
> che posson far lo cor volgere a Dio,
> a la mia caritate son concorsi'. (*Par.*, xxvi. 49–51; 55–57)

> ['But say again if you feel other cords drawing you toward him, so that you sound out with how many teeth this love bites you' [...] Therefore I began again: 'All the piercings that can turn our hearts to God have worked together in my charity'.]

Lino Pertile has explained the 'pulling of the heart' as one of the fundamental metaphors for the reciprocity between divine and human love in Heaven.[13] The 'biting of the heart' is less recognisably religious, and has an interesting past. It originates in Boethius, who employs it to describe the way the pleasures of the flesh hassle and sting those who indulge in them, eventually biting their smitten hearts.[14] With a similar meaning Dante employs such images in two songs which celebrate a 'lustful' and painful love: the 'stony rhyme' *Così nel mio parlar* ('la morte che ogni senso / co li denti d'Amor già mi manduca' [death which already is devouring all my senses with the teeth of Love]; ll. 31–32) and the late 'mountain song' *Amor da che conven ch'io pur mi doglia* ('per che l'armato cor da nulla è morso'

---

13 Lino Pertile, '"La punta del disio": storia di una metafora dantesca', *Lectura Dantis* 7 (1990), 3–28 (pp. 22–23). For the pulling of the heart with ropes, see also D. Pirovano, 'A la riva del diritto amore: Paradiso XXVI', in *Dante e il vero amore. Tre letture dantesche* (Pisa: Serra, 2009), pp. 91–126 (esp. pp. 111–12).

14 *De consolatione Philosophiae* iii, poem 7: 'habet hoc voluptas omnis / stimulis agit fruentes / apium par volantum, / ubi grata mella fudit, / fugit et nimis tenaci / ferit icta corda morsu'. In Boethius, *Theological Tractates; The Consolation of Philosophy*, ed. by H. F. Stewart and E. K. Rand, trans. S. J. Tester (Cambridge, MA: Harvard University Press, 1973).

[nothing bites through to her heart within its armour]; ll. 73–74).[15] Both songs can be viewed as part of Dante's own *trobar clus*, a celebration of harsh loves through difficult language and complex style, which includes, for the 'stony' sequence, the appropriation of the Provençal sestina. Thus, a rather resistant memory of Dante's own controversial lyric past is inscribed in the celebration of charity in *Paradiso*, a further testimony to both the creativity of the poetic vernacular and the irreducibility of desire.

In *Paradiso* xxvi, Dante registers another desire, much more akin to Ulysses' transgressive ardour. Adam's desire for the forbidden fruit is defined as trespassing — 'il trapassar del segno' [going beyond the mark] (*Par.*, xxvi. 117) — and almost automatically recalls the same injunction and defiance on the part of Ulysses in going beyond the geographical limits of the known world, the warnings ('riguardi', *Inf.*, xxvi. 108) posited by Hercules on the coasts of Spain and Africa. The trespassing of both Ulysses and Adam is impelled by their desire for the forbidden unknown. Incidentally, the lustful too have trespassed: they have forced open another crucial border, the limits that reason and the law impose on human passions: 'non servammo umana legge, / seguendo come bestie l'appetito' [we did not keep human law, following our appetite like beasts] (*Purg.*, xxvi. 83–84).

When looking at the canto Twenty-Sixes together, it is helpful to drop the distinction between intellectual and erotic desire, secular and divine love. Dante's long and thorny reflection on this topic shows that desire is initially one, only later bifurcating into intellectual and sensual; and that the possibility of swerving toward good or bad ends is inbuilt in desire, which comes to require the control of the will. Desire is trespassing: it is the force, drive, momentum that is in itself neither positive nor negative. It impels the self outside of its limits and borders, toward the other (the beloved, the object of knowledge, God) and both imbalances and satisfies the self, both imperils and saves it. Adam and Ulysses show that desire is both transgressive and necessary. Both lust and charity depend on a very primal, instinctual unbalancing of the self.

Trespassing towards the unknown by means of desire is also what Dante does in his *Comedy*, as a traveller who, like Ulysses, is concerned

---

15 In *Purgatorio*, this image recurs in a rather more obvious manner as the 'biting of remorse' (*Purg.*, xxxi. 88: 'Tanta riconoscenza il cor mi morse'), which Valentina Atturo has shown to be linked to the palinody of Dante's lyric past: see Valentian Atturo, 'Dalla pelle al cuore. La "puntura" e il "colpo della pietra", dai trovatori a Petrarca', *Studi romanzi* 8 (2012), 85–101. However, the image of the biting of the heart in Heaven retains the eroticism of the lyric image rather than the palinode of Purgatory.

about the madness of his enterprise, and as a poet who is aware that his great work is a flight towards the unknown and the forbidden. At the outset of the journey, Dante voices his fears of geographical and authorial trespassing in terms of folly: 'temo la mia venuta non sia folle' [I fear lest my coming may be folly] (*Inf.*, ii. 35). A comparative reading of the canto Twenty-Sixes offers the coordinates of Dante's position, by offering us two views of 'folly'. In *Inferno* xxvi, Ulysses, the epic hero, forcing his readers to gaze ahead, celebrates his 'folle volo' (l. 125), his mad and daring push through Hercules' pillars. In *Purgatorio* xxvi, Arnaut, the lyric poet, casts a somewhat melancholic backward gaze ('*consiros*', l. 123) to his past folly ('*pasada follor*', *ibid.*). Dante's present is in the encounter of these two forces; the forward drive of the future epic and the sweet call of the lyric past: one never overcomes the other, and both make the originality and greatness of the *Comedy*.

Ulysses-Adam-Dante

The theme of desire as trespassing fosters in these three cantos the moulding of the three-headed alias Ulysses-Adam-Dante. As mentioned above, the concept of 'il trapassar del segno' (*Par.*, xxvi. 117) establishes a firm link between Ulysses and Adam.[16] Throughout the poem, however, the equivalence between Dante and Ulysses (and between journey and poem) is also established on the grounds of folly and ambition, in the comparison between Dante's 'venuta folle' in *Inferno* ii. 35 and Ulysses's 'folle volo' in *Inferno* xxvi. 125, and throughout *Paradiso* ii. 1–9, where Dante describes himself as a new Ulysses (and us, his readers, as Ulysses's crew) embarking on a journey in uncharted seas.[17] Interestingly, Dante is also presented as

---

16 The identification of Ulysses and Adam is forcefully proposed in Bruno Nardi, *Dante e la cultura medievale* (Bari: Laterza, 1949), pp. 125–34, and it is widely, if not universally, accepted.

17 Compare the two 'short orations' to their sailors. *Inferno* xxvi. 112–20: '"O frati", dissi, "che per cento milia / perigli siete giunti a l'occidente, / a questa tanto picciola vigilia / d'i nostri sensi ch'è del rimanente / non vogliate negar l'esperïenza, / di retro al sol, del mondo sanza gente. / Considerate la vostra semenza: / fatti non foste a viver come bruti, / ma per seguir virtute e canoscenza"' ['O brothers', I said, 'who through a hundred thousand perils have reached the west, to this so brief vigil of our senses that remains, do not deny the experience, following the sun, of the world without people. Consider your sowing: you were not made to live like brutes, but to follow virtue and knowledge]. *Paradiso* ii. 1–9: 'O voi che siete in piccioletta barca, / desiderosi d'ascoltar, seguiti / dietro al mio legno che cantando varca, / tornate a riveder li vostri liti: / non vi mettete in pelago, ché forse, / perdendo me, rimarreste smarriti. / L'acqua ch'io prendo

Ulysses in *Purgatorio* xxvi, when the purging souls praise him as one who travels in order to acquire experience, literally to 'get experience on board', the words 'esperienza' and 'morir' pointing quasi-parodically to *Inferno* xxvi.

> 'Beato te, che de le nostre marche'
> ricominciò colei che pria m'inchiese,
> 'per morir meglio, esperïenza imbarche'. (*Purg.*, xxvi. 73–75)

> ['Blessed are you, who from these border lands of ours', began the shade who had inquired of me previously, 'are taking on a cargo of experience, so as to die better'.]

In *Paradiso* xxvi, Dante is linked to both Ulysses and Adam. To Ulysses, as mentioned before, when he describes himself in the discourse of charity as someone who has survived 'the sea of twisted love' and landed on the shore of divine love (ll. 62–63). To Adam, for the fact that Adam himself draws many parallels between himself and the traveller: not only it turns out that they have spent the same time in Eden (ll. 139–42), but he also pitches his own story in Dantean terms, whereby Eden where he first dwelled is 'l'eccelso giardino, ove costei / a così lunga scala ti dispuose' [the high garden where she there readied you for so long a stairway] (ll. 110–11), and Limbo, where he waited in anguish for Christ's harrowing of Hell, is just the place 'onde mosse tua donna Virgilio' [whence your lady sent Virgil] (l. 118). Moreover, Dante at the threshold of the Empyrean can be seen as a new Adam, a reformed first man.[18]

The equivalence between Adam, Ulysses and Dante begs one further question: if Adam stands for the biblical, and Ulysses for the epic, what does Dante stand for? According to the point of view of the canto Twenty-Sixes, he is a lyric poet (as illustrated by Guido and Arnaut), armed with

---

già mai non si corse; / Minerva spira, e conducemi Appollo, / e nove Muse mi dimostran l'Orse' [O you who in little barks, desirous of listening, have followed after my ship that sails onward singing: turn back to see your shores again, do not put out on the deep sea, for perhaps, losing me, you would be lost; the waters that I enter have never before been crossed; Minerva inspires and Apollo leads me, and nine Muses point out to me the Bears]. See also Maria Corti, *Percorsi dell'invenzione. Il linguaggio poetico e Dante* (Turin: Einaudi, 1993), pp. 147–63.

18 On this point, see in particular Giovanni Getto, *Canto XXVI. Lectura Dantis Scaligera, Paradiso* (Florence: Le Monnier, 1971).

his unruly and beautiful mother tongue (as sanctioned by Adam), facing his future madness (his own Ulyssean 'folle volo') with his past folly ('*la passada follor*'), the 'excess' of lyric poetry even in its most experimental and painful declensions.

In conclusion, I shall turn again to a quite minute textual point, which helps connect the several threads explored so far. As seen at the beginning of this reading, one very superficial link between the three cantos is the fact that the characters are represented as engulfed, surrounded, or appearing as flames. The keyword for the episode of Ulysses, 'ardore' (*Inf.*, xxvi. 97) is also related to burning. Although we do not find the word 'ardore' in the other canto Twenty-Sixes, we do find the verb 'ardo' [I burn], in both cases enclosed in a very similar rhyme scheme. At the beginning of *Purgatorio* xxvi, the lustful souls approach Dante and Guinizzelli addresses him:

> poi verso me, quanto potëan farsi,
> certi si fero, sempre con riguardo
> di non uscir dove non fosser arsi.
> 'O tu che vai, non per esser più tardo,
> ma forse reverente, a li altri dopo,
> rispondi a me che 'n sete e 'n foco ardo'. (*Purg.*, xxvi. 13–18)

[Then some approached me as closely as they could, always taking care not to come out where they would not be burned. 'O you who are walking behind the others, not because you are slower, but perhaps reverent, answer me, who am burning in thirst and fire'.]

At the beginning of the speech on charity, Dante recalls his very first meeting with Beatrice:

> 'perché la donna che per questa dia
> regïon ti conduce, ha ne lo sguardo
> la virtù ch'ebbe la man d'Anania'
> Io dissi: 'al suo piacere e tosto e tardo
> vegna remedio a li occhi, che fuor porte
> quand' ella entrò col foco ond' io sempr' ardo'. (*Par.*, xxvi. 10–15)

['for the lady who leads you through this bright region has in her glance the power of the hand of Ananias'. I said: 'At her pleasure, soon or late, let the remedy come for my eyes, which were the gates when she entered with the fire that always burns in me'.]

As I discuss elsewhere, 'sguardo: ardo: tardo' is a very common lyric rhyme.[19] In it, we find the memory of Dante's past: of the first encounters with Beatrice as recounted at the beginning of the *Vita nuova* (chapters 2 and 3), which Dante still chooses to record just at the outset of the discourse on *caritas*; of his two best friends, Guido Cavalcanti and Cino da Pistoia, who used this rhyme very conspicuously; and of his own wonderfully varied search for a new poetic language moulding the creativity of the maternal with the eloquence of the artificial — as they merge and melt with the severity of the *Convivio*'s desire for knowledge, and the grandiosity of Ulysses' epic ardour.

---

19 Elena Lombardi, 'Identità lirica e piacere linguistico', forthcoming.

27. Containers and Things Contained

Ronald L. Martinez

Three twenty-sevens make eighty-one. In the fourth book of *Convivio*, Dante observes that Christ, like Plato, would have lived eighty-one years if he had completed his span of life.[1] If Dante took this idea from Hugh of St Victor's *Didascalicon*, he might also have reflected on Hugh's comment that eighty-one, the fourth power of three, marks the return to unity.[2] Such a regress occurs at the cosmic level in the last of the canto Twenty-Sevens, when the pilgrim is torn from the constellation of Gemini and thrust into the *Primum Mobile*, the ninth Heaven — that is, eight plus one — so entering the sphere from which all the others take their single diurnal motion and in relation to which all time is measured and contained.[3] In a passage of *Convivio* rich in recurring terms for the articulation of time, Dante observes that this single motion is indispensable to life on earth, for without it 'there would be no

---

1   *Convivio*, IV. xxiv. 6, in Dante Alighieri, *Opere minori*, ed. by Cesare Vasoli and Domenico de Robertis, 3 vols (Milan and Naples: Ricciardi, 1988), vol. I/2, p. 823. All references to *Convivio* are to this edition.

2   *The Didascalicon of Hugh of St. Victor*, trans. Jerome Taylor (New York: Columbia University Press, 1961), p. 65: 'in a fourth progression, the soul, freed from the body, returns to the pureness of its simplicity, and therefore in the fourth multiplication, in which three times twenty-seven makes eighty-one, the number "one" reappears in the arithmetical product in order that it may be glowingly evident that the soul, after this life's end, designated by "eighty", returns to the unity of its simple state'. For Hugh in Dante, see Francesco Bausi, *Dante fra scienza e sapienza: esegesi dal canto XII del Paradiso* (Florence: Leo S. Olschki, 2009), pp. 192–97.

3   See also *Conv.*, Conv., II. iii. 5.

http://dx.doi.org/10.11647/OBP.0119.06

generation down here, nor any plant or animal life; there would be neither night nor day, nor any weeks nor months nor years, but the whole universe would be disordered, and the movement of the other Heavens in vain'.[4]

Indeed, temporal cycles, including the phases of human life, unfolded by Dante in detail through the fourth book of *Convivio*, prove an underlying theme for the Twenty-Sevens. In the case of *Inferno* xxvii. 67–68, Guido da Montefeltro intended his conversion as a right use of his time, like that which Dante — using Guido as an example — recommends in *Convivio* to those nearing the end of life.[5] Gabriele Muresu also points out that Guido's autobiography, including his gestation and birth as a mortal man ('mentre ch'io forma fui d' ossa e di polpe / che la madre mi diè' [the form of bone and flesh that my mother gave me]; *Inf.*, xxvii. 73–74), his military career, his conversion, his sparring with Boniface, and his final moments, yield almost a complete *vita e morte* (if not *miracoli*).[6] The first lines of *Purgatorio* xxvii mark dawn in Jerusalem, noon over the Ganges and midnight in Spain, suggesting how the arms of the Cross enfold all time and space,[7] and the canto is unique in the poem having its text be coterminous with — exactly contain — a half day, beginning with evening (l. 5), and continuing through the next day's sunrise (l. 133), epitomizing how on the mountain penitent souls perform distinct activities by day and by night.[8] Finally, if we supply, as Peter Armour suggests, the words Dante omits in the fully vernacular lesser Doxology ('Al padre, al figlio, a lo Spirito Santo / [...] Gloria' [To the Father, to the Son, to the Holy Spirit [...] glory']) that occupies the first lines of *Paradiso* xxvii,[9] we have indirect reference to the glory of the Trinity 'sicut erat in principio, nunc, et semper' [as it was in the beginning, now, and always]. At the other end of the canto, Beatrice details the corruption of humanity in terms of disordered temporal cycles, from the spoilage of fruits to the disrespect for Lenten privations ('divora qualunque cibo per

---

4   *Conv.*, II. xiv. 17. Unless otherwise specified, translations are my own.

5   Cf. *Conv.*, IV. xxiv. 8.

6   See Gabriele Muresu, 'La *rancura* di Guido da Montefeltro (*Inferno* XXVII)', in *L'orgia d'amor: Saggi di semantica dantesca (quarta serie)* (Rome: Bulzoni, 2008), pp. 51–91.

7   Pietro Calì, '*Purgatorio* XXVII', in *Dante Commentaries*, ed. by David Nolan (Dublin: Irish Academic Press, 1977), pp. 93–113 (pp. 94–95). The idea is based in part on Eph. 3.18; see Augustine, *In Joannis Evangelium Tractatus*, cxviii, ch. 19 (*PL* 35. 1949–1950).

8   See Luigi Blasucci, 'La dimensione del tempo nel *Purgatorio*', in *Studi su Dante e Ariosto* (Milan and Naples: Ricciardi, 1969), pp. 37–59 (pp. 54–57).

9   See Peter Armour, '*Paradiso* XXVII', in *Dante's Divine Comedy, Introductory Readings III: Paradiso*, ed. by Tibor Wlassics (Charlottesville, VA: University of Virginia Press. 1995), pp. 402–23 (p. 403).

qualunque luna' [devours whatever food in whatever month]; *Par.*, xxvii. 132). In her account infants grow up to hope for their parents's death (*Par.*, xxvii. 133–35), thus imitating one of the evil customs of the iron age from Ovid's influential account in the *Metamorphoses* of the four ages.[10] As Beatrice observes, 'che' n terra non è chi governi' [since on earth there is none who governs] (*Par.*, xxvii. 140), seas of cupidity submerge humankind, and only a tempest unleashed by the longest, most comprehensive cycle of the 'cerchi superni' [supernal spheres] can set the ships of state and Church on their right course (*Par.*, xxvii. 142–48). Secular time, then: its cause, its articulations, the effects of its passage, and the eternity that comprehends it, furnishes a unifying theme of the three canto Twenty-Sevens. The theme is fittingly concluded in the *Primum Mobile*, where the scattered leaves of time are traced back to their root in lines that express both reduction to the one and containment of what is below by what is above:

> e questo cielo non ha altro dove
> che la mente divina, in che s'accende
> l'amor che 'l volge e la virtù ch'ei piove.
>   Luce e amor d'un cerchio lui comprende,
> sì come questo li altri; e quel precinto
> colui che 'l cinge solamente intende.
>   Non è suo moto per altro distinto,
> ma li altri son mensurati da questo,
> sì come diece da mezzo e da quinto (*Par.*, xxvii. 109–17)

[this Heaven has no other where than the mind of God, in which is kindled the love that turns it and the power that it rains down. Light and love enclose it with one sphere, as this does all the others, and that girding only he who girds it understands. Its motion is not marked by another's but the others are measured by this one, as ten is measured by half and fifth].[11]

Dante's ternary of terms in these lines for containment — *comprende, precinto, cinge* — determines a chief emphasis of this vertical reading of Dante's poem.

---

10 Ovid, *Metamorphoses* I.148: 'filius ante diem patrios inquirit in annos' [the son inquires betimes into the father's years].

11 Texts and translations of Dante's poem are from Durling and Martinez. Translations of the Vulgate Bible are from the Douay version.

Both *Purgatorio* and *Paradiso* xxvii mark major thresholds in the pilgrim's journey. Stephen Botterill dubs *Purgatorio* xxvii 'supremely, literally liminal', since it transpires half in the circle of the lustful and half in the vestibule of the Earthly Paradise.[12] The pilgrim's coronation at the very end of that canto marks the conclusion of several actions of the poem: one is the passage of the seven levels where vices are unlearned and virtues instilled (cantos x–xxvii); another is the sequence of three dreams that concludes with the dream of Lia and Rachel. The invitation at line 58 of *Purgatorio* xxvii is the last in the series of angelic exhortations to proceed to the next terrace, five times using *venire* and three *intrare*,[13] drawing on Christ's encouragements at the final judgement adumbrated in Matthew 25: to the good servant, to enter into the joy of the Lord ('*intra in gaudium domini*'), and '*Venite* benedicti' to those whose compassion has earned them a place in the kingdom.[14] Indeed, the long journey with Virgil, understood as a visit to 'il temporal foco e l'eterno' [the temporal fire and the eternal], is completed here,[15] echoing the prospect laid out at *Inferno* i (ll. 115–19), where the two realms of fire, divided between the 'antichi spiriti dolenti' [ancient sorrowing spirits] and those 'contenti nel foco' [content in the fire] are presented as goals of the journey.[16]

Liminality and retrospection also characterize *Paradiso* xxvii. Dante in fact divides the canto's 148 verses *between* the eighth (given 99 lines) and ninth Heavens (given 49 lines). The lesser doxology that begins the canto is the sixth and last canto *incipit* to mention God, but the first to give us the entire Trinity in a single vernacular line. It celebrates joyfully the conclusion of the pilgrim's professions of faith, hope, and love, and his interview with Adam: in short, the content of cantos xxiv–xxvi. The stay in

---

12 Lines 70–71, halfway through the canto, record the sun's setting and the cessation of upward motion. See Stephen Botterill, 'Purgatorio XXVII', in *Dante's Divine Comedy, Introductory Readings II: Purgatorio*, ed. by Tibor Wlassics (Charlottesville, VA: University of Virginia Press, 1993), pp. 398–410 (pp. 399–400).

13 These are: *intrar, Purg.*, ii. 99; *intrate*, iii. 101; *Intrate*, ix. 131; *venite*, xii. 91–92; *intrate*, xv. 35; *venite*, xviii. 43; *intrate*, xxvii. 11; and '*Venite benedicti patris miei*', xxvii. 58.

14 Matthew 25.21, and Matthew 25.34–35, respectively.

15 Zygmunt G. Barański, 'Funzioni strutturali della retrospezione nella *Commedia*: l'esempio del canto XXVII del *Purgatorio*', in his '*Sole nuovo, luce nuova': Saggi sul rinnovamento culturale in Dante* (Turin: Scriptorium, 1996), pp. 221–53, details the canto's retrospectiveness.

16 The cluster 'foco [...] etterno' corresponding to the *ignem eternum* of Matthew 25.41 occurs only at *Inf.*, viii. 73 (of the fires of Dis) and at *Purg.*, xxvii. 127, 'il temporal foco e l'etterno', echoing *Inf.*, i. 114–18, 'trarroti di qui per loco eterno [...] e poi vedrai color che son contenti / nel fuoco'.

the constellation of Gemini, the longest of any in the spheres, nearly six full cantos in length, is also brought to a close. The closure is framed in both narrative and poetic terms — that is, with analogous gestures and exact verbal echoes — by the two looks back at the earth, in each case deemed an *aiuola*, a threshing-floor for human ferocity,[17] and by a pair of references, to be discussed below, to the sphere of the stars as aether. Matthew 25 plays a role in *Paradiso* xxvii (ll. 46–48) as well, when St Peter disavows 'that on the right hand of our successors one part of the Christian people should sit, and the other on the other side'.[18] A corresponding image is still visible in Dante's beloved San Giovanni on the Last Judgment wall, where are also found the words *Venite benedicti*, as in *Purgatorio* xxvii,[19] thus linking the two cantos through scenes familiar to the poet.

At first glance, it is less clear that *Inferno* xxvii concludes identifiable segments of the first cantica. But it is indubitably the last in the triptych of antihierocratic cantos in *Malebolge* (xix, xxiii, xxvii; two feature Boniface VIII) and the last infernal canto to adopt fire as a direct agent of punishment.[20] It is also the sole episode in the first cantica where the complete drama of death and damnation is recounted in the first person by one who suffers it, including his dying and being packed off to Minos for judgement.[21]

In short, the three canto Twenty-Sevens, the first less obviously, provide both retrospection and closure before a new phase of the journey. That is, each in some way *contains* what has *preceded*. In one sense of course this is true everywhere in the poem — in a linear narrative each subsequent episode can be said to contain the one preceding in narratological terms and in the reader's growing understanding of the work. Parallel-numbered cantos of the *Commedia* are themselves a special case of this kind of formal containment, for later cantos might be thought to be related to earlier ones as the outer curves of a spiral are related to inner.[22] As conceptual category

---

17 *aiuola* [threshing-floor] is at xxii. 151 and xxvii. 86.
18 See, Dante Alighieri, *Paradiso*, ed. by Anna Maria Chiavacci-Leonardi (Milan: Mondadori, 1997), p. 748; Matthew 25.33 has: 'And he shall set the sheep [*oves*] on his right hand, but the goats [*haedos*] on his left'.
19 More exactly, 'Venite, beneditti patris mei'. Cf. Matthew 25.34: 'Come, ye blessed of my Father, possess you the kingdom [*regnum*] prepared for you from the foundation of the world'.
20 Fire that as often observed refers both to Pentecost, in that the flames are like tongues, echoing Acts 2.3, and to the fire of Exodus 3.2–4 out of which God speaks to Moses, as Ulysses and Guido speak from their fiery enclosures.
21 Pier delle Vigna's episode almost qualifies, but he does not narrate in the first person.
22 E.g. *Inferno* vi discusses just Florence; *Purgatorio* vi, Italy, Rome, and Florence; *Paradiso* vi, the entire Mediterranean.

and as artistic device, containment demonstrably interested Dante across a wide spectrum of topics, including rhetorical colour (metonymy and synecdoche);[23] poetic form, as in the poet's account in *DVE* II. ix. 2 of the canzone stanza as the womb and receptacle of poetic art;[24] and the geocentric cosmology of the *Commedia*, where each level or sphere away from the geocenter contains the previous one. In the case of the Heavens as Dante understood them, such containment implies causal relationships: the pilgrim's upward journey takes him into spheres driven by angelic intelligences that possess increasing virtue, and thus causative power, in relation to the spheres preceding.[25]

Nonetheless, with the canto Twenty-Sevens this poetics of containment is both thematized and elaborated. All three cantos register vivid images of enclosure which in each instance function as metonymies for the content of the cantica as a whole and which further imply metapoetic reflection on their fashioning: that is, on the poetic act itself as an encircling and containing one, analogous to the shaping action of form on matter caused by the heavenly spheres moving over the sublunar world, as Dante sets it out in *Paradiso* when he compares the spheres to hammers wielded by the angels as *fabbri*, as smiths.[26] In the first two canto Twenty-Sevens the comprehensive image is a container of fire; in the last, it is a humble flowerpot, a *testo* — although fire is implicit, since in Dante's day as in our own such pots are made of fired earthenware.

On the heels of the Trojan horse mentioned in the previous canto, Dante in *Inferno* xxvii describes how Guido's voice emerges from his tongue-like

---

23 Metonymy and synecdoche are among the ten tropes of medieval rhetoric; metonymy, known as *denominatio*, is normally assigned to substitutions such as container for thing contained, or cause for effect (in each case, including vice-versa), while synecdoche, known as *intellectio*, to relations of part for whole and vice-versa. But there is significant overlap. See Geoffroi de Vinsauf, *Poetria nova*, lines 970–1037, in *Les arts poétiques du XIIe et du XIIIe siècle*, ed. by Edmond Faral (Paris: Champion, 1971), pp. 227–29, and also Geoffroi de Vinsauf, *Documentum de Arte Versificandi*, 44–46 in *ibid.*, p. 292.

24 For this passage, see Robert M. Durling and Ronald L. Martinez, *Time and the Crystal: Studies in Dante's* Rime petrose (Berkeley and Los Angeles, CA: University of California Press, 1990), pp. 26–32.

25 For a brief account of Dante's scheme, see Durling's Additional Note 11, 'Dante and Neoplatonism', in *The Divine Comedy*, III, pp. 744–49, and the next note.

26 *Par.*, ii. 127–38; see Stephen Bemrose, *Dante's Angelic Intelligences* (Rome: Edizioni di storia e letteratura, 1983), pp. 61–70. By virtue of the analogy between angels as secondary causes and human artistry, both the angels in *Par.*, ii. 128, and Arnaut Daniel in *Purg.*, xxvi. 117, can be identified as smiths, *fabbri*; their mutual archetype is God as *fabbro* (*Purg.*, x. 99). Dante's *fabbro* derives from Arnaut's smithing metaphors; see Maurizio Perugi, 'Arnaut Daniel in Dante', *Studi danteschi* 51 (1978), 59–152 (pp. 116–19).

flame by evoking the bronze bull that was designed to bellow with the screams of the victim cooked inside it. As deceptive containers, both horse and bull are emblems of fraud. Because Perillus, who devised and sculpted the bull, is immediately placed inside it ('*inbuit* auctor opus', Ovid quips), the story of the bull is especially vivid as an instance of fraud punished by its own device.[27] The bull is thus further notable in its icastic representation of the logic of *contrapasso*, which though first mentioned explicitly at the end of canto xxviii, is in cantos xxvi–xxvii foreshadowed in Virgil's account of the penalty of the *bolgia*: 'catun si fascia di quel ch'egli è inceso' [each is swathed in that which burns him inwardly] (*Inf.*, xxvi. 48).[28] Add Guido's reference, in speaking about his former career, to the sins of the lion and the fox, which tracks Virgil's observation that the malice punished in lower Hell 'injures someone either with force or with fraud' (*Inf.*, xi. 24), and a case can be made for the flaming enclosures as synechdochic emblems (*pars pro toto*) or metonymies (*contentum pro continente*) for all of Hell — what we saw Virgil call 'il fuoco etterno', contrasted to the 'temporal foco' of Purgatory. In a passage in the *Tusculan Disputations*, cited by George Corbett as a source for Farinata's apparent disdain for his fiery tomb,[29] Cicero mocks the ostentatious equanimity of an Epicurean sage who claims to find confinement in Phalaris' bull as comfortable as his own bed.[30] The Ciceronian intertext qualifies the brazen bull as an implicit image for the sarcophagi of the heretics, the first infernal torment that employs both enclosure and direct fire, 'hot as any metal-working art might require' (*Inf.*, ix. 119–20). The bull features thus in axial symmetry with the last of Hell's fiery torments, the tongue-shaped flames of *Inferno* xxvii, which are compared to the sculptor's work of art.

---

27 Pietro di Dante, followed by Benvenuto, recorded the Ovidian source (*Ars amatoria*, I, 655–56): 'neque enim lex aequior ulla est / quam necis artifices arte perire sua' [nor is there any law more equitable than for the artisan of murder to die by his own art].

28 For the *contrapasso*, see Justin Steinberg, 'Dante's Justice? A reappraisal of the *contrapasso*', *L'Alighieri* 44 (2014), 59–74.

29 See *Inf.*, x. 36, Farinata described 'com' avesse l'inferno a gran dispitto' [as if he had Hell in great disdain] and his words at x. 78 on hearing of the doom of his clan and political faction: 'ciò mi tormenta più che questo letto' [that torments me more than this bed]. See George Corbett, *Dante and Epicurus: A Dualistic Vision of Secular and Spiritual Fulfilment* (Oxford: Legenda, 2013), pp. 78–79, 87n20.

30 *Tusculan Disputations* II.vii.17–18: 'he [Epicurus] affirms somewhere that if a wise man were to be burned or put to the torture [...] even if he were in Phalaris's bull, would say, "How sweet it is! how little do I mind it" (*non curo*) [...] he would say that to be in Phalaris's bull was the same as to be in his own bed' (*lectulo*).

But not only the sculptor's craft. Although Dante gives credit to 'Highest Wisdom' for the crafting of infernal punishments,[31] the poem of Hell is inevitably an effect of Dante's verbal skill.[32] If Ovid's joke about the author filling the work applies with grim humour to Perillus, it also illustrates the late medieval understanding of the author as the efficient cause of his text: in causing his text, he contains it; in being caused, his text contains him.[33] There are in fact continuities between Guido's motives and Dante's: for example, Guido's curse of Boniface (*Inf.*, xxvii. 70: 'the high priest, may evil take him') is carried out by the poet, who has prepared Boniface's place in the third *bolgia*: indeed the whole *Inferno* realizes the malediction in Matthew 25:41 by which Christ assigns the reprobate to the 'eternal fire', a passage relevant, as we saw, to the other canto Twenty-Sevens as well. Such an overlap is potentially disturbing: by wrapping the counselors in tongue-shaped flames Dante suggests not only harmful uses of language, such as Guido's furnishing of stratagems to Boniface, but the ambiguous nature of verbal art in general, including the poet's, as Robert Durling argued: for example the 'allegory of the poets', with its 'bella menzogna' [beautiful lie] concealing ethical meaning (*Conv.*, II. i. 3), is itself structured like fraud, thus hard to distinguish from it.[34] As forms of artistic fraud, both bull and horse work in the poem as apotropaic charms for Dante as the fashioner of Hell's torments and of the vast but confining dwelling of Hell itself, variously described as a 'cieco carcere' [blind prison], a 'pozzo' [well], 'fossa' [ditch], and 'chiostro' [cloister], where Pope Nicholas III can 'bag himself' ('mi misi in borsa') and evil is 'ensacked' ('insacca'), and that is in lower regions divided into a series of 'bolge' [bags or pockets]. In short, a restrictive container.

In *Purgatorio* xxv–xxvii, it is again fire that functions as a container, both in the immediate sense, in that the souls must remain 'nel seno / al grande ardore' [in the bosom of the great fire] (*Purg.*, xxv. 121–22) in order to benefit from its therapeutic effect, and in the sense that the fiery barrier

---

31 *Inf.*, xix. 10–12. The 'art of Highest Wisdom' is executed, of course, with fire.

32 Phalaris had polished the bull with his file ('temperato con sua lima'), echoing the metaphorical *labor limae* recommended to the poet in Horace's *Ars poetica* 288–93, also there expressed in the terms of an analogy with sculpture.

33 See *Medieval Literary Theory and Criticism, c. 1100–c. 1375*, ed. by A. J. Minnis and A. B. Scott, with David Wallace (Oxford: Clarendon Press, 1988), pp. 198–99.

34 See Robert M. Durling, 'Deceit and Digestion in the Belly of Hell', in *Allegory and Representation: Selected Papers from the English Institute*, ed. by Stephen J. Greenblatt (Baltimore, MD and London: Johns Hopkins University Press, 1989), pp. 61–93 (pp. 74–75, 79–80).

screens the place immediately above, the Earthly Paradise. The barrier is in fact described as a wall (*Purg.*, xxvii. 36: 'questo *muro*') through which the pilgrim must pass to enter the garden of Eden (xxvii. 32: 'entra sicuro'). In analyses based on patristic sources, Bruno Nardi accordingly associated the wall that faces the pilgrim with the flaming sword of the angel placed outside Eden after the Fall.[35] And although Dante reserves fire for the extirpation of the habit of lechery, passage through and being tried in the fire seem to be required of all who wish to enter Eden: 'you go no further, holy souls, unless the fire bites first' (*Purg.*, xxvii. 10–11). As Nardi showed, moreover, texts such as I Corinthians 3.12–13 ('the fire shall try every man's work, of what sort it is') inform Dante's account of purgatorial fire not merely as punitive of those who pass through it, but — as in the last line of *Purgatorio* xxvi — 'il foco che li affina' [the fire that refines them].[36] Jacques Le Goff documents how the texts Nardi mentions such as Wisdom 3.6 ('as gold in the furnace he hath proved them'), recur in patristic and scholastic accounts distinguishing benign, 'probative' purgatorial fire from the fire of Hell, while another of these texts, Psalm 65.12 ('We have passed through fire and water') may be seen as prototypical of the pilgrim's *transitus per ignem*, and of his later drinking of Lethe and Eunoè.[37]

Sapegno observes that the fire in canto xxvii is a compendium — one could say as well a synechdoche or metonymy — of purgatorial discipline in general, which otherwise never uses fire at all;[38] those who will their suffering as the condition of their eventual liberation are 'content in the fire'. If as Simona Bargetto argues we see in the wall of flames the second baptism with fire announced by John the Baptist (Matthew 3:16), we can also think of the fire as an incubator,[39] along with Virgil, who calls it 'l'alvo / di questa fiamma' [the womb of this flame] (*Purg.*, xxvii. 25–26), echoing traditional figuration of the baptismal font as the womb (*uter*)

35 Bruno Nardi, 'Il mito dell' Eden', in *Saggi di filosofia dantesca* (Milan: Società anonima editrice Dante Alighieri, 1930), pp. 347–74 (pp. 352–55).
36 *Pace* Gianfranco Contini, 'Alcuni appunti su *Purgatorio* 27', in *Un'idea di Dante* (Turin: Einaudi, 1970), pp. 171–90 (pp. 174–76). Gabriele Muresu, 'Virgilio, la corona, la mitria (*Purgatorio* XXVII)', *Rivista di letteratura italiana antica* 8 (2007), 223–61 (p. 229), rejects the association with the angel of Genesis, but treats the fire as both expiatory and cathartic.
37 Jacques Le Goff, *The Birth of Purgatory*, trans. by Arthur Goldhammer (Chicago, IL: University of Chicago Press, 1981), pp. 237–88 (pp. 245–48, 260–61, 281–86).
38 'compendio e simbolo'; see *Purgatorio*, ed. by Natalino Sapegno (Florence: La Nuova Italia, 1968), p. 295.
39 Simona Bargetto, 'Memorie liturgiche nel XXVII Canto del *Purgatorio*', *Lettere italiane* 49 (1997), 185–247.

through which the Church brings forth her regenerate children:[40] another powerful image of containment, both temporary and liminal.

Dante's references to the penitent lustful singing the metrical hymn *Summae Deus clementiae* in the fire evoke further images of containment in alluding to the episode from the Book of Daniel of Shadrach, Meshach, and Abednego cast into the fiery furnace by King Nebuchadnezzar. Reassuring the pilgrim that he will not be harmed by the flames (*Purg.*, xxvii. 27: 'non ti potrebbe far d'un capel calvo' [it could not make you bald by one hair]), Virgil shows confidence in the divine protection that shielded the three boys.[41] The fiery furnace recalls at once Phalaris' bull as a simile for Guido's torment in Hell and the fact that Christian saints such as Eustace were martyred within brazen bulls.[42] Indeed, the three boys are remembered in the prayer *Suscipe, domine*, part of the commendation for the dying: 'Free, O lord, the soul of your servant as you freed the three boys from the furnace of burning fire (*de camino ignis ardentis*)'.[43]

Again, given Dante's career as a poet of Amor, there are inescapably metapoetic dimensions to the fire on the terrace of the lustful. Gianfranco Contini observed that the purgatorial fire is a homeopathic penance, like applied to like, in that the fire's heat reenacts the ardent passion that love poets describe as their condition.[44] Fire, a radically polysemous signifier in the poem, stands for both the past ardour of sinful loves, and for the present fire that transmutes *ardore* into charity. The fire is further metapoetic in that the suffering that refines Arnaut Daniel is a traditional metaphor for the love poet's quest for artistic perfection, as well as character building, in fulfilling the strictures of *fin'amors*.[45] No accident then that just one

---

40 Cf. the thirteenth-century Roman pontifical (44.18), 'immaculato divini fontis utero' [from the unstained womb of the divine fount]. See *Le pontifical de la curie romaine au XIIIe siècle*, ed. by Monique Goullet, Guy Lobrichon and Eric Palazzo (Paris: Cerf, 2004), pp. 302–03.

41 Daniel 3.19–27 and 92–94 ('not a hair of their head had been singed') were linked by exegetes (e.g. Rupert of Deutz, *De Trinitatis et operibus eius*, 42.7, in *PL* 167.1506–1507C) with Luke 21.18 ('But a hair of your head shall not perish'. That they walk unharmed (Daniel 3.24), was previously echoed by Dante's 'spirits walking within the flames' (*Purg.*, xxv. 124)

42 William R. Cook and Ronald Herzman, 'St. Eustace: A Note on *Inferno XXVII*', *Dante Studies* 94 (1976), 137–39.

43 For Daniel 3 in the liturgy, see Philippe Bernard, 'Le cantique des trois enfants (Dan. III, 52–90): Les répertoires liturgiques occidentaux dans l'antiquité tardive et le haut moyen age', *Musica e storia* 1 (1996), 232–76.

44 Contini, 'Alcuni appunti', pp. 176–78 ('per antitesi omeopatica').

45 *Ibid.*, pp. 178–79, citing the lyric *topos* of the salamander thriving in fire, as fish thrive in water.

canto back (*Purg.*, xxvi. 41, 86–87) Dante mentions Pasiphae's 'false cow' fashioned by Daedalus and reminiscent of the hollow horse and bull of *Inferno* xxvi–xxvii. They are deceptive containers all, apotropaic instances of art gone bad, and thus warnings to poetic makers whose lyric stanzas, like the sexually charged sestina *cambra* fashioned by Arnaut Daniel, might have once been conducive to the heterosexual form of trespass Dante's Guinizzelli calls *ermafrodito* (*Purg.*, xxvi. 82).[46]

Among the fixed stars in *Paradiso* xxvii we find numerous references to fire: the four souls who dialogue with the pilgrim (Peter, James, John, Adam) are 'face / [...] accese' [burning torches], and St Peter says 'arrosso e sfavillo' [I redden and spark] (*Par.*, xxvii. 54) as he denounces corruption in the Church, taking on the aspect of the planet Mars, traditionally associated with fire (as it is in Dante's *Convivio*), rather than temperate Jupiter.[47] The crimson of both wrath and shame then spreads from Peter to besprinkle the entire Heaven ('vid' ïo allora tutto' l ciel cosperso' [I then saw all Heaven suffused]; l. 30), including Beatrice, whose deep blush is compared to the darkening of the whole universe at the crucifixion. On a brighter note, we find the metaphysical idea of the love that moves the sun and the stars, by virtue of its contiguity with the mind of God in the circumambient Empyrean, 'igniting' the *Primum Mobile*: 'e questo cielo non ha altro *dove* / che la mente divina in che s'accende / l'amor che 'l volge' [and this Heaven has no other *where* than the mind of God, in which is kindled the love that turns it] (*Par.*, xxvii. 109–12). The Empyrean itself, too, as Dante knew, means 'Heaven of fire', suggesting a spiritual conflagration kindled by Empyrean *caritas*.[48] If in Dante's famous simile of the resting *villano* the flames of the eighth *bolgia* of Hell are discrete, scattered lights like fireflies seen on a summer evening (*Inf.*, xxvi. 25–33), and the ring of fire in *Purgatorio* xxvii walls Purgatory off from Eden all the way around, in *Paradiso* xxvii, in an incandescence that emphasizes the urgency of Peter's invective, Dante imagines a whole celestial sphere becoming incarnadine.

Substituting with rhetorical *tapinosis* a humble for a lofty image, the poet, as we saw, in *Paradiso* xxvii conceives of the *Primum Mobile*, the all-containing sphere of the physical universe, as an earthenware

---

46 See *The Divine Comedy*, II, pp. 454–55.
47 *Conv.*, II. xiii. 21: 'Its heat is similar to that of fire'; for Jupiter, see *Conv.*, II. xiii. 25: 'Jupiter is a star of temperate complexion'.
48 *Conv.*, II. iii. 8: 'the Catholics posit the empyrean Heaven, which is to say Heaven of fire, or luminous Heaven'.

flowerpot — which might allow us to imagine Dante's entire physical cosmos as nested spherical pots. This metaphorical *testo*, housing the roots of temporal processes that unfold beneath it, anchors several other images of containment in the last canto xxvii. By calling the constellation of Gemini in the starry sphere 'il nido di Leda' [Leda's nest] (l. 98), Dante echoes the use of *alvo* for the gestational fire in Purgatory and recalls the mythological *vacca* containing Pasiphae used to discourage the lustful in Purgatory.[49] Dante makes his natal constellation the birthplace of Helen of Troy, whose egg, as Horace recalls in the *Ars poetica*, originated the Trojan war: Leda's nest is thus the remote beginning of the Roman nation.[50] The nest harbours these meanings by virtue of multiple verbal figures. Metaphorically, the nest is Leda's womb because it sheltered the eggs that contained her offspring; Helen, born from the egg, is the thing contained. These implications are joined to serial metonymies of cause for effect: Helen, 'per cui tanto reo / tempo si volse' [who brought such evil times] (*Inf.*, v. 64–65), was a cause of the war; Leda, and the seed of the swan, Jupiter, were causes of Helen, and so on.[51] The ultimate effect of this series of causes is the pilgrim himself, a descendant of the Trojans and born under Gemini.

The looks back at earth also frame an encapsulating *vision*: the pilgrim's tenure in Gemini, spanning six hours of time, in spatial terms a celestial arc of 90 degrees, beginning on the meridian of Jerusalem and ending on the meridian of Gades, when added to the previous look back in *Paradiso* xxii, permits a complete prospect of the habitable portion of the world, between the Ganges and Gades and slightly beyond. Given the pilgrim's location in Gemini, this prospect reflects Dante's conclusion to the *Questio de aqua et terra*, where he argues that the emergence of the wedge of land over the level of the ocean, so making terrestrial life possible, was effected by the Heaven of the Fixed Stars acting upon the earth immediately after Creation.[52] But the poet's gaze also defines his own scope over the course of the poem:

49 Also the Trojan horse and brazen bull of *Inf.*, xxvi and xxvii; Virgil refers to the former as 'feta armis' [pregnant with arms] (*Aen.* II. 238).

50 *Ars poetica*, lines 147–49. Compare how, in 'Leda and the Swan', W. B. Yeats compresses the futures of Troy and Argos entirely within the moment of Zeus' insemination of Leda: 'a shudder in the loins engenders there / the broken wall, the burning roof and tower, / and Agamemnon dead' (ll. 9–11).

51 Cf. Dante's account in *Epist.* v. 24 of Rome's whole history, founded remotely in Laomedon's refusal of hospitality to the Argonauts, which led to the first sack of Troy under Hercules, and to the rape of Helen.

52 Cf. Dante Alighieri, *Epistole, Ecloge, Questio de situ et forma aque et terre*, ed. M. P. Stocchi (Padua: Antenore, 2002), p. 267 (*Questio* 70–73). See Armour, 'Canto XXVII', p. 407.

from his perch he sees Ulysses' 'mad track', identifying an episode largely
of his own invention, as well as the rape of Europa, which set in motion the
fractious history of Thebes, one of the failed cities of the *Inferno*.[53] The look
back is thus metapoetic, capturing at a glance what Dante has contemplated
within the space and time of human history, within 'l'aiuola che ci fa tanto
feroci' [the little threshing floor that makes us so ferocious], but within the
formal boundaries of the poem as well. This comprehensive glance justifies
Dante's use of *etera* for the starry sphere, the 'rounded aether' (*Par.*, xxii.
132) and the 'etera [...] adorno' [aether [...] adorned] (*Par.*, xxvii. 71).[54] The
term is used in Proverbs 8:27–28, describing how God and Wisdom first
traced the limits of the universe. Dante translated the passage: 'quando
con certa legge e certo giro vallava li abissi, quando suso fermava [l'etera]
e suspendeva le fonti dell' acque' [when with certain law and certain
compass he walled the depths, when he fixed the sky (*etera*) above, and
poised the fountains of waters].[55] Dante has thus placed his pilgrim in a
position analogous to that of the divine artificer gazing on his creation. The
adoption of *etera* along with mention of Ulysses's path beyond Cádiz ('di là
da Gade') confirms the metapoetic moment, as the notion of Gades as the
boundary of a literary work is set out at the end of the *Poetria nova*, marking
the limits of Geoffroi de Vinsauf's didactic enterprise.[56]

What subjects are contained, then, in these explicitly capacious cantos?
Necessarily juxtaposed from the canto Twenty-Sevens are Boniface VIII's
famously deceptive absolution of Guido da Montefeltro in *Inferno* and St
Peter's denunciation in *Paradiso* of several papacies contemporary with
Dante. In a recent essay, Ronald Herzman and William Stephany correlate
the episodes in which Boniface appears in the poem, including the two
canto Twenty-Sevens dealt with here, arguing that Dante's treatment of

53 Cf. the pyre of Eteocles and Polynices in *Inf.*, xxvi. 52–54, and *Purg.*, xxvi. 94–96, referring
to Statius' Hypsipyle (*Thebaid* IV. 718–V. 752). The Europa reference alludes to Statius'
exordium to the *Thebaid*, an epic reference. See Franco Fido, 'Writing like God, or Better?:
Symmetries in Dante's 26th and 27th Cantos of the *Commedia*', *Italica* 63 (1986), 250–64 (p.
257), who notes the georgic episode in *Inf.*, xxvi. 25–30 and the bucolic one in *Purg.*, xxvii.
76–84. *Par.*, xxvii completes the *rota Virgilii*.

54 'etera tondo' and 'etera addorno' are metrically equivalent and assonant, with *tondo* and
addorno partial anagrams into the bargain.

55 *Conv.*, III. xv. 16. As is well known, *etera* is present by emendation, highly likely given
the Scriptural source. Dante arguably knew passages in Aristotle's *De caelo et mundo* i.3
(270 b 24) and iii.3 (302 a 31) that identified the *aether* with fire (supposedly Anaxagoras'
view).

56 *Poetria nova*, line 2066, in *Les arts poétiques*, p. 261.

Boniface systematically repudiates the hierocratic claims visible — posted, so to speak — in the frescoes in the chapel of the Quattro Coronati in Rome. The paintings illustrate concessions by Constantine of imperial insignia and privileges to Pope Sylvester, concessions that were fabricated by the author of the fraudulent *Donatio constantini*.[57] The authors underline how the Pope's use of the keys to threaten Guido, a former Ghibelline warlord and promoter of imperial authority in northern Italy, established the high-water mark of papal corruption first set into motion by the Donation, consequences also deplored in *Paradiso* xxvii in the words of St Peter himself, who delivers the tenth and penultimate invective in the *Paradiso*.[58]

The Quattro Coronati frescoes were intended to counter the threat posed to the papacy by Frederick II. Dante's campaign in dispraise of the popes responds in turn to steps taken later in the century to widen the reach of papal power. Perhaps the most significant appropriation, as illustrated in the Quattro Coronati frescoes, was the presumed concession to the Pope of the conical *phrygium* or *regnum*, headgear formerly imperial. In 1273 Gregory X shifted the crowning of the Pope with the *tiara*, or *regnum*, from the Lateran to the Vatican, implicitly enlarging his scope of authority; so that, beginning in the late thirteenth century, ceremonials and pontificals refer to the crowning not as the pope's consecration, but his coronation. This tendency blossomed with the full-scale *imitatio imperii* advanced by Boniface VIII. Pipino's chronicle relates that upon his coronation in 1294, Boniface sat on his throne crowned with the tiara and deemed himself a Caesar and an emperor. Later he made a point of publishing important bulls on 22 February, the feast of Peter's chair, the *cathedra Petri*, while his court theologian and apologist, Giles of Rome, tailored the symbolism of the tiara's topknot so that it could be affirmed that Boniface embodied the Church itself: '*Papa potest dici ecclesia*'.

In addition to insulting imperial dignities, Boniface enhanced his status at the expense of Peter, and of Christ himself: he had himself sculpted

---

57 For this and the next two paragraphs I rely on Agostino Paravicini-Bagliani, *Le chiavi e la tiara: immagini e simboli del papato medievale* (Rome: Viella, 1998), pp. 13–23, 45–97, 107–08, and Ronald Herzman and William Stephany, 'Dante and the Frescoes at Santi Quattro Coronati', *Speculum* 87 (2012), 95–146; for the *cathedra Petri* as implicitly present in *Inf.*, xix, see John A. Scott, 'The Rock of Peter and *Inferno*, XIX', *Romance Philology* 23 (1970), 462–79.

58 On the invectives, see Reto R. Bezzola, '*Paradiso* XXVII', *Letture dantesche*, vol. 3, *Paradiso*, ed. by Giovanni Getto (Florence: Sansoni, 1964), pp. 551–66 (pp. 553–54).

holding Peter's keys in the same pose as the Arnolfo di Cambio bronze of St Peter in the Vatican, and topped it all off by ordering a funeral monument within the Vatican — Peter's sepulchre — representing Boniface, rather than Peter, holding the keys. This programme of arrogance and usurpations plausibly underlies the violence of Peter's outburst in *Paradiso* xxvii referring to Boniface:

> 'Quelli ch' usurpa in terra il luogo mio,
> il luogo mio, il luogo mio, che vaca
> ne la presenza del Figliuol di Dio' (*Par.*, xxvii. 22–24)

['He who on earth usurps my place, my place, my place, which is vacant in the presence of the Son of God'].

But why should the utterance be tripled?

Dante's accounts of papal-imperial relations in the canto Twenty-Sevens of *Inferno* and *Paradiso* focus appropriately on two principal symbols of papal pretension: the keys, the power of opening and closing in Heaven and earth; and the papal throne or seat, broadly understood to include the Vatican, which is St Peter's temple as head of the whole church and, possibly, his gravesite (*cimitero*). Dante's Boniface uses the keys to threaten Guido with damnation,[59] while Dante's St Peter waxes indignant that the keys, which should liberally open the purgatorial gates, are instead brandished as insignia on the battle standards of armies ranged against fellow Christians who oppose papal political ambitions: 'che contra battezzati combattesse' [warring against the baptized] (*Par.*, xxvii. 51). These included the Hohenstaufens, Aragonese, Colonnesi, and Ghibellines in general, or indeed the Forlivesi once defended by Guido da Montefeltro against papal and Angevin troops sent by Martin IV in 1282.[60] In this sense, Peter alludes to the 'Italian' crusades preached in order to affirm papal authority, from Alexander IV through Benedict XII.[61]

---

59 *Inf.*, xxvii. 104–05: 'però son due le chiavi, / che il mio antecessor non ebbe care' [for that reason the keys are two, which my predecessor did not prize].

60 *Inf.*, xxvii. 44; see Donald L. Galbreath, *Papal Heraldry* (London: Heraldry Today, 1972), p. 6; also Paravicini Bagliani, *Le chiavi*, pp. 46 and 111 on Innocent III and the papal gonfalon, the *vexillum*.

61 See Norman Housley, *The Italian Crusades: The Papal-Angevin Alliance and the Crusades Against Christian Lay Powers, 1254–1343* (Oxford: Clarendon Press, 1982), pp. 13–70.

In short, the *Inferno* and *Paradiso* Twenty-Sevens dramatize Dante's view of the crises afflicting the two chief powers of the medieval world during the papacies of Boniface, Clement V, and John XXII. In *Inferno* xxvii Empire and Church are represented, in a negative light, by Constantine's supposed concessions to Sylvester and by the bargain Boniface strikes with Guido that follows from those concessions. In *Paradiso* xxvii Peter speaks for the Church, while the Empire is implicit in Peter's reference to Scipio, who saved Rome, 'the glory of the world', from Carthage so that it could become the seat 'di madre Roma e di suo impero' [of mother Rome and her empire] (*Inf.,* ii. 20). But the corruption of Boniface, whose place yawns vacant in the presence of Christ, and the crisis of governance decried by Beatrice — which might refer both to the vacancy of 1300 created by Boniface's unworthiness, and the vacancy of the imperial office after the death of Henry VII — has created a deficit of both the spiritual and the temporal authorities that should rightly sit in Rome. As Benvenuto da Imola relates, neither temporal nor spiritual authority was to be found, because Boniface had usurped both.[62]

More specifically, Peter's *luogo*, usurped by Boniface, can be correlated both with Peter's chair and with the Vatican cemetery as the place of his burial. Peter's triple exclamation can be linked back to *Inferno* xxvii, where Guido da Montefeltro's advice shows Boniface the way to prevail over the Colonna on his *alto seggio* [high throne],[63] an expression that echoes accounts in consecration ceremonials of the papal seat as a *solium glorie* [glorious threshold].[64] As we know, the Pope's triple iteration of 'il luogo mio' in *Paradiso* xxvii recalls the thrice-mentioned *templum domini* in Jeremiah 7:4, also referred to there as *in loco isto* and *in hoc loco* [in this place] and *in locus meus* [in my place].[65] Significantly, *locus iste* also appears in Antiphons for

---

62 Thus Benvenuto da Imola: 'quia Bonifacius usurpat utramque potestatem' [for Boniface usurps both powers]. References to Dante's old commentators in this and the next note are taken from the *Dartmouth Dante Project* http://dante.darmouth.edu/. Dante's epistle to the cardinals of 1314 refers to the city as 'deprived of both its lights' (*Epist*. xi.10).

63 *Pace* Mirko Tavoni, 'Guido da Montefeltro dal *Convivio* a Malebolge (*Inferno* XXVII)', in *Qualche Idea su Dante* (Bologna: Il Mulino, 2015), pp. 251–94 (pp. 264–65), who makes a case for the 'alto seggio' as the citadel of Penestrina Boniface conquers. *Inf.,* ii. 24; xvii. 111 and *Par.,* xxvii. 22–24 are linked by Francesco Torraca's commentary on *Par.,* xxvii. 22–24. If only the citadel is meant, the force of Dante's irony is diminished.

64 *Le pontifical,* XIIIB.41, p. 114, specifically in words from I Samuel 2:8, describing how the elected pope is lifted from the dung (*de stercore*) and placed on the threshold of glory (*solium glorie*).

65 See Jeremiah 7:3 and 7 ('in loco isto'), also 7:12 ('ad locus meus', of the altar at Shiloh).

the dedication of a Church (*'locus iste* est domus dei' [this place is the house of God]), the texts for which are drawn from Jacob's vision at Beth-el of angels rising and descending on a ladder, traditionally the account of the origin of the Church.[66] These words inform St Peter's 'luogo mio', as well as the pilgrim's original reference to Rome in *Inferno* ii. 22–24 as 'established to be the holy place [*loco santo*] where the successor to Peter is enthroned'. And when St Peter announces that Boniface has turned the Vatican *cimitero* into a sewer, a *cloaca*, his meaning includes, again, *Peter's* burial place — located according to tradition under the *aedicula* in St Peter's — but also possibly alluding to the funeral chapel in the Vatican, erected by Boniface during his lifetime and supplemented with Arnolfo di Cambio's lifelike effigy of the Pope holding the keys.[67] Peter's *luogo* is thus at once the *cathedra Petri*, the Temple of the Vatican, and his sepulchre, all occupied illicitly and unworthily by Boniface: it is also, as Peter says, his mystical headship of the Church, which becomes void (*vaca*) in the presence of Christ.

Where then are Church and Empire to be located in *Purgatorio* xxvii, the midmost of our Twenty-Sevens? They are, if anywhere, in the metaphorical crown and mitre that Virgil sets on the pilgrim's head at the canto's end (*Purg.*, xxvii. 139–42). For Kantorowicz, Virgil, in a laicized liturgy modelled on baptism, confers the 'crown of honour and glory' (Psalms 8:6) that attests to the perfection of natural virtue and reason in a superindividual *humanitas* embodied by the pilgrim. As John Scott observes, Virgil's coronation of the pilgrim on the threshold of Eden — or of that earthly felicity that Eden can allegorically represent — certifies his possession of the directive authorities of Empire and Church originally instituted as 'remedies for sin'. As both crown and mitre enclose the head, the Empire and papacy might be said to have devolved within the pilgrim, who is now

---

Jeremiah 7:11 ('is this house then [...] become a den of robbers?') originates from the New Testament (see note below), specifically the idea of the Church transformed from a house of prayer into a den of thieves. See Rachel Jacoff, 'Dante, Geremia, e la problematica profetica', in *Dante e la Bibbia*, ed. by Giovanni Barblan (Florence: Olschki, 1988), pp. 113–23 (p. 115), and Armour, 'Canto XXVII', pp. 413–14.

66 Genesis 28:10–22. For the dedication liturgy, see *Sources of the Modern Roman Liturgy; The Ordinals by Haymo of Faversham and Related Documents (1243–1307)*, ed. by S. J. P. Van Dijk, 2 vols (Leiden: Brill, 1963), 2, pp. 317–18.

67 Note how Peter's phrasing, 'fatt' ha del cimitero mio cloaca / del sangue e de la puzza' [He has made my burial place a sewer of the blood and stench] (*Par.*, xxvii. 22, 25–26), follows that of Christ on the defilement of his house in Matthew 21:13: 'Domus mea domus orationis vocabitur; vos autem fecistis illam speluncam latronum' [My house was called a house of prayer; you have made it a den of thieves].

ruler over himself ('te sovra te', *Purg.*, xxvii. 139–42).[68] Further associations
have been offered for Virgil's ritual. Simona Bargetto sees the crowning in
relation to the pilgrim's second baptism of fire, and recalls that for Catholic
liturgy baptism is a coronation, and 'all true Christians can be called kings
and priests'[69] — indeed Christ's invitation in Matthew 25:34, beginning
with *Venite, benedicti*, in fact promises a kingdom, a *regnum*.[70] Michelangelo
Picone sees the ritual as a transfer of poetic authority from Virgil to Dante,
and offers a metapoetic reading of Virgil's lines, 'fuor sei de l'erte vie, fuor
sei de l'arte' [you are beyond the steep ways, beyond the narrow] (*Purg.*,
xxvii. 132), as a reference to the stern discipline of art, topical in rhetorical
manuals.[71]

I would hazard, however, that if we exclude the historical struggles of
the contemporary papacy and empire, which are implicit in the contested
symbols of mitre and tiara, Virgil's ritual cannot be fully understood:
the crowning, too, may arguably be seen as a refutation of the Quattro
coronati frescoes in which Constantine grants the tiara to Sylvester. As
often observed, in contemporary ceremonials both popes and emperors
were sequentially crowned both with the two-horned mitre, standing
for ecclesiastical authority, and with the *regnum* or diadem, later tiara,
associated with temporal power.[72] In light of Boniface's ostentatious
insignia it is difficult to overlook Dante's polemical intentions in having
the pilgrim crowned not by a pope, who held the prerogative of crowning
the emperor, nor indeed by any of the prelates charged with crowning the

---

68 See Ernst H. Kantorowicz, *The King's Two Bodies: A Study in Political Theology* (Princeton,
NJ: Princeton University Press, 1957), pp. 451–95 (pp. 491–95), and John A. Scott, *Dante's
Political Purgatory* (Philadelphia, PA: University of Pennsylvania Press, 1996), pp. 180–
81. Justin Steinberg, *Dante and the Limits of the Law* (Chicago, IL: University of Chicago
Press, 2015), pp 54–63, argues that the pilgrim possesses *arbitrium* in the sense of judicial
discretion subject to law, rather than unconstricted freedom. See also Albert R. Ascoli,
Dante and the Making of a Modern Author (Cambridge: Cambridge University Press, 2008),
pp. 329–57.

69 Bargetto, 'Memorie liturgiche', pp. 239–41; see also Mira Mocan, *L'arca della mente,
Riccardo di San Vittore in Dante* (Florence: Olschki, 2012), pp. 141–56 (pp. 143–46).

70 The *regnum* prepared for the righteous 'from the foundation of the world' (Matth. 25.34).

71 Michelangelo Picone, '*Purgatorio* 27: Passaggio rituale e *translatio* poetica', *Medioevo
romanzo* 12 (1987), 389–402 (p. 391), quoting Geoffroi de Vinsauf, *Poetria nova*, lines 149–
50: 'Thus the way that lies open is more restricted [*artior*] [...] its art superior' [*ars major*]
(*Les arts poétiques*, p. 201).

72 For the double coronations, see Joan M. Ferrante, The *Political Vision of the Divine Comedy*
(Princeton, NJ: Princeton University Press, 1984), pp. 243–45, and Peter Armour, *Dante's
Griffin and the History of the World: A Study of the Earthly Paradise* (Purgatorio, cantos *xxix–
xxxiii*) (Oxford: Clarendon Press, 1989), pp. 143–48.

pope — there are of course none such in Purgatory — but rather by the Roman layman and poet Virgil (although, as Muresu observes, Virgil is anachronistically well informed regarding the Christian dispensation).[73] As several readers take it, given the vacancies in papal and imperial authority this office must fall to Virgil, because only a representative of natural reason, classical ethics ('they left morality to the world', *Purg.*, xviii. 69) and Roman law (e.g. *Inf.*, xi. 22–66)[74] has sufficient status to confer mitre and crown.[75] Not only does Virgil supplant the authorities of Empire and Church, which Dante felt to be lacking, but the Roman poet corrects the absorption by the papacy of imperial insignia. Furthermore, in light of Paola Rigo's account of the poet's hoped-for *cappello* (*Par.*, xxv. 1–12), which she identifies with the *pilleum*, the freedman's cap, this poetic coronation dispels the spectre of Dante forced to wear the defamatory fool's cap (*mitra*) in the ritual imposed on exiles reconciled with the Florentine government.[76] The poetic vector is crucial: Virgil has expertise in poetic coronations, given his own triumphal olive crown in the elaborate ceremonial that begins the third *Georgic* (ll. 1–22). Certainly the emphatic final hemistich of *Purgatorio* xxvii, *corono e mitrio*, acquires considerable resonance through *poetic* means, by the narrower way of art (*via* […] *artior*). The rhyme of *mitrio* with *arbitrio*, which occurs elsewhere in *Purgatorio* only at viii. 113, xvi. 71 and xviii. 74 (the last two exactly framing the center of the poem, as Singleton showed[77]) articulates a fundamental principle of human dignity: the freedom that the pilgrim seeks as he enters Purgatory (*Purg.*, i. 71), which Dante refers to in *Monarchia* as God's greatest gift to humankind and the basis of human happiness in this life and in the next.[78] Just as Dante prospectively assigns to his poem the task of overcoming the cruelty of his fellow citizens in

73 Muresu, 'Virgilio', pp. 256–58. Muresu denies any association with Church and Empire and argues that Virgil's words are derived from Ecclesiastes 45:14 (Moses crowning Aaron as high priest) and Exodus 29:6–7. Both texts contributed to the medieval coronation orders.

74 Amedeo Quondam, 'Corona', in *Enciclopedia dantesca*, ed. by Umberto Bosco, 6 vols (Rome: Istituto della Enciclopedia Italiana, 1970–1978), II, pp. 212–13 and Domenico Consoli, 'Mitriare', in *Enciclopedia Dantesca*, III, p. 979, offer contrasting views.

75 Ferrante, *Political Vision*, p. 43; Ascoli, *Dante and the Making*, p. 356, Steinberg, *Dante and the Limits*, pp. 107, 172, 186n12.

76 Paola Rigo, 'Prenderò il cappello', in *Memoria classica e memoria biblica in Dante* (Florence: Olschki, 1984), pp. 135–63 (pp. 142–51). The *pilleum* is related to the *phrygium*, or *tiara*: see Isidore of Seville, *Etymologiae*, XIX. 31.4: 'The mitre is a phrygian cap, protecting the head' (Migne, *PL* 82.699A).

77 Charles S. Singleton, 'The Poet's Number at the Center', *Dante Studies* 80 (1965), 1–10.

78 See *Par.*, v. 19–25 and *Mon.*, I. xii.6.

Paradiso xxv. 1–12, and anticipates a future coronation as a poet, it is, more than anything, the *poetry* that fills up the space vacated by other authorities: this is perhaps the benign sense of the author entering and filling his work, '*inbuit auctor opus*'.

Indeed, the political invective of the canto Twenty-Sevens displays poetic, that is, verbal correspondences, linking fire and blood by their common colour. Both the *Inferno* and *Paradiso* Twenty-Sevens register bloodletting by tyrannical violence. In the Romagna that Dante's pilgrim describes to Guido, a 'sanguinoso mucchio' [bloody heap] ensued from Guido's victory over the papal Guelph army besieging Ghibelline Forlì in 1283, with the papal keys as their 'signaculo in vessillo' [emblem on a standard] (*Par.*, xxvii. 50). Romagnole tyrants such as the Malatesta suck blood with teeth sharpened into gimlets ('fan dei denti succhio', *Inf.*, xxvii. 48).[79] In Paradise, Peter returns to the blood-sucking conceit when accusing the Gascon Bertrand de Got (Clement V), and the Cahorsin Jacques Duèse (John XXII), of preparing to drink the blood of the faithful (*Par.*, xxvii. 57–58), in a eucharistic parody that echoes the apocalyptic 'woman drunk on the blood of the saints'.[80]

But the blushing of the crystalline Heaven as if reddened by the setting sun ('il ciel *cosperso*', *Par.*, xxvii. 30) announces as well the shedding of blood in sacrifice. Peter avows that he and other early popes nourished the Church, the bride of Christ, 'del sangue mio, di Lin, e di quel di Cleto' [by my blood, by Linus's, by that of Anacletus],[81] as did Sixtus and Pius and Calixtus and Urban, who 'sparser loro sangue dopo molto fleto' [shed their blood after much weeping] in the agonies of martyrdom (*Par.*, xxvii. 45). For the purpose of this vertical reading, scattered blood and blushes take us back to *Purgatorio* xxvii, which begins, as we saw, by establishing the time with reference to Jerusalem, the world's center, as the place where Christ shed his blood ('lo sangue sparse'). The word rhyming there with *sparse* is *riarse* [scorched], which associates shed blood with the burning noonday

---

79 Cf. *Epist.*, XI 7:14–15, and the Latin used there for the 'daughters of the horseleech' (*filiae sanguisugae*), that is, daughters of cupidity, who espouse apostaste bishops and cardinals. These prelates may in their turn be called 'sons to shame', *filios ad ruborem*, so collating bloodletting with blushing.

80 See *Apoc.* 17.6: 'And I saw the woman drunk with the blood of the saints, and with the blood of the martyrs of Jesus'. *Par.* xxvii uses *sangue* three times in eighteen lines.

81 Cf. *Epist.*, XI 2, of the sacrifices of Peter and Paul for Rome: 'that Rome [...] which the same Peter and Paul [...] consecrated as the Apostolic See by the shedding of their own blood'. On blushing and blood in *Paradiso* xxvii see also Jacoff, 'Dante, Geremia', p. 116.

sun on the Ganges, and marks the centre of the system of references to blood, blushes, fire, and sacrifice.

The comparison of the hesitant pilgrim to the dying Pyramus (*Purg.*, xxvii. 37–39) means that shed blood is also present, albeit inexplicitly, in the text of the midmost of our canto Twenty-Sevens: Dante's echo of the fable about why the 'mulberry turned crimson' (*Purg.*, xxvii. 39) references the copious bloodletting at the end of Ovid's tale. Bargetto refurbishes Francis Fergusson's claim that the reference to Pyramus and Thisbe and their sanguinary end recalls Christ's blood shed on the cross in the first verses of the canto.[82] As the cross of Christ traditionally extends to the four cardinal points, and in Dante's treatment marks the four articulations of the solar day, it may be taken, as we saw, as a figure embracing the whole of space and time. 'Christ's blood streams in the firmament', is how Marlowe's Faustus put it, which may point again to the most comprehensive container of all for Dante's pilgrim, one also suggested by eighty-one, the sum of three twenty-sevens: Christ's age had he lived out his natural life, circumscribing the fullest extent of the human lifespan.

---

82 Bargetto, 'Memorie liturgiche', pp. 227–28; see Francis Fergusson, *Dante's Drama of the Mind, A Modern Reading of the Purgatorio* (Westport, CT: Greenwood Press, 1981), pp. 162–63, 67. For Pyramus and Thisbe in *Purgatorio*, see Durling's Additional Note 13 in *The Divine Comedy*, II, pp. 618–20.

28. Cosmographic Cartography of the 'Perfect' Twenty-Eights

Theodore J. Cachey Jr.

Besides its intrinsic interest for the interpretation of the poem, the Cambridge vertical readings project raises many intriguing, and indeed, fundamental methodological questions. This chapter takes as its point of departure one of these: the numerological system that evidently informed the design of the poem. It is likely, in fact, that when many readers of the poem first heard of the vertical readings project their minds went directly to perhaps the most widely recognized and commented upon case of Dante's clearly aligning a set of three cantos distributed across three canticles in the same position along the poem's vertical axis according to a thematic criterion: the Sixes. But how many readers would think of relating this structural feature to the fact that the number six is the first perfect number?

Simply put, perfect numbers are those numbers that equal the sum of their divisors. The first number to fulfil this condition is 6, which can be divided by 1, by 2, and by 3, with the sum of these divisors adding up to 6; and the second perfect number is 28, with the divisors 1, 2, 4, 7, and 14, which add up to 28. Perfect numbers are extremely rare. Arithmetic, as taught during the medieval period in the tradition of Boethius, was acquainted with only four perfect numbers: 6, 28, 496, and 8128.

In an important paper on perfect numbers, medieval number theory and their relation to biblical exegesis and medieval compositional practices, Otfried Lieberknecht discussed the practical application of the arithmetic of perfect numbers by medieval exegetes of the Bible, who applied it to

 http://dx.doi.org/10.11647/OBP.0119.07

more or less every biblical occurrence of the number six and twenty-eight, and in particular to the six days of the creation, including Augustine in his biblical commentaries.[1] Lieberknecht offered in his paper a largely persuasive interpretation of *Inferno* xxviii in which he argued that the canto is structured in its parts and as a whole according to the concept of the *numerus perfectus*. Lieberknecht did not concern himself with the cartographic dimensions of *Inferno* xxviii that will be the focal point of this essay. Indeed, I do not think that before the vertical readings project it would have occurred to anyone to argue as I would like to do here, that the *numerus perfectus* informed the macro structure of the three canticles, according to a design in which the Sixes and the Twenty-Eights played a key structural role.

For beyond the political thematic that the Sixes share and that has been the focus of critical commentary, their vertical disposition within the poem's macrostructure appears to be informed by an overlooked and understudied geospatial criterion. That is to say, the political theme is parsed according to spatial parameters: those associated with the city of Florence in *Inferno* vi, the Italian peninsula in *Purgatorio* vi, and the inhabited world or *oikumene* in *Paradiso* vi. Just as the 'perfect' Sixes parse the body politic according to a geographical criterion that progressively maps the distribution of the human community in space, Dante offers us in the 'perfect' Twenty-Eights a mapping programme that establishes the cosmological setting of each of the three canticles and, cumulatively, of the entire poem in a progression that goes from a *mappamundi* of the inhabited world in *Inferno* xxviii to a *descriptio orbis* encompassing the entire terrestrial sphere in *Purgatorio* xxviii (including the discovery or 'invention' of the Earthly Paradise), to the contemplation of the divine plan of the entire cosmos in *Paradiso* xxviii. Moreover, beyond number theory there are fundamentally metaphysical motivations that inspire the mapping programme of the 'perfect' Twenty-Eights that go to the very heart of the poetics of the cosmographical poem and its truth claim. These will be the subject of some reflections in the last part of this *lectura*.

But first, the methodological digression on numerology needs to be developed a bit further, for there is some evidence to suggest that perhaps

---

1   Otfried Lieberknecht, *Dante's Historical Arithmetics: The Numbers Six and Twenty-eight as 'numeri perfecti secundum partium aggregationem' in Inferno XXVIII*, paper given at the 32nd International Congress on Medieval Studies, 8–11 May 1997, Western Michigan University (Kalamazoo), during the session n. 322 (Problems in Dante's *Inferno*, dir. Christopher Kleinhenz, sponsored by the Dante Society of America), http://www. lieberknecht.de/~diss/papers/p_np_txt.htm

the Fourteens might also play a role in a numerological macro structure, held together as it were, by a cosmological and geographical thematic. In fact, Virgil's account in *Inferno* xiv of the river system of Hell and its sources in the tears of the giant or 'veglio' of Crete is vital for an understanding of the geospatial parameters of the first two canticles. As we will learn in *Purgatorio* xxviii, the river Lethe at the summit of Mount Purgatory, which washes away the memories of the sins of the repentant at the end of their penitential journeys, is continuous with the river system of Hell (*Inf.*, xiv. 136–38). We will see in more detail below how the Lethe connects with the Earthly Paradise in a global system that converges at the earth's center at the bottom of the universe. Moreover, the connection between *Inferno* xiv and *Purgatorio* xxviii is an important one for the overall mapping programme of the poem for the way that it situates the island of Crete at the center of the *oikumene*, in opposition to the island of Purgatory, as part of a global triangle of juxtapositioning that involves as its third element Jerusalem at the antipodes from the Mountain of Purgatory.[2]

A linkage between *Inferno* xiv and *Purgatorio* xiv, on the other hand, is not hard to discern. The latter is dedicated to a cartographically inflected review of the degraded ethical state of the central regions of the Italian peninsula that were crucial to the poet's biographical experience, the first part of which, dedicated to Tuscany, is focused by a description of the Arno river and its course. *Inferno* xiv and *Purgatorio* xiv ostentatiously share a riverine thematic. Dante alludes very clearly to the river system of Hell in the account of the downward course of the Arno River and the inhabitants along its banks, whose moral and ethical qualities go from bad to worse in a way that parallels the further down is worse character of the river system of Hell that descends from Acheron to Styx, to Phlegeton, to Cocytus.[3] In her vertical reading of the Fourteens, Catherine Keen noted this connection between *Inferno* xiv and *Purgatorio* xiv, but was stymied as to any further parallels linking these cantos to *Paradiso* xiv.[4] Given the connections between *Inferno* xiv and *Purgatorio* xxviii, one might wonder

---

2 These observations are informed by Ambrogio Camozzi, 'Il veglio di Creta alla luce di Matelda — Una lettura comparativa di *Inferno* XIV e *Purgatorio* XXVIII', *The Italianist* 29.1 (2009), 3–49.

3 Regarding *Purgatorio* xiv see Catherine M. Keen's insightful '"A Local Habitation and a Name": Origins and Identity in *Purgatorio* XIV', *L'Alighieri* 49 (gennaio-giugno 2017), 69–90.

4 Catherine M. Keen, 'The Patterning of History: Poetry, Politics and Adamic Renewal', in *Vertical Readings in Dante's 'Comedy': Volume 2*, ed. by George Corbett and Heather Webb (Cambridge: Open Book Publishers, 2016), pp. 55–76, http://dx.doi.org/10.11647/OBP.0100

whether considering the 'perfect' Twenty-Eights as a set in relation to the Fourteens might enable us to make some further connections. The linkages between the Fourteens of the first two canticles and *Purgatorio* xxviii are indeed intriguing, and I will return to the question of whether there might be further structural resonances to uncover between the Fourteens and the Twenty-Eights below.

A Cartographic Reading of *Inferno* xxviii

In what sense is our reading cartographic? The mapping impulse in Dante corresponded and was in response to the transition from medieval place to early modern space that was occurring during the time that Dante was writing.[5] The cartographic manifestation of this transition (for which the shipwrecked voyage of Ulysses, foreshadowing the discovery of the New World, is perhaps the best-known expression in Dante's oeuvre) was the emergence of the empirically based nautical charts of the Mediterranean basin, as exemplified by the Carta Pisana, the earliest of this type of map to survive, and by the Dulcert chart dated 1339 (see Figs. 1 and 2). These nautical charts or portolans came alongside medieval *mappaemundi*, ranging from the canonical Hereford map to a less well-known eighth century map in the Vatican Library, which features Dante's Crete-centered *oikumene* (see Figs. 3 and 4). The empirical charts were eventually to overtake the *mappaemundi* and render them obsolete.[6]

---

5   Pierre Duhem, *Medieval Cosmology: Theories of Infinity, Place, Time, Void, and the Plurality of Worlds*, ed. and trans. by Roger Ariew (Chicago, IL: University of Chicago Press, 1985), pp. 139–268; Edward S. Casey, *The Fate of Place. A Philosophical History* (Berkeley, CA: University of California Press, 1998), pp. 103–15; Alexander Murray, 'Purgatory and the Spatial Imagination', in *Dante and the Church: Literary and Historical Essays*, ed. by Paolo Acquaviva and Jennifer Petrie (Dublin: Four Courts Press, 2007), pp. 61–92; Theodore J. Cachey, Jr., 'Cosmology, Geography and Cartography', in *Dante in Context*, ed. by Zygmunt G. Barański and Lino Pertile (Cambridge: Cambridge University Press, 2015), pp. 221–40; idem, 'Cartographic Dante: A Note on Dante and the Greek Mediterranean', in *Dante and the Greeks*, ed. by Jan M. Ziolkowski (Washington, D.C.: Dumbarton Oaks Research Library and Collections, 2014), pp. 197–226.

6   For the tradition of medieval *mappaemundi*, see the studies of Evelyn Edson, including *Medieval Views of the Cosmos*, with E. Savage-Smith (Oxford: Bodleian Library, 2004); *Mapping Time and Space: How Medieval Mapmakers Viewed their World* (London: British Library, 1999); and *The World Map, 1300–1492: The Persistence of Tradition and Transformation* (Baltimore, MD and Santa Fe, NM: Johns Hopkins University Press, 2007); for the portolan chart, see Tony Campbell, 'Portolan Charts from the Late Thirteenth Century to 1500', in *The History of Cartography, Volume one, Cartography in Prehistoric, Ancient, and Medieval Europe and the Mediterranean*, ed. by J. B. Harley and David Woodward (Chicago, IL: University of Chicago Press, 1987), pp. 371–463.

Fig. 1 *Carta Pisana*, late 13th century, © Bibliothèque nationale de France,
Rés. Ge. B. 1118, all rights reserved.

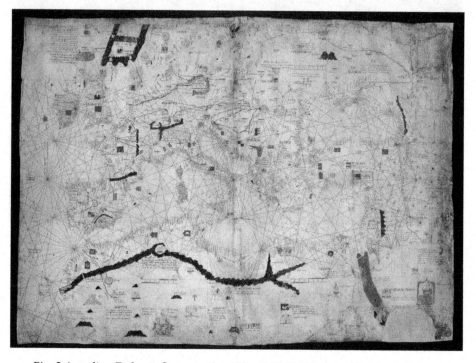

Fig. 2 Angelino Dulcert, *Carta nautica*, 1339, © Bibliothèque nationale de France,
Rés. Ge. B 696, all rights reserved.

Fig. 3 *Hereford Mappamundi, ca.*1300, © The Dean and Chapter of Hereford
Cathedral and the Hereford Mappamundi Trust, all rights reserved.

contrast ?

Fig. 4 *Mappamundi*, 8th century. This *mappamundi* represents a Crete-centered *oikumene*. © Biblioteca Apostolica Vaticana, Vat. lat. 6018 ff. 63v-64r., all rights reserved.

Dante is highly sensitive to these developments in the history of cartography. He is aware of the principal genres of cartographic representation and utilizes them in a metaliterary, or rather, a meta-cartographic manner during the course of the poem.[7] In the same way that Dante absorbs, synthesizes, and transcends his literary sources he transforms prior and contemporary traditions of mapping. Dante was especially attuned to the epistemological and representational issues raised by mapping, no less than he was to those raised by writing, especially as regards the relationship between literary representation and truth. The mapping programme of the poem ultimately serves Dante as a means of reinforcing both the truth claim, made most explicitly in *Inferno* xvi, and the metaphysical foundations of the poem.

---

7   See Theodore J. Cachey, Jr., 'Title, Genre, and Metaliterary Aspects of Dante's *Commedia*', in *Cambridge Companion to the Divine Comedy*, ed. by Zygmunt G. Barański and Simon Gilson (Cambridge: Cambridge University Press, forthcoming).

In the *Inferno* Dante utilizes three principal cartographic genres characteristic of his age, including the medieval *mappaemundi* or T-O maps, the nautical or portolan chart, and the regional or chorographic map of a territory. Very few regional maps of any territory survive from the age of Dante other than maps of the Holy Land, and only a couple of regional maps of Italy survive, from just after Dante.[8] The poet's detailed mappings of Italy throughout the three canticles are among his most innovative contributions to cartographic writing. Indeed, arguably the most detailed and compelling cartographic representation of the peninsula to survive from Dante's time is found in the *Commedia* itself. The strikingly modern cartographic mode of conceiving of Italy as a unity of language and culture was of course foreshadowed in Dante's linguistic treatise, the *De vulgari eloquentia*, whose birds-eye territorialization of the peninsula represented in its own right an important chapter in the history of cartography.[9]

Inferno xxviii is the culmination of the mapping programme of the first canticle and it establishes the premises for a cartographic programme that plays out in the rest of the poem along the axis of the Twenty-Eights. The canto presents a kind of analogy to the most advanced cartographic practices of the time, as exemplified by the Vatican map by Pietro Vesconte (*ca*.1320; see Fig. 5), the most sophisticated cartographer of the period, which brings together the nautical map and the *mappamundi*. In fact, in *Inferno* xxviii Dante fashions a kind of palimpsest of cartographic genres. The canto represents the culmination of the cartographic programme of the first canticle together with other culminating or cumulative aspects of that canto which have been noted before. These range from the emphasis on the rhetorical figure of *accumulatio*[10] to the synthetic articulation of the principle of the *contrapasso* which had guided the system of justice and representation of the entire canticle. The explicit definition of *contrapasso* is given by the sower of discord Bertran de Born who can be said to 'reap what he sows', in an episode which also includes an emphatic assertion by the poet that he is telling the truth. Dante's claim that he is telling the truth, as we will see, is an important sub-theme of the perfect Twenty-Eights.

---

8   See Michelina Di Cesare, 'Il sapere geografico di Boccaccio tra tradizione e innovazione: *l'imago mundi* di Paolino Veneto e Pietro Vesconte', in *Boccaccio geografo, Un viaggio nel Mediterraneo tra le città, I giardini e… il 'mondo' di Giovanni Boccaccio*, ed. by Roberta Morosini and Andrea Cantile (Florence: Maura Paglia Editore, 2010), pp. 67–88.

9   See Franco Farinelli, 'L'immagine dell'Italia', in *Geografia politica delle regioni italiane*, ed. by Pasquale Coppola (Turin: Einaudi, 1997), pp. 33–59.

10   See Edoardo Sanguineti, *Interpretazione di Malebolge* (Florence: Olschki, 1961), pp. 284–85; and Pietro G. Beltrami, 'Metrica e sintassi nel canto XXVIII dell'*Inferno*', *Giornale storico della letteratura italiana* 162 (1985), 1–26.

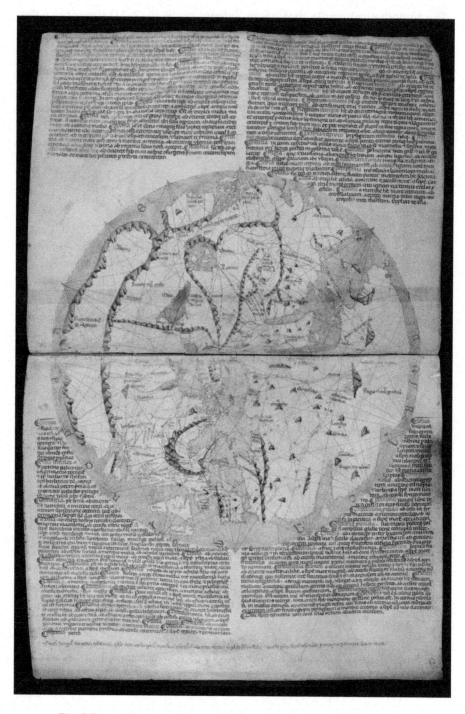

Fig. 5 Pietro Vesconte, *Mappamundi, ca.*1320, © Biblioteca Apostolica
Vaticana, Pal.lat.1362A_0008_fa_0001v-2r, all rights reserved.

The hypothetical simile that opens *Inferno* xxviii (ll. 7–21) describing the 'fortunata terra / di Puglia' [Apulia, land laid low by war] (ll. 8–9), which is a synecdoche for the whole south of Italy, completes within the realm of the *Malebolge* of fraud a cartographical outline of the Italian peninsula that the poet had drawn in a series of geographical similes that started in the circle of violence (*Inf.*, ix. 112–16; *Inf.*, xii. 4–10; *Inf.*, xvi. 91–105). The Mediterranean basin of the nautical or portolan charts is synthetically captured by the tercet:

> Tra l'isola di Cipri e di Maiolica
> non vide mai sì gran fallo Nettuno,
> non da pirate, non da gente argolica. (*Inf.*, xxviii. 82–84)

[Between the islands of Cyprus and Majorca Neptune never witnessed so terrible a crime, whether one committed by pirates or by Greeks.]

Dante not only recapitulates the previously outlined cartographic parameters of Italy in the canto, but by means of this synecdoche reiterates the eastern and western ends of the Greek Mediterranean that had been traversed in earlier cantos of the eighth circle, by the voyage of Jason and the Argonauts in the eastern Mediterranean (*Inferno* xviii) and by Ulysses's voyage in the farthest west (*Inferno* xxvi). At the same time, however, through the reference, in the same tercet, to Neptune who never witnessed such a crime, the poet establishes a link forward to the farthest limits of the poem and the vision of God at the end of *Paradiso*, so that Dante can be seen to utilize the parameters of the Greek Mediterranean to chart the journey of the poem itself:

> Un punto solo m'è maggior letargo
> che venticinque secoli a la 'mpresa
> che fé Nettuno ammirar l'ombra d'Argo (*Par.*, xxxiii. 94–96)

[My memory of that moment is more lost than five and twenty centuries make dim that enterprise when, in wonder, Neptune at the Argo's shadow stared.]

But finally, the *contrapasso* of the sowers of discord can itself be seen to figure an inverted *mappamundi* of the T-O type like the twelfth-century *mappa orbis terrae* that illustrates Isidore of Seville's *Etymologiae* or Goro Dati's *Mappamundi* at the Laurenziana Library in Florence (*Inf.*, xxviii. 22–33 and 118–23; see Figs. 6 and 7). Within the circular 'dolente strada' or pathway of the sinners at either end of the canto's series of sinners, the vertical cut on the bodies of Mohammed, 'rotto dal mento infin dove si trulla' [cleft from the chin right down to where men fart] (l. 24) and Ali, 'fesso nel volto dal mento al ciuffetto' [his face split open from his chin to forelock] (l. 33), intersects with the horizontal separation of Bertran de Born's' head from his body, 'par ch'io 'l veggia, / un busto sanza capo andar' [I truly saw, and seem to see it still, a headless body make its way] (ll. 118–19), according to an iconographic programme no doubt inspired by a sub genre of *mappamundi* representing the body of Christ projected upon or embracing the *oikumene* (see Figs. 8 and 9). Beyond *Inferno* xxviii a connection can be drawn between the inverted T-O map figured there and the celestial Greek Cross upon which Christ flashes in the Heaven of Mars in *Paradiso* xiv, perhaps inspired by the Cross that Dante would have seen in St Apollinare in Classe (see Figs. 6 and 10).

Fig. 6 *Mappa orbis terrae* (T-O), illustration of a copy from the twelfth-century manuscript of the *Etymologiae* by Isidore of Seville,

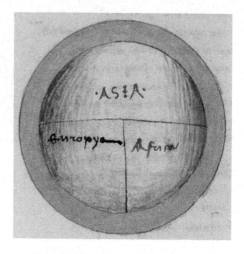

Fig. 7 Goro Dati, *T-O mappamundi*, fifteenth century, Firenze,

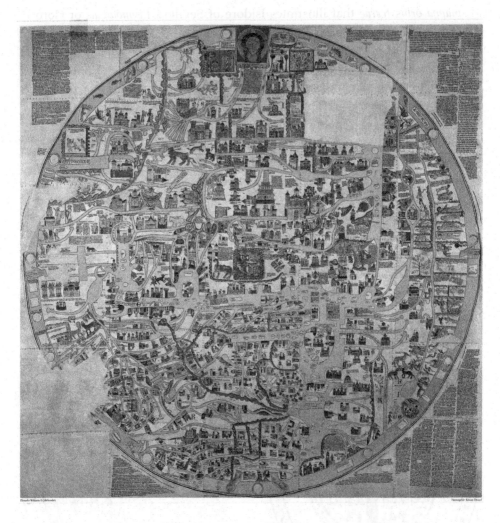

Fig. 8 *Ebsdorf mappamundi*, 1235–1239. The map was destroyed during the
Second World War. © Kloster Ebstorf, all rights reserved.

Fig. 9 *Mappamundi, English Psalter,* © British Library Board, Add. MS 28681, f.9r, all rights reserved.

Fig. 10 *Apse mosaic cross*, Ravenna, 6th century, Church of St Apollinare in Classe,

> Come distinta da minori e maggi
> lumi biancheggia tra ' poli del mondo
> Galassia sì, che fa dubbiar ben saggi;
>   sì costellati facean nel profondo
> Marte quei raggi il venerabil segno
> che fan giunture di quadranti in tondo.
>   Qui vince la memoria mia lo 'ngegno;
> ché quella croce lampeggiava Cristo,
> sì ch'io non so trovare essempro degno;
>   ma chi prende sua croce e segue Cristo,
> ancor mi scuserà di quel ch'io lasso,
> vedendo in quell' albor balenar Cristo. (*Par.*, xiv. 97–108)

[As the Milky Way, arrayed with greater and lesser lights, glows white
between the universal poles, making even sages wonder how and why,
these rays, thus constellated, made, deep within Mars, the venerable
sign that the crossing of its quadrants fixes in a circle. Here my memory

outstrips my skill, for that cross so flamed forth Christ that I can find no
fit comparison. But he who takes his cross and follows Christ shall yet
forgive me what I leave untold, for shining in that dawn I did see Christ.]

The parodic T-O map, figured by the *contrapasso* inflicted on the bodies of the
sowers of discord, Mohammed and Ali and Bertran de Born, is juxtaposed
with the Greek Cross of Christ formed by the souls of the martial heroes of
the faith celebrated in the Heaven of Mars. This comparison could not be
more pointed. It also represents an illustration of the way that the 'perfect'
Twenty-Eights reverberate and ramify among the Fourteens, producing a
broader system of resonances.

Inventing the Map of Purgatory in *Purgatorio* xxviii

While Dante brings together all the threads of contemporary cartographic
representation in his dystopic picture of the inhabited world in *Inferno*
xxviii, he goes off the map, so to speak, and sails uncharted waters in
Purgatorio xxviii. Dante goes beyond his alter ego Ulysses, whose voyage
of oceanic discovery beyond the pillars had ended in shipwreck, and
beyond the imaginations of the classical poets who 'forse in Parnaso esto
loco sognaro' [dreamed on Parnassus of perhaps this very place] (*Purg.*,
xxviii. 141). As Bruno Nardi first illustrated in a famous 1922 essay on 'the
myth of Eden',[11] Dante modified, conflated and altered in a highly original
manner traditions surrounding the location of the Eden of the church
fathers, the scholastics and centuries of medieval cartography in order
to arrive at his original 'invention' or 'discovery' (as a kind of Colombus
ante litteram) of the 'true' location of the Earthly Paradise at the summit of
Mount Purgatory, situated at the antipodes of Jerusalem, thereby placing
in geometrical opposition the location of the first man Adam's original sin
and the site of Christ's redemptive sacrifice on Golgotha.

The second part of *Purgatorio* xxviii (ll. 85–148) dedicated to Matelda's
lesson on the supernatural cosmology of Eden, which foreshadows
the cosmological and metaphysical seminars conducted by Beatrice in
Paradise, is essential for the cosmographic cartography of the poem, and
anticipates the culminating map of the cosmos of *Paradiso* xxviii. *Purgatorio*
xxviii is fundamental for the cartography of the poem in both physical

---

11 Bruno Nardi, 'Intorno al sito del "Purgatorio" e al mito dantesco dell'"Eden"', *Il giornale
dantesco* 25 (1922), 289–300.

and metaphysical senses in so far as it maps the physical reality of the cosmos at the same time that, by giving an account of God's providential design, it presages the account of the angelic hierarchy in *Paradiso* xxviii that is ultimately responsible, from a metaphysical perspective, for the implementation of that design.

Purgatorio xxviii, in particular, charts the joining or bond between Heaven and earth, in keeping with the overall theme of the canto that describes an earthly paradise that is both of this world and not of this world. For instance, a direct link is established with 'la prima volta' [the first circling] (l. 104):

> Or perché in circuito tutto quanto
> l'aere si volge con la prima volta,
> se non li è rotto il cerchio d'alcun canto... (*Purg.*, xxviii. 103–05)

> [Now, since all the air revolves in a circuit with the first circling, unless its revolution is at some point blocked...]

The 'first' or 'primal' revolution ('la prima volta') is that of the *Primum Mobile* or ninth Heaven. The *Primum Mobile* will be the setting for *Paradiso* xxviii, and Dante establishes here a direct topographical link between *Purgatorio* xxviii and *Paradiso* xxviii by virtue of this cosmological joining of the ninth Heaven and the Earthly Paradise. In its diurnal revolution the ninth Heaven sweeps the other spheres or Heavens with it around the earth and at the same time causes the atmosphere to circle the earth with it.

The breeze that caresses the Earthly Paradise is limited, however, to the highest reaches of the mountain. In his commentary to *Purg.*, xxviii. 103–04 Charles Singleton noted that:

[i]n *Meteor.* I, 3, 341ᵃ, Aristotle states that the air flows in a circuit since it is carried along in the total circulation, and Thomas Aquinas [*Exp. Meteor.* I, lect. 5], commenting on Aristotle, had noted: 'Et sic ille aer, qui excedit omnem altitudinem montium, in circuitu fluit; aer autem qui continetur infra montium altitudinem, impeditur ab hoc fluxu ex partibus terrae immobilibus'. ('And accordingly that air, which exceeds the altitude of all the mountains, flows in a circuit; but the air which is contained in the midst of high mountains is impeded in its flow by the immobile parts of the earth'.)[12]

---

12 Charles Singleton, gloss to *Purg.*, xxviii. 103–04, *Dartmouth Dante Project* (https://dante.dartmouth.edu).

The precision of the 'scientific' dimensions of Dante's account of the supernatural sources of the breeze and the waters of the Earthly Paradise, reminiscent of Dante's cosmographical treatise, the *Questio de aqua et terra*, are worthy of note. Meteorological details are intermingled, as a kind of terrestrial counterpoint to the overall supernatural nature of Eden, in the account of the breeze and the source of the rivers.[13] These scientific asides serve as an essential support for the truth claim of Dante's account.

Matelda's lecture about the physical and metaphysical properties of the Earthly Paradise and their source, are aimed, moreover (just as Beatrice's discourse will be in the *Paradiso*) at 'unclouding' Dante's mind: 'che puote disnebbiar vostro intelletto' [that may disperse the clouds within your minds] (*Purg.*, xxviii. 81), 'e purgherà la nebbia che ti fiede' [and thus disperse the fog assailing you] (*Purg.*, xxviii. 90). These passages prepare for the culminating use of this figure in *Paradiso* xxviii that comes at the end of Beatrice's explication of the most difficult problem of Dante's cartographical poetics, as I discuss below:

> Come rimane splendido e sereno
> l'emisperio de l'aere, quando soffia
> Borea da quella guancia ond' è più leno,
>   per che si purga e risolve la roffia
> che pria turbava, sì che 'l ciel ne ride
> con le bellezze d'ogne sua paroffia;
>   così fec'io, poi che mi provide
> la donna mia del suo risponder chiaro,
> e come stella in cielo il ver si vide. (*Par.*, xxviii. 79–87)

[As the vault of our air is left serene and shining when Boreas blows from his gentler cheek and the dark refuse of the sky is cleared and purged away so that the Heavens smile as all their quarters fill with loveliness, just so did I feel when my lady bestowed on me her lucid answer, and, like a star in Heaven, the truth shone clear.]

---

13 Respectively, *Purg.*, xxviii. 97–99: 'Perché 'l turbar che sotto da sé fanno / l'essalazion de l'acqua e de la terra, / che quanto posson dietro al calor vanno...' [So that the turbulence below, created by the vapors rising both from land and sea toward the sun's heat as far as they can rise]; and *Purg.*, xxviii. 121–23: 'L'acqua che vedi non surge di vena / che ristori vapor che gel converta, / come fiume ch'acquista e perde lena...' [The water you see here does not spring from a vein that is restored by vapor when condensed by cold, like a river that gains and loses flow'].

Purgatorio xxviii also establishes a vital connection with the geography of this world through the hydrological connection that it establishes between the river Lethe and the river system of Hell that traces its origins to the island of Crete as described in *Inferno* xiv. It was there that in response to Dante's query, 'Maestro, ove si trova / Flegetonta e Letè?' [Master, where are Phlegethon and Lethe?] (*Inf.*, xiv. 130–31), Virgil had told Dante that he would eventually encounter Lethe:

> 'Letè vedrai, ma fuor di questa fossa,
> la dove vanno l'anime a lavarsi
> quando la colpa pentuta è rimossa'. (*Inf.*, xiv. 136–38)

> [Lethe you shall see: not in this abyss but where the spirits go to cleanse themselves once their repented guilt has been removed.]

When Dante finally arrives in the Earthly Paradise and encounters Lethe, Matelda leaves the pilgrim in no doubt about its source:

> 'esce di fontana salda e certa,
> che tanto dal voler di Dio riprende,
> quant' ella versa da due parti aperta'. (*Purg.*, xxviii. 124–26)

> [issues from a sure, unchanging source, which by God's will regains as much as it pours forth to either side.]

Concerning its destination, however, there has been less certainty, although a general consensus has emerged that Lethe, according to Dante's cosmographic cartography, descends to the center of the earth.[14] Thus all of Lucifer's works, even the recollection of sin that survives the penitential ascent, finally flow back to the originator on the icy lake. At the earth's center two streams converge from opposite directions. From Mount Ida on the Mountain of Crete, located in the middle of the inhabited world, descend the tears of the Old Man of Crete. From the Earthly Paradise, situated at the antipodes from Mount Ida, descends the Lethe. The breeze that shakes the trees of the Earthly Paradise, which shower the world with the *virtù* that produces the vegetation of the earth, and the rivers of the Earthly Paradise

---

14 At least since Daniel J. Donno, 'Moral Hydrography: Dante's Rivers', *Modern Language Notes* 92 (1977), 130–39.

trace their origin to a supernatural source in God's providential design of the universe. Both play vital roles in salvation history, as illustrated by Matelda's cosmological lesson.

The truth claim that Dante makes at the end of the canto for his distinctive and highly original *mappamundi* that locates Eden at the top of Mount Purgatory at the antipodes of Jerusalem is especially worth underscoring. The truth of Dante's poetry of the Earthly Paradise, according to Matelda, surpasses that of the classical poets:

> 'Quelli ch'anticamente poetaro
> l'età de l'oro e suo stato felice,
> forse in Parnaso esto loco sognaro.
>
> Qui fu innocente l'umana radice;
> qui primavera sempre e ogne frutto;
> nettare è questo di che ciascun dice'.
>
> Io mi rivolsi 'n dietro allora tutto
> a' miei poeti, e vidi che con riso
> udito avëan l'ultimo costrutto (*Purg.*, xxviii. 139–47)

['Those who in ancient times called up in verse the age of gold and sang its happy state dreamed on Parnassus of perhaps this very place. Here the root of humankind was innocent, here it is always spring, with every fruit in season. This is the nectar of which the ancients tell'. I turned around then to my poets and saw that they had listened to her final utterance with a smile.]

In recognition of their error the poets smile, just as Gregory the Great smiled when he reached Paradise and realized that he had been mistaken about the order of the celestial hierarchy, according to the account that Dante gives in *Paradiso* xxviii. The true account of the *Commedia* gives the correct order, which corresponds to that of Pseudo-Dionysius:

> E Dïonisio con tanto disio
> a contemplar questi ordini si mise,
> che li nomò e distinse com'io.
>
> Ma Gregorio da lui poi si divise;
> onde, sì tosto come li occhi aperse
> in questo ciel, di sé medesmo rise.
>
> E se tanto secreto ver proferse
> mortale in terra, non voglio ch'ammiri:

>ché chi 'l vide qua sù gliel discoperse
>   con altro assai del ver di questi giri. (*Par.*, xxviii. 130–39)

[Dionysius with such passion set his mind to contemplate these orders that he named them and arranged them as do I. But later Gregory took a different view, so that, opening his eyes here in this Heaven, he saw his errors, laughing at himself. And if a mortal man on earth set forth such hidden truth, you need not wonder: for he who saw it here above revealed it then to him, along with many other truths about these circlings.]

While Dionysius had received his information according to the tradition from St Paul, the poet Dante, like St Paul, gains his knowledge of the celestial order first-hand. It is not by accident that the ends of these two cantos correspond so perfectly. We are supposed to connect them as regards the poem's truth claim. The theme of the smile of recognition at one's error is linked in both cantos to the mapping programme of the 'perfect Twenty-Eights' and to the overarching truth claim that Dante makes for the *Commedia*.[15]

The truth claim made by the poet in connection with the Bertran de Born episode of *Inferno* xxviii (ll. 118–42) had inaugurated this theme along the trajectory of the Twenty-Eights. The culminating canto for this theme, however, along the axis of the Twenty-Eights, is *Paradiso* xxviii, which as Gianfranco Contini observed in his famous *lectura* of that canto, features as its primary structuring verbal motif the word 'vero' and its derivatives.[16] What is the relationship between the truth claim of the poem and the mapping of the *oikumene* in *Inferno* xxviii, of the terrestrial globe in *Purgatorio* xxviii, and of the cosmos in *Paradiso* xxviii? Or to put it another way, as stated at the outset: why cartography? We will return to this in the conclusion.

---

15 See Theodore J. Cachey, Jr., 'Una nota sugli angeli e l'Empireo', *Italianistica. Rivista di letteratura italiana.* 44.2 (2015), 149–60. For Gregory's smile, see Vittorio Montemaggi, 'Dante and Gregory the Great', in *Reviewing Dante's Theology*, ed. by Claire Honess and Matthew Treherne (Bern: Peter Lang, 2013), I, pp. 209–62.

16 Gianfranco Contini, 'Un esempio di poesia dantesca (Il canto XXVIII del '*Paradiso*')', in *idem, Un'idea di Dante* (Turin: Einaudi, 1976), pp. 191–213: '[...] la parola che qui Dante insegue e ripete, il *vero*, è talmente palese da sottostare alla più vivida illuminazione anzi dell'intenzionalità' (p. 192).

Mapping the Cosmos in *Paradiso* xxviii

Paradiso xxviii, 'in which the pilgrim will come to understand the nature and origin of space', represents, in fact, the crowning achievement of the poem's cosmological mapping.[17] Simply put, Dante completes here the cosmographic cartographical programme of the 'perfect' Twenty-Eights by offering the reader a map of the cosmos from the perspective of the ninth Heaven at the top of the created world. The poet, in fact, conducts himself like a mapmaker in the canto by first setting down the figure or model of the cosmos in *Paradiso* xxviii. 13–45. In Beatrice's commentary in the next section, in lines 46–87, the poet provides essential information concerning the projection and scale of the map. On the one hand, Beatrice translates the latitudes and longitudes, so to speak, of the cosmos in terms of their spatial representation in the model, while on the other she provides the ratio or proportion of distances on the map to the corresponding distances 'in reality'. Finally, Beatrice provides the map's legend, the key to understanding the symbols used on any map, by identifying the nine orders of the angels in lines 97–139.

Dante's map of the cosmos as presented in the figure of nine concentric rings circling around a point of light in verses 13–45 is a special kind of map:

> E com' io mi rivolsi e furon tocchi
> li miei da ciò che pare in quel volume,
> quandunque nel suo giro ben s'adocchi,
>   un punto vidi che raggiava lume
> acuto sì, che 'l viso ch'elli affoca
> chiuder conviensi per lo forte acume;
>   e quale stella par quinci più poca,
> parrebbe luna, locata con esso
> come stella con stella si collòca.
>   Forse cotanto quanto pare appresso
> alo cigner la luce che 'l dipigne
> quando 'l vapor che 'l porta più è spesso,

---

17 See Christian Moevs, *The Metaphysics of Dante's 'Comedy'* (Oxford: Oxford University Press, 2005), p. 140. See also for this canto, Alison Cornish, 'The Sufficient Example: *Paradiso* 28', in her *Reading Dante's Stars* (New Haven, CT and London: Yale University Press, 2000), pp. 108–18.

distante intorno al punto un cerchio
d'igne si girava sì ratto, ch'avria vinto
quel moto che più tosto il mondo cigne;
   e questo era d'un altro circumcinto,
e quel dal terzo, e 'l terzo poi dal quarto,
dal quinto il quarto, e poi dal sesto il quinto.
   Sopra seguiva il settimo sì sparto
già di larghezza, che 'l messo di Iuno
intero a contenerlo sarebbe arto.
   Così l'ottavo e 'l nono; e chiascheduno
più tardo si movea, secondo ch'era
in numero distante più da l'uno;
   e quello avea la fiamma più sincera
cui men distava la favilla pura,
credo, però che più di lei s'invera.
   La donna mia, che mi vedëa in cura
forte sospeso, disse: 'Da quel punto
depende il cielo e tutta la natura.
   Mira quel cerchio che più li è congiunto;
e sappi che 'l suo muovere è sì tosto
per l'affocato amore ond' elli è punto'. (*Par.*, xxviii. 13–45)

[When I turned back and my eyes were struck by what appears on that
revolving sphere — if one but contemplates its circling — I saw a point
that flashed a beam of light so sharp the eye on which it burns must
close against its piercing brightness. The star that, seen from here below,
seems smallest would seem a moon if put beside it, as when one star
is set beside another. As near, perhaps, as a halo seems to be when it
encircles the light that colours it, where the vapor that forms it is most
dense, there whirled about that point a ring of fire so quick it would have
easily outsped the swiftest sphere circling the universe. This point was
encircled by another ring, and that by the third, the third by the fourth,
the fourth by the fifth, and the fifth by the sixth. Higher there followed
the seventh, now spread so wide that the messenger of Juno, in full circle,
would be unable to contain its size. And so, too, the eighth and ninth,
each one revolving with diminished speed the farther it was wheeling
from the first. And that one least removed from the blazing point of light
possessed the clearest flame, because, I think, it was the one that is the
most intruthed by it. My lady, who saw me in grave doubt yet eager to
know and comprehend, said: 'From that point depend the Heavens and
all nature. Observe that circle nearest it, and understand its motion is so
swift because it is spurred on by flaming love'.]

The poet's description of nine rings circling the *punto* can be understood in cartographic terms as a mandala, that is, a diagram, chart or geometric pattern that represents the cosmos metaphysically and symbolically. Such devices used for ritual purposes by Indian religions focus the attention of practitioners and adepts and act as an aid to meditation and even trance induction. In a similar manner, the geometric pattern or model that Dante presents in verses 13–45 of *Paradiso* xxviii is meant to serve the reader as an object of contemplation and a tool to focus the attention. In contemplating it, with Beatrice's guidance, we as readers are meant to achieve a transformed perspective on the nature and origin of space, just as the pilgrim's perspective is transformed. This is the deepest sense and purpose of those verses at the beginning of the passage cited that have puzzled the critics: 'E com' io mi rivolsi e furon tocchi / li miei da ciò che pare in quel volume, / quandunque nel suo giro ben s'adocchi' [When I turned back and my eyes were struck by what appears on that revolving sphere — if one but contemplates its circling] (*Par.*, xxviii. 13–15).[18] By contemplating the poet's map of the cosmos as projected on the sphere of the *Primum Mobile* one can achieve insight into the nature and origin of space, that is, by focusing upon the point ('un punto vidi che raggiava lume', l.16) that transcends the finite mind. The point is the first ontological principle for Aristotle, the reflexivity of pure awareness upon which 'depend Heaven and the world of nature' (*Metaphysics* 12.71072b14). In fact Beatrice says the same things as Aristotle about the *punto*: 'Da quel punto / depende il cielo e tutta la natura' [From that point depend the Heavens and all of nature] (*Par.*, xxviii. 41–42).[19]

To complement and transcend the cartography of the *oikumene* of *Inferno* xxviii and the plan of the terrestrial globe in *Purgatorio* xxviii, Dante provides in *Paradiso* xxviii nothing less than a mandala of the cosmos, as well as an account of its projection and a legend. Dante's picture of the spatial temporal universe includes, also, an account of the angelic hierarchy that providentially governs the universe. Indeed, the geometrical figure or model of the cosmos that Dante employs was probably inspired by a passage from Boethius's *Consolation of Philosophy*

---

18 See Moevs, p. 141: 'In absolute terms, to turn from the reflection to the source is to turn from the world to its ground; it is to focus the light of awareness on itself in a single point. What is thus revealed is there to be seen whenever (quandunque) one turns upon oneself and looks well'.

19 *Idem*, p. 142.

that described the means by which divine providence expresses its intention through the created world:

> For as the innermost of several circles revolving round the same centre approaches the simplicity of the midmost point, and is, as it were, a pivot round which the exterior circles turn, while the outermost, whirled in ampler orbit, takes in a wider and wider sweep of space in proportion to its departure from the indivisible unity of the centre — while, further, whatever joins and allies itself to the centre is narrowed to a like simplicity, and no longer expands vaguely into space — even so whatsoever departs widely from primal mind is involved more deeply in the meshes of fate, and things are free from fate in proportion as they seek to come nearer to that central pivot [...]. (Boethius, *The Consolation of Philosophy*, IV, 6)[20]

Dante's utilization of the figure of the circle serves an analogous and parallel purpose to Boethius's. The same principle by which greater proximity to the divine at the centre implies greater adherence to the divine characterizes both Dante's plan of the angelic hierarchy in lines 97–139, and the will of providence in Boethius's formulation. But the metaphysical stakes are higher for Dante insofar as he aims to bring the pilgrim and the reader to an understanding of the nature and the origin of space. For the 'punto' which radiates light represents nothing less than 'the nexus between spatial temporal extension and self-subsistent conscious being'.[21] Nevertheless it is clear from the question that the pilgrim next poses to Beatrice that he still regards spatial extension as an ontological reality:

> E io a lei: 'Se 'l mondo fosse posto
> con l'ordine ch'io veggio in quelle rote,
> sazio m'avrebbe ciò che m'è proposto;
>   ma nel mondo sensibile si puote
> veder le volte tanto più divine,
> quant' elle son dal centro più remote.
>   Onde, se 'l mio disir dee aver fine
> in questo miro e angelico templo
> che solo amore e luce ha per confine,

---

20 'Nam ut orbium circa eundem cardinem sese vertentium, qui est intimus, ad simplicitatem medietatis accedit ceterorumque extra locatorum veluti cardo quidam, circa quem versentur, exsistit, extimus vero maiore ambitu rotatus quanto a puncti media individuitate discedit, tanto amplioribus spatiis explicatur, si quod vero illi se medio conectat et societ, in simplicitatem cogitur diffundique ac diffluere cessat, simili ratione, quod longius a prima mente discedit, maioribus fati nexibus implicatur ac tanto aliquid fato liberum est, quanto illum rerum cardinem vicinius petit...'

21 Moevs, p. 141.

udir convienmi ancor come l'essemplo
e l'essemplare non vanno d'un modo,
ché io per me indarno a ciò contemplo'. (*Par.*, xxviii. 46–57)

[And I to her: 'If the universe were arranged in the order I see here
among these wheels I would be content with what you've set before me.
However, in the world of sense we see the farther from the centre they
revolve the more divinity is in their orbits. And so, if my desire to know
shall gain its end in this rare temple of the angels, which has but light
and love for boundaries, then I still need to learn exactly why model and
copy fail to follow the same plan, or, using my own powers, I reflect on
this in vain'.]

The pilgrim has realized that the model (essemplo) he has seen (the self-
subsistent point projecting concentric reflected rings about itself) is the
precise inverse of the copy (essemplare) that is the sensible world, in which
the Empyrean contains the concentric spheres of creation. In explaining the
projection and scale of the map Beatrice effectively resolves the question
for Dante and the reader:

Così la donna mia; poi disse: 'Piglia
quel ch'io ti dicerò, se vuo' saziarti;
e intorno da esso t'assottiglia.
    Li cerchi corporai sono ampi e arti
secondo il più e 'l men de la virtute
che si distende per tutte lor parti.
    Maggior bontà vuol far maggior salute;
maggior salute maggior corpo cape,
s'elli ha le parti igualmente compiute.
    Dunque costui che tutto quanto rape
l'altro universo seco, corrisponde
al cerchio che più ama e che più sape:
    per che, se tu a la virtù circonde
la tua misura, non a la parvenza
de le sustanze che t'appaion tonde,
    tu vederai mirabil consequenza
di maggio a più e di minore a meno,
in ciascun cielo, a süa intelligenza'. (*Par.*, xxviii. 61–78)

[My lady said this, then went on: 'Take what I shall tell you if you would
be fed, and see you sharpen your wits on it. The material Heavens are
wide or narrow according as power, greater or less, is diffused through
all their parts. Greater goodness makes for greater blessedness, and

greater bliss takes on a greater body when all its parts are equal in perfection. This sphere, therefore, which sweeps into its motion the rest of the universe, must correspond to the ring that loves and knows the most, so that, if you apply your measure, not to their appearances but to the powers themselves of the angels that appear to you as circles, you will see a marvelous congruence, larger with more, smaller with less, in each sphere according to its celestial Intelligence.]

The size of the heavenly spheres, according to Beatrice's explanation (*Par.*, xxviii. 61–78) is caused by the causal-formative influence (virtù) they embody. In effect, Beatrice explains, if you 'measure' virtù and not appearances ('la parvenza / de le sustanze') you will find that there is no contradiction between the source and its mirror-image, between the intelligible order and its spatiotemporal reflection. As a result of Beatrice's explanation the pilgrim, and potentially the reader as well, experience a radical shift of perspective. Rather than seeing the ontological hierarchy of being through the reflected image that is space-time, and ascending from the material, located at the centre, to the divine, located at the periphery, we see its truth or source as beginning from the reflexivity of conscious being, at the centre, radiating out as spatial extension.[22]

But to conclude we must return, finally, to consider the representational issues raised by *Paradiso* xxviii and the relationship between cartography and Dante's truth claim for the poem. For commentators have justly called attention to the ambiguity of the verses we have just discussed:

> '… udir convienmi ancor come l'essemplo
> e l'essemplare non vanno d'un modo,
> ché io per me indarno a ciò contemplo' (*Par.*, xxviii. 55–57)

[then I still need to learn exactly why model and copy fail to follow the same plan, or, using my own powers, I reflect on this in vain.]

The usual interpretation is that the *essemplo* is the model, that is, the supersensory invisible world of the Empyrean and the *essemplare* is the copy, that is, the sensible world. The ambiguity is located in the question of which word refers to the copy and which to that which is being copied, or to put it another way, which (*l'essemplo* or *l'essemplare*) is the map and which the thing mapped. The Bosco-Reggio commentary notes that the

---

22 *Idem*, p. 144.

majority of the ancient commentators understood *l'essemplo* to be the copy, that is, the physical world, and *l'essemplare* to be the model, the supersensible world, while many modern commentators invert the terms. Bosco-Reggio conclude that it is perhaps best to follow the interpretation of the ancients;[23] Sapegno notes the same ambiguity and reversibility of the terms while observing that either way 'il senso non cambia' [the meaning does not change].[24]

It seems unlikely that Dante would not have been aware of the interchangeability of *l'essemplo* and *l'essemplare* and that he is using it to indicate that the model or map and the reality are both, in the end, representations of a truth that transcends the space-time realm of representation. In fact, in *Paradiso* xiv, as noted earlier, in counterpoint to the T-O map of *Inferno* xxviii, Dante described the vision of Christ's flashing cross as outstripping his representational resources:[25]

> Qui vince la memoria mia lo 'ngegno;
> ché quella croce lampeggiava Cristo,
> sì ch'io non so trovare essempro degno;
>   ma chi prende sua croce e segue Cristo,
> ancor mi scuserà di quel ch'io lasso,
> vedendo in quell' albor balenar Cristo. (*Par.*, xiv. 103–08)

> [Here my memory outstrips my skill, for that cross so flamed forth Christ that I can find no fit comparison. But he who takes his cross and follows Christ shall yet forgive me what I leave untold, for shining in that dawn I did see Christ.]

Dante's mappings of the cosmos, while truthful, are ultimately inadequate to represent 'the knot or nexus between self-subsistent Intellect-Being and spatiotemporal contingency, which is the knot of the incarnation, or

---

23 See Umberto Bosco and Giovanni Reggio, glossa to *Par.*, xxviii. 55–57, *Dartmouth Dante Project*, https://dante.dartmouth.edu

24 See Natalino Sapegno, gloss to *Par.*, xxviii. 55–56, *Dartmouth Dante Project*, https://dante.dartmouth.edu

25 The passage anticipates the failure of memory and imagination that will occur at the end of *Paradiso* xxxiii when the poet will attempt to recall and represent his face to face encounter with the triform divinity, likening himself to a mapmaker trying to project the sphere on the flat surface of a map, 'qual è 'l geomètra che tutto s'affige per misurar lo cerchio, e non ritrova, pensando, quel principio ond' elli indige' [Like the geometer who fully applies himself to square the circle and, for all his thought, cannot discover the principle he lacks] (*Par.*, xxxiii. 133–35).

revelation, of Christ and of the *Comedy*'s poetics'.[26] For the poet 'can find no fit comparison' ('non so trovare essempro degno') for a truth that lies beyond the representational capabilities of the map and of writing.

Why cartography, then? Historians of cartography Denis Wood and John Fels observe in *The Natures of Maps* that: 'Insisting that something is there is a uniquely powerful way of insisting that something is. Mapped things — no matter how conceptually daunting — possess such extraordinary credibility that they're capable of propelling into popular discourse abstruse abstractions cantilevered from abstruse abstractions: high pressure cells, El Niño, seafloor spreading, thermohaline circulation'.[27] I believe that Dante, on the cusp of the transition from a medieval place-based cosmos to early modern space, between the representational genres of the ideological mythopoetic cartography of medieval *mappamundi* and the empirical 'scientific' mappings of modern nautical charts, recognized the power of maps of whatever genre or representational idiom to assert a truth that lay behind and beyond them. He therefore made cosmographic cartography on the axis of the 'perfect' Twenty-Eights one of the pillars of his rhetorical programme in support of the truth claim of the poem. In the variety of cartographic writing that features so prominently along the axis of the 'perfect' Twenty-Eights, in the *sermo humilis* mappings of the Italian peninsula, including even the humblest and most obscure of places; in the poem's Global Positioning System that tags and triangulates the locations of Crete, Jerusalem, and Purgatory; and in the mandala-like mapping of the cosmos in *Paradiso* xxviii, the *Commedia* came to possess something of the extraordinary credibility of maps.

---

26 Moevs, p. 144.
27 Denis Wood and John Fels, *The Natures of Maps: Cartographic Constructions of the Natural World* (Chicago, IL: University of Chicago Press, 2008), p. 7.

29. Truth, Untruth and the Moment of Indwelling

John Took

In what follows I shall come as quickly as I can to the notion of verticality as a way of reading the *Commedia* and of discerning and celebrating the symmetry at work within it — something which, in the case of *Purgatorio* and *Paradiso* xxix, can be done by way of stressing the nature and function of each alike as a moment of reconfigured consciousness preliminary to the soul's entry into the immediate presence of God, and in that of *Inferno* xxix by way of precisely the opposite, of the soul's captivity to the alternative project. But I have to confess that what really interests me about Dante and verticality is not so much the opportunity it affords for reading one canto in the light of another as its usefulness as a way of confirming, with Dante himself, the now essentially layered structure of his mature spirituality. For Dante was nothing if not an enthusiast, each successive encounter — be it Beatrician, Aristotelian or Virgilian — tending for a while at least to take over his existence lock, stock and barrel as a means both of world-interpretation and of self-interpretation. Each successive encounter, in other words, in taking him over, took him over entirely, a situation making not so much for their mutual inherence as for their successionality, for their organization on the plane, so to say, of the horizontal: first nature then grace, first philosophy then theology, first reason then revelation, these things tending within the economy of the whole to relate one with the other by way less of their *height and depth* than of their *before and after*, of their either *preceding* or *following on* as orders of concern.

   http://dx.doi.org/10.11647/OBP.0119.08

This situation — this surrendering on Dante's part lock, stock and barrel to the successive encounter and thus a sense of human experience as but a matter of its successive moments — is readily verifiable from the text, especially from the *Convivio* and the *Monarchia* where it is a question, precisely, of the periodization of human experience for the purposes of resolving high-level issues in the areas respectively of moral and political philosophy. So, then, in the case of the *Convivio*, where it is a question of defining the ways and means of properly human happiness for the benefit of 'those many men and women in this language of ours burdened by domestic and civic care',[1] Dante's commitment to an order of activity both moral and intellectual in kind and sufficient to its own ends, accomplishable here and now, is subject to the unqualified supervision of Aristotle, who is, before ever we reach the *Commedia*, the 'master of those who know'. As far as the *Monarchia* is concerned, it is a question of separating out papal and imperial jurisdiction this side of death, Dante's commitment to the notion of 'two ends' ('duo ultima') again presupposing the sharpest possible distinction between the ways and means of properly human happiness here and hereafter, in this life and the next. Now Dante, it is true, both in the *Convivio* and in the *Monarchia* has some doubt about all this, all men, in the *Convivio*, desiring here and now to seek out their maker as the final cause of all desiring, and human happiness here and now, in the *Monarchia*, being in some sense ('quodammodo') ordered to human happiness hereafter.[2] But

---

1 *Conv.*, I. i. 4 and I. ix. 5. For Dante's sense of ethics — theology apart — as pre-eminent among the human sciences, *Conv.*, II. xiv. 14–18; for his sense of our wishing to know here and now only what we *can* know here and now, III. xv. 7–10; for Aristotle as, if not the founder, then the finisher of moral philosophy and the guide to human happiness here and now, IV. vi. 6–16; and as exemplary in its sense of man's turning to God as a matter of what comes next, IV. xxviii. 3: 'It should therefore be understood here that, as Cicero says in his book *On Old Age*, a natural death is for us like reaching a port after a long journey and coming finally to rest. And that indeed is right, for just as a good sailor, on approaching port, lowers his sails, and, gently steering his ship, slips in gently, so ought we to lower the sails of our worldly affairs and turn to God with our whole heart and mind so that we too might come to that port with the utmost gentleness and calm'. For Aristotle as the 'master of those who know', *Inf.*, iv. 130–32, and, as the 'glorious philosopher to whom nature has most completely revealed her secrets', *Conv.*, III. v. 7.

2 *Mon.*, III. xv. 17–18: 'But the truth concerning this last question should not be taken so literally as to mean that the Roman Prince is not in some sense subject to the Roman Pontiff, since this earthly happiness is in some sense ordered towards immortal happiness. Let Caesar therefore show that reverence towards Peter which a firstborn son should show his father, so that, illumined by the light of paternal grace, he may the more effectively light up the world, over which he has been placed by Him alone who is ruler over all things spiritual and temporal'. For the *Convivio*, III. ii. 7 and IV. xii. 14: 'And since most natural to God is the will to be (for as we read in the aforesaid text "first

for all that, there is here a species of horizontality answering to something deeply rooted in Dante's nature; at every point there is a desire to give each and every cultural encounter its head before turning to how, precisely, it might be integrated within the economy of the whole. It is, then, only in the context of the *Commedia* and of the greater philosophical and theological maturity thereof that the *horizontality* of human experience, its unfolding sequentially or in terms of the *before and after* of its key components, is resolved in terms of its verticality, of the *height and depth* of that experience, of its layered substance and dimensionality. It is, in other words, only in the context of the *Commedia* and of all it represents by way of a spiritual coming of age that we have a developed sense of the theological as but the encompassing of the philosophical, of grace as operative from out of the depths, and of the ἔσχατος as but the *innermost* as distinct from the *aftermost* truth of this or that instance of specifically human being.[3] And it is this sense of the revised geometry of human being under the conditions of time and space that brings us to our three cantos, to *Purgatorio* xxix and *Paradiso* xxix as each, in its way, pausing in a moment of stillness to contemplate the kind of mutual indwelling of the human and the divine into which the pilgrim poet is called as the final cause of his every significant striving of the spirit, and to *Inferno* xxix as, whatever else it is, an essay in denial, in self as, despite self, ranged over against self in respect of its high calling.

But to get back now to verticality in the sense of a vertical reading of the text, and taking first the twenty-ninth canto of the *Inferno*, we are now in the last *bolgia* or ditch of the fraudulent — not as yet of those guilty of breaking or of reneging on a relationship of mutual trust (for these are still further down in the pit) but of the counterfeiters and impersonators, of those falsifying the customary means of exchange or else assuming a false identity. The spectacle is indeed forlorn, any number of scabrous souls

---

of all comes being, prior to which there is nothing") the human soul too wishes above all things to be. And since its being depends on God and is preserved by him, it naturally desires and wills to be united with him for the purposes of strengthening its own being […] and since, further, God is the first cause of our souls and fashions them after his own likeness, the soul desires first and foremost to return to him'.

3 Eloquent and I think exact in respect of Dante's theological coming of age in the *Commedia*, Kenelm Foster in *The Two Dantes* (London: Darton, Longman & Todd, 1977) at p. 246: 'Theologically speaking, this brilliant work [the *Convivio*] is immature. And if it a sign of growing maturity that a man takes stock of the tensions and contradictions latent in himself then certainly the *Comedy* marks a great advance, in this respect on the *Convivio*'. Fundamental still, Etienne Gilson, *Dante and Philosophy*, trans. David Moore (New York and Evanston, IL and London: Harper Row, 1963; originally *Dante et la philosophie*, Paris: Vrin, 1939).

picking away at scales as big as those of a fish and confirming as they do so their unrecognizability as creatures of orderly seeing, understanding and doing. The sick of the Valdichiana and of the Maremma, Dante says — malarial wastes neither of them very far from Florence — have nothing on this, the bleak imagery of it all confirming the notion, and with it the truth, of spiritual decay and lovelessness. Coming down, then, into the last cloister of the *Malebolge* (the terminology, incidentally, is Dante's own),[4] he and Virgil are able at last to see and smell through the darkling air something of the wretchedness of it all, whereupon Virgil enquires of two souls propped up one against the other whether or not there be here a Latin spirit, both, as it turns out, being precisely that — a Griffolino and a Capocchio each burnt alive, the one in Arezzo and the other in Siena, for wizardry and alchemy respectively. The matter, clearly, is grave, but as the canto goes on the tone becomes more and more burlesque and the style more and more comic, Griffolino for his part offering a spirited account of how he exacted large sums of money from the bishop's son by teaching him how to fly, and of how the good bishop, smelling a rat, had him hunted down and put to the stake. Capocchio, who had in his time cultivated something of a reputation as, as he himself puts it, an 'ape of nature' (possibly a mimic or caricaturist of some kind), then gives a no less lively account of the goings on in what appears to have been something approaching the Drones Club of Siena, remarkable only for its cultivation of every kind of fatuous pastime. And it is with this that a canto notable only for its account of the systematic dismantling in human experience of every kind of trust and concern (and indeed for its severing the bond of love or 'vinco d'amore' ideally binding one man to another within the domestic and civic context generally) comes to rest, its gradual shading off into something close to buffoonery registering, as the *stilus comicus* usually does in Dante, the fundamental indignity of it all.[5]

---

4   *Inf.*, xxix. 40–45: 'Quando noi fummo sor l'ultima chiostra / di Malebolge, sì che i suoi conversi / potean parere a la veduta nostra, / lamenti saettaron me diversi / che di pietà ferrati avean li strali; / ond' io li orecchi con le man copersi'. [When we were above the last of the *Malebolge* so that the fresh brethren were plainly in view, diverse wailing, the shafts thereof barbed by pain, assailed me, whence I put my hands to my ears].

5   For Dante and the 'comic style', Alfredo Schiaffini, 'A proposito dello stile comico di Dante', in *Momenti di storia della lingua italiana* (Rome: Studium, 1953), pp. 47–51; Zygmunt G. Barański (ed.), '"Libri poetarum in quattuor species dividuntur". Essays on Dante and "Genre"', *The Italianist* 15 (1995), and, more recently, 'Language as Sin and Salvation: A *Lectura* of *Inferno* XVIII' (Binghamton, NY: Centre for Medieval and Renaissance Studies, 2014). More generally, C. S. Baldwin, *Medieval Rhetoric and Poetic*

Looked at in the round, the *Purgatorio* — the beautiful *Purgatorio* — has to do with the struggle, by way of a commingling of nature and grace at the still centre of personality, to affirm one way of loving over another. Having, in other words, taken into self the guilt of self and embarked on the way of sorrowing (on what Bernard of Clairvaux used to call the way of assiduous tears: '*assiduitas lacrymarum*'), the soul sets about bringing home the kind of love generated by the sights and sounds of the world round about to the kind of love given with the act itself of existence, to the kind of connatural loving whereby the soul seeks out, so to speak, from beforehand, before it ever thinks about it, communion with the One who *is* as of the essence.[6] At the summit of Mount Purgatory, situated for Dante in the southern seas at the antipodes of Jerusalem, is the Earthly Paradise, the place of man's first disobedience in Adam. Both for the penitent spirits of Purgatory proper and for Dante himself as one merely passing through, this is a moment of clear-sightedness, a moment in which, having lived out the agony of self-confrontation and of self-reconfiguration on the plane of loving, the soul sees and understands as never before the course both of its own history and of world history. This clarity of seeing and understanding constitutes both the necessary condition and the point of departure for everything coming next by way of its proper ecstasy, of its knowing itself in the kind of spiritual self-transcendence proper to it as the most immanent of its immanent possibilities. It is, then, at this point, in canto xxix of the *Purgatorio*, that, having come forth from the upward way and rejoicing now in the sylvan freshness and fragrance of the Earthly Paradise, Dante sees unfolded before him, in a magnificent pageant, the entire course of God's self-revelation in scripture, a procession consisting of the poets, prophets and chroniclers of the Old Dispensation and of the evangelists, preachers

---

(Gloucester, MA: Peter Smith, 1959; originally 1928); Franz Quadlbauer, *Die antike Theorie der 'Genera dicendi' im lateinischen Mittelalter* (Vienna: Herman Böhlaus, 1962). For the 'vinco d'amor' motif, *Inf.*, xi, 55–57.

6   For the bringing home of one kind of love to another and the role in this respect of free will as the power to significant choice, see cantos xvi–xviii generally of the *Purgatorio*. Otello Ciacci, 'La teoria dell'amore: Canto XVII del *Purgatorio*', in *Nuove interpretazioni dantesche* (Perugia: Volumina, 1974), pp. 75–95; Italo Borzi, 'L'analisi dell'anima: amore e libertà (*Purgatorio* XVII)', in *Verso l'ultima salute. Saggi danteschi* (Milan: Rusconi, 1985), pp. 139–76; Giuseppe Frasso, '*Purgatorio* XVI–XVIII: una proposta di lettura', in *Contesti della Commedia. Lectura Dantis Fridericiana 2002–2003*, ed. Francesco Tateo and Daniele Maria Pegorari (Bari: Palomar, 2004), pp. 65–79. For Bernard on an assiduity of tears, *In festo omnium sanctorum* I. x (*PL* 183, 458A): 'Equum indomitum flagella domant; animam immitem contritio spiritus et assiduitas lacrymarum' [Just as a whip tames a wild horse, so also does a contrite spirit and an assiduity of tears tame a restive soul].

and pastors of the New Dispensation, a cloud of witnesses testifying between them to the substance and continuity of God's purposes in history. Glimpsing in the distance the golden candelabra of the Book of Revelation ('And being turned, I saw seven golden candlesticks [...] and there were seven lamps of fire burning before the throne, which are the seven spirits of God'),[7] he then sees, following in its wake, the twenty-four elders of the Old Testament clothed, as again the Book of Revelation has it, in white raiment and with crowns of white lilies — the colour of faith. Next come four living creatures, each with a crown of green leaves (the colour of hope) and with six wings apiece (Ezekiel at this point, Dante notes, has but four wings apiece but John, he says, 'is with me on this').[8] These, evidently, are the four evangelists, one at each corner of something truly spectacular, namely a chariot more resplendent than that of the sun itself and drawn along by a creature half-lion and half-eagle — to wit, by a griffin — the whole representing the Church as led by the Christ in his own twofold nature as man and God.[9] On the right-hand of the chariot, and treading

---

7   Revelation 1:12 and 4:5. Dino Bigongiari, 'The Pageant on the Top of Purgatory; Virgil's Departure; the Appearance of Beatrice', in *Readings in the Divine Comedy: A Series of Lectures*, ed. by Anne Paolucci (Dover, DE: Griffon House, 2006), pp. 312–25; Peter Armour, 'Canto XXIX. Dante's Processional Vision', in *Lectura Dantis. Purgatorio*, ed. by Allen Mandelbaum *et al.* (Berkeley and Los Angeles, CA and London: University of California Press, 2008), pp. 329–40; Aldo Coppa, 'La mirabile processione', in *L'Eden di Dante*, ed. by Anonio d'Elia (Cosenza: Giordano, 2012), pp. 109–66; Sergio Cristaldi, 'Simboli in processione', in *Lectura Dantis Romana. Cento canti per cento anni. II. Purgatorio*, vol. 2, ed. by Enrico Malato and Andra Mazzucchi (Rome: Salerno Editrice, 2014), pp. 867–97. More generally on the Earthly Paradise, Peter Dronke, 'The Phantasmagoria in the Earthly Paradiso', in *Dante and the Medieval Tradition* (Cambridge and New York: Cambridge University Press, 1986), pp. 55–81; Richard Lansing, 'Narrative Design in Dante's Earthly Paradise', *Dante Studies* 112 (1994), 101–13; Lino Pertile, *La puttana e il gigante. Dal* Cantico dei Cantici *al Paradiso Terrestre di Dante* (Ravenna: Longo, 1998).

8   *Purg.*, xxix. 105: 'Giovanni è meco e da lui si diparte' [John, departing from him, is with me]. Peter Hawkins, 'John is with me', in *Dante's Testaments. Essays in Scriptural Imagination* (Stanford, CA: Stanford University Press, 1999), pp. 54–71. Ezekiel 1:5–6 and Revelation 4:6–8.

9   Decisive historically for an interpretation of the griffin image are the further allusions of canto xxxi with its account both of the dual nature of the animal (the 'ch'è sola una persona in due nature' moment of line 81) and of its twofold and constantly shifting aspect (the 'doppia fiera dentro vi raggiava, / or con altri, or con altri reggimenti' of lines 122–23), though for an alternative interpretation, taking its cue now from Dante's particular brand of moral and political dualism, see Peter Armour, *Dante's Griffin and the History of the World. A Study in the Earthly Paradise* (Purgatorio, *cantos XXIX–XXXIII*) (Oxford: Clarendon, 1989). See too John A. Scott, *Dante's Political Purgatory* (Philadelphia, PA: University of Pennsylvania Press, 1996), especially pp. 185–89. Representative of a now increasingly sophisticated literature in the area of Dantean Christology, Claudio Gigante, '"Adam sive Christus"; creazione, incarnazione, redenzione nel canto VII del

between them in an exquisite *pas de trois*, are three maidens representing
the theological virtues, themselves arrayed in red, green and white, while
to the left are the four cardinal virtues indispensable to good order on earth,
and, inasmuch as good order on earth means for Dante good *imperial* order
on earth, suitably attired in purple. Then, following on from the evangelists,
comes the beloved physician of *Acts* together with the sword-bearer of the
Pauline epistles, 'sword-bearer', doubtless, in respect of Paul's exhortation
to put on the whole armour of God including the 'gladium spiritus quod est
verbum Dei' [the sword of the Spirit which is the word of God] (Ephesians
6:17). And then, finally, there are four more figures of humble mien, the
authors of the catholic epistles, together with an elderly gentleman, solitary
and at first sight somnambulant, his countenance, however, lit up and
more than ever radiant by way of the vision and of the rapture to which he
is party. The seven of them, Dante says, — Luke, Paul, Peter, John, James,
Jude and John of the Apocalypse — wear crowns of red roses and other
blossoms, red being the colour of love as, following on from faith and hope,
but the greatest of these. With a thunderous roar — confirmation from
on high with respect to the twofold truth and magnificence of it all — the
procession comes to a halt, the next part of the pageant bearing on what in
Dante's view of it amounts to the latter-day prostitution of the Church by
those to whom it has been most signally entrusted. But just for the moment
it is a question of God's original plan, of the chariot of the Church in its
pristine state with Christ at its head:

> Lo spazio dentro a lor quattro contenne
> un carro, in su due rote, trïunfale,
> ch'al collo d'un grifon tirato venne.
> Esso tendeva in sù l'una e l'altra ale
> tra la mezzana e le tre e tre liste,
> sì ch'a nulla, fendendo, facea male.
> Tanto salivan che non eran viste;
> le membra d'oro avea quant' era uccello,
> e bianche l'altre, di vermiglio miste.

Paradiso', *Rivista di studi danteschi* 8.2 (2008), 241–68; Oliver Davies, 'Dante's *Commedia* and the Body of Christ', in *Dante's Commedia. Theology as Poetry*, ed. by Vittorio Montemaggi and Matthew Treherne (Notre Dame, IN: University of Notre Dame Press, 2010), pp. 161–79; Antonio d'Elia, *La cristologia dantesca logos-veritas-caritas: il codice poetico-teologico del pellegrino* (Cosenza: Pellegrini, 2012); Paolo Fedrigotti, '"La verità che non soffera alcuno errore e la luce che allumina noi ne la tenebra". L'intonazione anagogica della *Divina Commedia* ed il suo fondamento cristico', *Divus Thomas* 115.3 (2012), 17–44.

Non che Roma di carro così bello
rallegrasse Affricano, o vero Augusto,
ma quel del Sol saria pover con ello. (*Purg.*, xxix. 106–17)

[The space between these four contained a triumphal chariot upon
two wheels, which came drawn along by the neck of a griffin. And he
stretched up the one and the other of his wings between the midmost
stripe, and the three and three others, so that he did harm to no one of
them by cleaving it. So high they rose that they were lost to sight. His
members were of gold so far as he was bird, and the rest were white
mixed with crimson. Not Africanus, or indeed Augustus, gladdened
Rome with so beautiful a chariot, but even that of the Sun would be poor
beside it.]

Canto xxix of the *Paradiso* takes its cue from, and stands to be interpreted
in the light of, the dramatic substance of canto xxviii where, in anticipation
of his coming into the presence of God as but a simple light, a 'semplice
lume' perfectly undifferentiated and therefore perfectly irreducible to
anything more fundamental than itself, Dante proposes a fresh model of
the universe, an alternative way of seeing and understanding it. Where,
then, up to now it has been a question of God as the *encompassing*, as
containing everything proceeding from him in consequence of the original
let it be, now, by contrast, it is a question of his subsisting at the centre of
the universe as but the infinitesimal focal point of all being whatever. And
it is from this infinitesimal point, a point having about it neither space nor
time nor polarity nor material referentiality of any kind, that, in Dante's
account of it, everything that *is* in the universe came forth in an instant,
including pure form, pure matter and the amalgamation of these things in
the starry Heavens, together with the intelligences whereby those Heavens
are moved. This coming forth, however, leaves the Godhead, impatient
as it is either of addition or of subtraction, just as it always was, is and
ever will be. The key passage here, as rapt in expression as it is exact in
conception, runs as follows:

Non per aver a sé di bene acquisto,
ch'esser non può, ma perché suo splendore
potesse, risplendendo, dir '*Subsisto*',
  in sua etternità di tempo fore,
fuor d'ogne altro comprender, come i piacque,
s'aperse in nuovi amor l'etterno amore.

Né prima quasi torpente si giacque;
ché né prima né poscia procedette
lo discorrer di Dio sovra quest' acque.
  Forma e materia, congiunte e purette,
usciro ad esser che non avia fallo,
come d'arco tricordo tre saette.
  E come in vetro, in ambra o in cristallo
raggio resplende sì, che dal venire
a l'esser tutto non è intervallo,
    così 'l triforme effetto del suo sire
ne l'esser suo raggiò insieme tutto
sanza distinzïone in essordire.
  Concreato fu ordine e costrutto
a le sustanze; e quelle furon cima
nel mondo in che puro atto fu produtto;
    pura potenza tenne la parte ima;
nel mezzo strinse potenza con atto
tal vime, che già mai non si divima. (*Par.*, xxix. 13–36)

[Not for the gaining of good unto himself, which cannot be, but that his splendour might, in its resplendence, say '*Subsisto*', in his eternity, outside of time and of every other limit, as it pleased him, the eternal love opened out in new loves. Nor before, as though inert, did he lie, for neither before nor after did the moving of God upon these waters proceed. Form and matter, conjoined and simple, came forth flawless into being which had no defect, as three arrows from a three-stringed bow; and as in glass, in amber, or in crystal a ray shines so that there is no interval between its coming and its being complete, so did this threefold effect ray forth from its Lord into its being all at once, without discrimination at the point of origin. Concreate was order and structure in all things, with pure form at the summit of the world, pure potentiality in its lowest part, and, between them, these things bound up one with the other in such a way as never to be separated.][10]

---

10 For the now revised geometry of the universe (the simple light at the centre model), Christian Moevs, *The Metaphysics of Dante's 'Comedy'* (Oxford: Oxford University Press, 2005), especially p. 161ff. For Dante on creation and cosmic order, Attilio Mellone, *La dottrina di Dante Alighieri sulla prima creazione* (Nocera: Convento di Santa Maria degli Angeli, 1950); *idem*, 'Emanatismo neoplatonico di Dante per le citazioni del *Liber de causis*', *Divus Thomas* 54 (1951), 205–12; *idem*, 'Il concorso delle creature nella produzione delle cose secondo Dante', *Divus Thomas* 56 (1953), 273–86; Marc Cogan, *The Design in the Wax* (Notre Dame, IN and London: University of Notre Dame Press, 1999); Piero Boitani, 'La creazione nel *Paradiso*', *Filologia e critica* 33.1 (2008), 3–34; Bruno Basile, 'Canto II. La luna e l'ordine del cosmo', in *Lectura Dantis Romana. Cento canti per cento anni*, ed. by Enrico Malato and Andrea Mazzucchi, vol. 3 (Rome: Salerno Editrice, 2015), pp. 61–84.

For the Dante, then, of *Paradiso* xxix it is a question of God's opening out in ever fresh channels of love to fashion pure actuality (the separate substances or pure Intelligences responsible in turn for informing things here below), pure potentiality (the as yet undetermined matter upon which the separate substances get to work) and the fusion of these things in the perfect stability and unchangeability of the starry Heavens. Alas, he goes on (in the person of Beatrice), you could not count to twenty before a not insignificant part of creation thus conceived rebelled, Lucifer the light-bringer now living on in the darkest reaches of the pit where life, light and love are forever stilled — all this prefiguring the fall of man himself as similarly unwilling to bear the yoke of his creatureliness. True, the greater part of the heavenly host, Dante maintains, remained faithful to its maker and was accordingly rewarded with an ever deeper insight into his essential nature, a position which allows him to register the notion that grace may in a certain sense be said to be merited by those disposed in love to seek it out: 'e non voglio che dubbi, ma sia certo, / che ricever la grazia è meritorio / secondo che l'affetto l'è aperto' [and I'd have you not doubt, but rather be assured, that in the degree to which the heart is open to it, there is merit in the receiving of grace].[11] But this, overflowing as it is with implications for Dante's theology both of grace and of salvation, at once gives way in this twenty-ninth canto of the *Paradiso* to an indictment of those preachers and philosophers who, indifferent to the majesty of creation as but a matter of the love-extrinsication or overflowing of the Godhead, are content to feed the flock with mere silly stories and tittle-tattle. Happy to settle for a laugh ('e pur che ben si rida'), they are, in truth, no better than impostors, nay blasphemers and traducers of the gospel to a man:

> 'Voi non andate giù per un sentiero
> filosofando: tanto vi trasporta
> l'amor de l'apparenza e 'l suo pensiero!

---

11 *Par.*, xxix. 64–66 (cf. Thomas, in much the same spirit on the greater part, at least, of his fellow Dominican preachers at xi. 124–39). Marina Marietti, 'I moderni pastori fiorentini (*Paradiso* XXIX 103–26). La parola di Beatrice nel Primo Mobile', *Letteratura italiana antica* 7 (2006), 249–55; Giuseppe Ciavorella, 'La creazione, gli angeli e i "moderni pastori" (*Paradiso* XXIX)', *Letteratura italiana antica* 13 (2012), 181–207. For Dante on nature and grace, see A. C. Mastrobuono, *Dante's Journey of Sanctification* (Washington, D.C.: Regnery Gateway, 1990); Norberto Cacciaglia, '"Per fede e per opere" (una lettura del tema della salvezza nella *Divina Commedia*)', *Critica Letteraria* 30.2–3 (2002), 265–74 (also in *Annali dell'Università per Stranieri di Perugia* 29 (2002), 123–31); Christopher Ryan, *Dante and Aquinas. A Study of Nature and Grace in the* Comedy (London: UCL Arts and Humanities Publications, 2013).

E ancor questo qua sù si comporta
con men disdegno che quando è posposta
la divina Scrittura o quando è torta.

Non vi si pensa quanto sangue costa
seminarla nel mondo e quanto piace
chi umilmente con essa s'accosta.

Per apparer ciascun s'ingegna e face
sue invenzioni; e quelle son trascorse
da' predicanti e 'l Vangelio si tace.

[...]

Non ha Fiorenza tanti Lapi e Bindi
quante sì fatte favole per anno
in pergamo si gridan quinci e quindi:

sì che le pecorelle, che non sanno,
tornan del pasco pasciute di vento,
e non le scusa non veder lo danno.

Non disse Cristo al suo primo convento:
"Andate, e predicate al mondo ciance";
ma diede lor verace fondamento;

e quel tanto sonò ne le sue guance,
sì ch'a pugnar per accender la fede
de l'Evangelio fero scudo e lance.

Ora si va con motti e con iscede
a predicare, e pur che ben si rida,
gonfia il cappuccio e più non si richiede'. (*Par.*, xxix. 85–96 and 103–17)

['You there below — so much does the love of show and indeed the very thought of it carry you away — do not follow a strict path in your philosophizing, though even this, here above, is borne with less anger than when divine scripture is neglected or perverted. Not the least thought is given among you to the blood it cost to sow the world with it or how prized is the one drawing nigh to it in humility. Everyone instead is out for appearance and his own fabrications, this, the gospel now silent, being the stuff of preachers [...] There aren't in Florence so many Lapos and Bindos as tales such as this proclaimed on this hand and that, day in day out throughout the year, from the pulpit, the poor benighted sheep coming in from the pasture being fed on nothing but wind (their having no sense of their loss by no means excusing them). For Christ did not say to those first gathered around him: "Be away and preach idle tales to the world", but furnished, rather, a sure foundation. That alone, then, sounded on their lips, they, in their struggle to kindle the faith, making of the gospel their shield and spear. But now they preach with but jests and gibes, seeking no more than a good laugh to inflate their cowls'.]

How, then, might these cantos be said to come together as part of one and the same meditation? How might we set up a 'vertical' reading designed to identify a common core of concern? In terms, I think, of their status as preliminary in respect of what Dante himself refers to as the soul's movement into God (the 'indiarsi' of *Par.*, iv. 28) and of all this entails by way of a constant redrawing both of the perimeters and of the parameters of consciousness, both of the boundaries and of the substance of spiritual awareness. More exactly, it stands to be set up by way of what in the *Purgatorio* and *Paradiso* Twenty-Nines amounts to a fresh contemplation of those moments when the maker and the made, the creator and the creature, were indeed but one, of the *cosmic* moment in which the Godhead opened out in ever fresh channels of creative concern and of the *Christic* moment in which it contracted by way of the Son to take on the flesh for the purposes of making man sufficient for his own uplifting. All this serves to prepare the spiritual wayfarer for a re-enactment of this situation, this mutual indwelling of the creator and the created as but the first and final cause of his own spiritual striving. Now this, as a way of seeing and understanding what is going on here, requires careful statement, for to speak in this way of a constant redrawing of the perimeters and of the parameters of historical selfhood as the soul draws nigh (the 'E io ch'al fine di tutt' i disii / appropinquava [...]' of *Paradiso* xxxiii) is by no means to suggest an abandoning of the properties of personality, a leaving behind of everything that confirms the individual in the uniqueness of his or her presence in the world; for nothing, in Paradise, is left behind by way of the particularity of self, Paradise for Dante being in this sense no more than the sum total of its parts, the elect, so to speak, in the aggregate. But for all that, it *is* a question of transfiguration, of 'transhumanization' (the 'trasumanar' of *Paradiso* i), of, inasmuch as the soul is party now to the very life of the Godhead, its living out on its own account something of the *always and everywhereness* thereof, of its knowing itself in a manner transcending every material and indeed every spiritual contingency of its being. Here, then, as I see it, lies the deep meaning of these two cantos and their function within the economy of the poem as a whole, each alike busying itself about the substance and psychology of ultimate *inyouing* and *inmeing*, ultimate in the sense that it is a question now of the *inyouing* and *inmeing* not of man and man but of man and God.[12] First, then, in *Purgatorio* xxix, comes the kind of

---

12 The terminology is decisive for any account of the sociology of the *Paradiso* and indeed for the fundamentally Trinitarian substance of that sociology: the 'O luce etterna che sola in te sidi, / sola t'intendi, e da te intelletta / e intendente te ami e arridi!' [O light eternal,

mutual indwelling accomplished and confirmed in the person of the Son, a species of indwelling into which every man and every woman as but the adopted sons and daughters of the Most High are in turn summoned. Never mind then, Dante says, the illustrious cloud of witnesses preceding it or even the evangelists themselves with their six wings apiece one at each corner of the chariot of the church, for what matters here, he insists, is the chariot itself and the Christ by which it is drawn:

> A descriver lor forme più non spargo
> rime, lettor; ch'altra spesa mi strigne,
> tanto ch'a questa non posso esser largo;
> [...]
> Lo spazio dentro a lor quattro contenne
> un carro, in su due rote, trïunfale,
> ch'al collo d'un grifon tirato venne. (*Purg.*, xxix. 97–99 and 106–08)

[For the purposes of describing how they were, dear reader, I have no more rhymes to spare, for other commitments constrain me such that I cannot here be more open-handed [...] The space between these four contained a triumphal chariot upon two wheels, which came drawn along by the neck of a griffin.]

---

alone seated in yourself, alone knowing yourself, and, known and knowing, alone loves and smiles upon yourself] (*Par.*, xxxiii. 124–26). It is once again Dante's own, the key passage here being *Par.*, ix. 73–81, neologism, here as throughout, being the way of philosophical and theological intensification: '"Dio vede tutto, e tuo veder s'inluia", / diss' io, "beato spirto, sì che nulla / voglia di sé a te puot' esser fuia. / Dunque la voce tua, che 'l ciel trastulla / sempre col canto di quei fuochi pii / che di sei ali facen la cocolla, / perché non satisface a' miei disii? / Già non attendere' io tua dimanda, / s'io m'intuassi, come tu t'inmii"'. ['God sees all', I said, 'and you see in him, blessed spirit, such that no wish may from you be hidden. Why, then, does your voice, which ever delights in Heaven with the song of those devout fires that made their cowl of six wings, not satisfy my desires? I would not, were I in you as you are in me, await your question'.] To the fore here, both notionally and expressively, the farewell discourses of John's gospel: 'Ut omnes unum sint, sicut tu, Pater, in me, et ego in te, ut et ipsi in nobis unum sunt' [that all of them may be one, Father, just as you are in me and I am in you, that in us they may be one]. For the 's'aperse in nuovi amori' moment of the argument, see Andrea Romano, '"S'aperse in nuovi amori l'etterno amore". Appunti sull'idea di Dio in Dante', *La Panarie. Rivista Friulana di Cultura* 152 (2007), 55–58, while for the 'per far l'uom sufficiente a rilevarsi' moment of *Paradiso* vii, see Alessandro Ghisalberti, '*Paradiso*, canto VII. Dante risponde alla domanda: perché un Dio uomo', in *Lectura Dantis Scaligera 2009–2015*, ed. by Ennio Sandal (Rome and Padua: Antenore, 2016), pp. 141–58 as well as my own 'The Twin Peaks of Dante's Theology in the *Paradiso*', in *Conversations with Kenelm. Essays on the Theology of the* Paradiso' (London: UCL Arts and Humanities Publications, 2013), pp. 49–79. For the 'trasumanar' moment of *Paradiso* I, see Steven Botterill, 'From *deificari* to *trasumanar*? Dante's *Paradiso* and Bernard's *De diligendo Deo*', in *Dante and the Mystical Tradition. Bernard of Clairvaux in the* Commedia (Cambridge: Cambridge University Press, 1994), pp. 194–241.

But that is not all, for preceding and encompassing the co-presencing of Father and Son in the person of the Christ is the presence of all things to the Father before all ages, this sense of the referability to the Godhead of every material and spiritual contingency of existence here and now dominating absolutely the first half of *Paradiso* xxix: Beatrice's apprehending in an instant that same Godhead in the twofold aspatiality and atemporality thereof (l. 12);[13] the subsistence of the One as impatient of all addition (ll. 13–15);[14] God's knowing neither time nor any other species of material referentiality (ll. 17, 20);[15] the instantaneity of it all, there being no gap between the coming forth and the completeness of things (ll. 25–27);[16] the concreation or simultaneity of being and order (l. 31);[17] with, at the very end of the canto, and more than ever sublime, these lines on the — for all its forever opening up in fresh channels of love — never less than perfect simplicity of the Godhead:

> La prima luce, che tutta la raia,
> per tanti modi in essa si recepe,
> quanti son li splendori a chi s'appaia.
>   Onde, però che a l'atto che concepe
> segue l'affetto, d'amar la dolcezza
> diversamente in essa ferve e tepe.
>   Vedi l'eccelso omai e la larghezza
> de l'etterno valor, poscia che tanti
> speculi fatti s'ha in che si spezza,
>   uno manendo in sé come davanti. (*Par.*, xxix. 136–45)

[The primal light which irradiates it all is received in as many modes as are the splendours with which it twins. Wherefore, since love follows

---

13 *Par.*, xxix. 12: 'là 've s'appunta ogne *ubi* e ogne *quando*' [there where every *ubi* and every *quando* is centred].

14 *Par.*, xxix. 13–15: 'Non per aver a sé di bene acquisto, / [...], ma perché suo splendore / potesse, risplendendo, dir "*Subsisto*"' [Not for the sake of gaining good for himself, [...] but in order that his splendour, shining forth, might say '*I am*'].

15 *Par.*, xxix. 17: 'fuor d'ogne altro comprender' [beyond every other parameter]; l. 20: 'ché ne prima né poscia procedette' [for [until God's moving upon these waters] there was neither before nor after].

16 *Par.*, xxix. 25–27: 'E come in vetro, in ambra or in cristallo / raggio resplende sì che dal venire / a l'esser tutto non è intervallo [...]' [just as, in glass, amber or crystal a ray shines such that there is no gap between its coming and its completion [...]].

17 *Par.*, xxix. 31: 'concreato fu ordine e costrutto' [concrete was order and being [among the Intelligences].

upon the act of understanding, then nature here [that of the separate substances] glows and warms each after its manner. Behold now, therefore, the infinite bounty of the Eternal Goodness, which fashioning as it does so many mirrors upon which it is divided, yet remains as before but one in itself.]

Throughout, then, the pattern is the same, for everywhere to the fore in these twenty-ninth cantos of the *Purgatorio* and the *Paradiso* (but especially here in the twenty-ninth of the *Paradiso*) it is a question of the resolution of the many and the one in the moment of ultimate homecoming. Everywhere — but again supremely here in the *Paradiso* — it is a question of the mutual immanence of creature and creator as the final cause of every integral striving of the spirit, an immanence, however, by no means abolishing the properties of personality, but, rather, confirming them in their now transfigured substance.

What, then, of the counterfeiters, the deceivers and the spinners of silly stories, no less prominent in the paradisal than in the infernal phase of Dante's discourse in the *Commedia*? Well, here too there is continuity of a kind, for both in *Inferno* xxix and in *Paradiso* xxix it is a question of those who, alert if only hazily to the *what might be* of their existence and, in the case of the preachers, to their responsibility to the flock, nonetheless settle less for *in-Godding* than for *in-selfing* as a way of seeing, understanding and implementing their humanity, less for a movement of self into the One who *is* as of the essence than for an installation of self at the centre of its own universe. True, Dante's tone both in the *Inferno* and in the *Paradiso* shades off hereabouts into the clownish, the comic and the downright ludicrous, but — again as always in the *Commedia* — the clownish, the comic and the downright ludicrous contain a sense of the catastrophic and of the infinite sadness thereof; for when it comes to posturing and imposturing, to silly stories and strategies, it is a question of captivity to the merely ready-to-hand, to the self-consciously inauthentic project. For them, then, no opening out of self on the other and the greater than self, no seeing and understanding of self as but part of the love-economy of the whole, no *inyouing* and *inmeing* as, again, among the most radiant emphases of the *Paradiso* and of what, in Dante's view, it means for man as man *to be* as a creature 'capax Dei, 'capable of God'. Simply self in the narrow confines and unfreedom of self, the falsifiers of *Inferno* xxix, like the preachers and philosophers of *Purgatorio* xxix (happy one and all provided only they can raise a laugh) being but far-wanderers, souls busy about wasting their substance in a far-off country. Continuity indeed, then, and a link of sorts between the twenty-ninth of Heaven and the twenty-ninth of Hell, but continuity making upon reflection (as continuity generally does in the *Commedia*) for an ever fresh sense of the matter to hand, for a sense now — certainly as far as the silly preachers with their jesting and gibing are concerned — of the effrontery of it all.

30. Brooks, Melting Snow, River of Light

Piero Boitani

The itinerary through our three cantos can be seen as a straight vertical ascent from falseness (*Inferno* xxx) to the human (*Purgatorio* xxx) and then to the divine revelation of truth (*Paradiso* xxx), but this itinerary also takes the form of a change in the nature of poetry itself. Consider, for instance, the opening of the three cantos. Apparently, there is no difference in register between the solemn mythological references of *Inferno* xxx. 1–21, on the one hand, and, on the other, the astronomical passages of *Purgatorio* xxx. 1–6 and *Paradiso* xxx. 1–9. The stories of Athamas and Hecuba, that is, of Thebes and Troy, recalled in *Inferno* xxx are eminently tragic ones and as such need the high style. But the coming of Beatrice in *Purgatorio* xxx is more than that — it is, as we shall see, an event presented as if it were a scene from the Bible or the liturgy, and therefore it requires a 'sublime' elevation. Finally, the immaterial Empyrean and Beatrice's full beauty are the first completely trans-human scenes of the poem and will therefore employ the language of ineffability. Significantly, the stars which shine in the opening of *Purgatorio* xxx begin to disappear in *Paradiso* xxx, in one of the most moving images of a canticle which up to that point has constantly used stars in wonderful similes to describe the heavenly scenery. It is presented in deliberate contrast with an image of *Paradiso* xiv:

> E sì come al salir di prima sera
> comincian per lo ciel nove parvenze,
> sì che la vista pare e non par vera. (*Par.*, xiv. 70–73)

    http://dx.doi.org/10.11647/OBP.0119.09

[When early evening hours are drawing in, new things begin to show across the sky so that the sight both seems and seems not true.][1]

The beautiful evening of *Paradiso* xiv is replaced, in *Paradiso* xxx, by a beautiful dawn. There, 'nove parvenze', the stars, begin to be visible, each of them 'perde il parere' until they all, including the most beautiful, disappear:

> Forse semilia miglia di lontano
> ci ferve l'ora sesta, e questo mondo
> china già l'ombra quasi al letto piano,
>   quando 'l mezzo del cielo, a noi profondo,
> comincia a farsi tal, ch'alcuna stella
> perde il parere infino a questo fondo;
>   e come vien la chiarissima ancella
> del sol più oltre, così 'l ciel si chiude
> di vista in vista infino a la più bella. (*Par.*, xxx. 1–9)

[Maybe, around six thousand miles away, the sixth hour, close to noon, flares out, while earth inclines its shadow-cone to rest, near level. At this same time, the mid-point of the sky will start, so deep above us, to transform, and some stars lose their semblance in those depths. Then brightest Aurora who serves the sun advances and, dawning, the skies, vista by vista, are closed till even the loveliest is gone.]

Athamas and Hecuba, ancient and noble as they might be, cannot even come close to this. And indeed the tragic register itself of *Inferno* xxx's opening terzinas contains as it were the seeds of its own destruction. Both Athamas and Hecuba are going mad, the former 'insano', the latter 'forsennata', the pain wrenching her mind askew to the point of making her bark like a dog. The rest of the canto presents a literal going to the dogs of the high style, replaced in turn by the 'comic' and the novella-like ones.[2] As to the former, the two souls which first appear in *Inferno* xxx, those of Gianni Schicchi and Capocchio, race around the circle, gnashing and goring, 'as swine do when their pigsty is unbarred' (l. 27). As to the latter, the story of Gianni Schicchi disguising himself as Buoso Donati on his deathbed in order to get, by the will he dictated, the best mare of the herd, sounds exactly like one

---

1   The text of the *Comedy* used in this essay is that established by G. Petrocchi for *La Commedia secondo l'antica vulgata*, 2nd edn (Florence: Le Lettere, 1994); English translation by Robin. Kirkpatrick (London: Penguin, 2006–2007).
2   See G. Contini, 'Sul XXX dell'*Inferno*', now in his *Un'idea di Dante* (Turin: Einaudi, 2001 [1970]), pp. 159–70.

of Boccaccio's narratives in the *Decameron*.[3] Later in the canto, the amazing quarrel between Master Adam and Sinon — a quarrel which culminates with Sinon's punch on Adam's belly and Adam's riposte by means of a momentous slap on Sinon's face — sounds precisely like one of Dante's *tenzoni* with Forese Donati or with Cecco Angiolieri.

The central piece of *Inferno* xxx focuses on a man whom the dropsy of Dante's justice has almost turned into a lute — Master Adam, most likely an Englishman provided with the title of Magister Artium who, following instructions from the Counts of Romena, coined false Florentine florins by mixing three carats of dross with twenty-one of gold to reach the prescribed twenty-four, and who was burnt at the stake for this in Florence in 1281, when Dante was sixteen.[4] His individual sin — individual, that is, as distinct from the economic and political error committed by most European governments ever since antiquity — is punished by Dante's *contrappasso* with literal inflation (the lute-like shape), monetary inflation of course being the dire consequence of debasing a gold currency. Adam the counterfeiter, who bears the name of Adam, mankind's father, appears neither comic nor tragic. If anything, he sounds pathetic when, consumed by thirst, he recalls the brooks that trickle down from the Casentine, and terribly angry because he cannot move an inch when he curses the Romenas and Sinon.

For Dante, counterfeiting money is as bad as counterfeiting people, as Gianni Schicchi and ancient Myrrha have done, or falsifying words, the prerogative of Potiphar's wife in Genesis and of Sinon, the Greek who, according to Virgil, followed Ulysses' instructions to deceive the Trojans into bringing the fatal Wooden Horse into the city.[5] Thus, *Inferno* xxx sums up Dante's view of fraudulence or falseness, which has been the poem's theme ever since canto xviii. It is the only theme which *Inferno* xxx might perhaps be seen to share with *Purgatorio* xxx, where Dante the pilgrim is reproached by Beatrice for having, after her death, 'turned his steps to paths that were not true' and followed '*false images of good*' (ll. 130–31). Dante the pilgrim would thus appear to be not an active counterfeiter, but as one

---

3   I have examined these episodes in *Dante's Poetry of the Donati*, now in *Dante e il suo futuro* (Rome: Edizioni di Storia e Letteratura, 2013), pp. 223–88.

4   Historical information and bibliography about Maestro Adamo is to be found s.v. 'Adamo' in the *Enciclopedia dantesca*, I (Rome: Istituto dell'Enciclopedia Italiana, 1974). Also available at http://www.treccani.it/enciclopedia/adamo_res-a2d44ac8-87ee-11dc-8e9d-0016357eee51_(Enciclopedia-Dantesca)/

5   *Inf.*, xxx. 37–45; and see R. Dragonetti, 'Dante et Narcisse ou les faux monnayeurs de l'image', in *Dante et les mythes. Tradition et rénovation, Revue des Etudes Italiennes* (Paris: Didier, 1965), pp. 85–146.

who deceived himself into believing those images true (*Purg.*, xxx. 127–32). What, on the other hand, this canto might mean to Dante the poet, or what the relationship is between truth and non-truth in Dante's own poetry, is a question which, only noting that *Inferno* xxx casts a disquieting shadow, I must leave open for the moment.

Inferno xxx shares with its cognate thirties of *Purgatorio* and *Paradiso* an image which revolves around water. The sinners of the tenth *bolgia* suffer unquenchable thirst, and water is, to one of them at least, a dream. Master Adam has the icy cold, sweet streams which flow into the Arno from the green hills of Casentine always before his eyes. Water has, in him, turned into the putrid humour that blows up his belly. The contrast could not be starker. In *Purgatorio* xxx, on the other hand, it is the melting snow of the Apennines that, as we shall see, turns into water when the warm wind from Africa blows on the mountains (*Purg.*, xxx. 85–99), and this corresponds perfectly to (in fact, it is the simile the poet uses for) the feelings of Dante the pilgrim, who sheds copious tears at the angels' chant. Finally, in *Paradiso* xxx a river of light becomes visible, and the pilgrim bends down to drink from it with his eyes. The river immediately becomes a lake, or an ocean — a circular figure, in any case, greater than the sun — and the image of the brooks falling from the Casentine returns, after sixty cantos, to describe the way in which thousands of blessed souls are mirrored in that light:

> E come clivo in acqua di suo imo
> si specchia, quasi per vedersi addorno,
> quando è nel verde e ne' fioretti opimo,
>   sì, soprastando al lume intorno intorno,
> vidi specchiarsi in più di mille soglie
> quanto di noi là sù fatto ha ritorno. (*Par.*, xxx. 109–14)

> [It is as though the incline of some hill were mirrored in a lake below, as if to view itself adorned in flower and richest green. Above that light, and standing round, I saw a thousand tiers or more as mirrorings of those of ours who've now returned up there.]

Thus, from *Inferno* xxx to *Paradiso* xxx the water icon runs full circle, but with a varying degree of homogeneity in the relationship between nature and the human being. The tragic contrast between them in Master Adam gives way to perfect harmony between Dante and the melting snow in *Purgatorio* xxx, and finally turns, as it were, upside down in the image of the hill contemplating itself in the mirror of the brook that flows from it — for the river and the lake of light of the Empyrean are, as the poet says of all he sees up there, shadowy prefaces of their truth, and 'where God rules without some means between, / the law of nature bears no weight at all' (*Par.*, xxx. 122–23).

Purgatorio xxx, the next canto in my sequence, brings us closer to an answer to the question I asked earlier on about the nature of the relationship between false and true in Dante's own poetry.[6] This is, as we all know, Beatrice's canto, the canto in which Dante the poet stages his encounter with the long lost lady of his heart by means of one of the most momentous recognition scenes of all Western literature, one with which only three or four stand on a par — Odysseus and Penelope in the *Odyssey*; Pericles, Marina and Thaisa in Shakespeare's *Pericles*; Hermione and Leontes in Shakespeare's *The Winter's Tale*; Pierre Bezuhov and Natasha in *War and Peace*. Elsewhere, I have examined this passage as a recognition scene.[7] What I will therefore do at this point is pick up a few details that seem significant.

First and foremost, there is the general orchestration of the passage, where Beatrice appears as the climax of the long allegorical procession that takes place on the summit of Purgatory. The passage opens with the astronomical image I mentioned at the beginning, and immediately afterwards it is widened and deepened by three proclamations and two similes. In the former, Beatrice is announced as the Bride of the Song of Songs, and hence, as interpretations of that Biblical book would have it, as Wisdom or the Church (*Veni, sponsa, de Libano*); as David and/or Christ entering Jerusalem in the Psalms and the Gospels, but at the same time as Christ about to be present in the Eucharist during Mass (*Benedictus qui venis*); and finally as Augustus' nephew and heir apparent, Marcellus, in Virgil's *Aeneid* (*manibus date lilia plenis*).[8]

---

6 The best essays on *Purgatorio* xxx are E. Sanguineti, 'Il Canto XXX del *Purgatorio*', in *Letture dantesche*, vol. 2, ed. by G. Getto (Florence: Sansoni, 1965), pp. 605–23; C. J. Ryan, 'Virgil's Wisdom in the *Divine Comedy*', *Medievalia et Humanistica* II (1982), 1–38; R. Jacoff, 'At the Summit of Purgatory', in *Lectura Dantis. Purgatorio*, ed. by A. Mandelbaum, A. Oldcorn, C. Ross (Berkeley and Los Angeles, CA and London: University of California Press, 2008), pp. 341–52.

7 See Piero Boitani, in *Riconoscere è un dio. Scene e temi del riconoscimento nella letteratura* (Turin: Einaudi, 2014), pp. 367–408.

8 *Purg.*, xxx. 11: Song of Songs 4:8; *Purg.*, xxx. 19: Matthew 21:9 and Psalms 117: 25 (Vulgate); *Purg.*, xxx. 21; *Aeneid*, VI, 883.

The first simile compares the rising of the angels on the chariot to the rising of the blessed on Doomsday. In the second simile, the rising of the sun veiled by mist at dawn is the image by which Dante presents the appearance of the lady herself. Within a cloud of flowers which rises and falls from the angels' hands, she in the end materializes, olive-crowned over a white veil, and clad, under a green mantle, in the colour of living flame.

All this is quite extraordinary as a sequence, a real explosion of fireworks, but one terzina stands out among the others to show us the ultimate quality of Dante's poetry. Dante compares the rising on the chariot of the ministers and messengers of eternal life, the angels, to the rising of the blessed on Doomsday:

> Quali i beati al novissimo bando
> surgeran presti ognun di sua caverna,
> la revestita voce alleluiando,
>   cotali in su la divina basterna
> si levar cento, *ad vocem tanti senis*,
> ministri e messagger di vita etterna. (*Purg.*, xxx. 13–18)

> [As when the Last New Day is heralded, and happy souls will rise keen from their caves, dressed in new voice, to echo 'Alleluia' so now, *ad vocem tanti senis*, there arose above the hallowed chariot a hundred angels, bearing news of eternal life.]

We accept this as a perfectly normal kind of simile the way we take the sun veiled by vapours and the lady within the cloud of flowers, but in fact it is quite surprising. The resurrection of the flesh is a scene neither Dante nor we have ever witnessed. Dante, followed by some of his readers, might conceive it on the basis of cryptic messages in the Gospels of Mark and Matthew or of what Paul says in the First Letter to the Corinthians ('In a moment, in the twinkling of an eye, at the last trumpet [...] the dead shall be raised incorruptible'),[9] but the actual visualization of the blessed celebrating with halleluias their 'new-clad voice' — or the 'new-clad voices' simply chanting halleluias — is wholly Dantean, as in fact is the verb 'alleluiare' in its wonderful gerund. We are suddenly transported into the imaginative world found in the mosaics on the ceiling of the Florence Baptistry or in Giotto's frescoes in the Scrovegni Chapel at Padua, or later in Signorelli's

---

9   Mark 13:27; Matthew 24:31; 1 Corinthians 15:52.

fresco of the Resurrection of the Flesh in Orvieto, and in Michelangelo's Sistine Chapel Judgment.[10] The amazing thing about the passage is that Dante is authenticating an invention (the rising of the angels on the chariot) by means not of something out of ordinary, common experience, but by means of another invention, namely the pictures of Doomsday spread in churches all over Italy at the time — and, ultimately, by means of faith.

When she sees her husband after the slaying of the Suitors, Penelope looks at him both knowing and not recognizing Odysseus. When Pierre Bezuhov returns to Moscow and to Natasha at the end of *War and Peace*, he does not recognize her 'because of the immense change in her' and above all because there is no trace of the old smile in her eyes.[11] Neither Pericles nor Leontes recognize their wives because they believe they are dead. It is this phenomenon that Proust describes with marvellous precision and insight towards the end of *Time Regained*, when Marcel fails to recognize his old friends during the 'Matinée' at the Guermantes:

> For to 'recognise' someone, and, *a fortiori*, to learn someone's identity after having failed to recognise him, is to predicate two contradictory things of a single subject, it is to admit that what was here, the person whom one remembers, no longer exists, and also that what is now here is a person whom one did not know to exist; and to do this we have to apprehend a mystery almost as disturbing as that of death, of which it is, indeed, as it were the preface and the harbinger.[12]

Dante overcomes this terrible contradiction with a magnificent leap. He does not recognize Beatrice, but himself and his old love for her. Before having visual cognition of her, his soul feels the same wonder and trembling it used to feel in adolescence:

> E lo spirito mio, che già cotanto
> tempo era stato ch'a la sua presenza
> non era di stupor, tremando, affranto,
>   sanza de li occhi aver più conoscenza,
>   per occulta virtù che da lei mosse,
>   d'antico amor sentì la gran potenza. (*Purg.*, xxx. 34–39)

---

10 The frescoes by Signorelli and Michelangelo were directly inspired by Dante's *Comedy*.

11 Homer, *Odyssey*, 94–95; L. Tolstoy, *War and Peace*, IV, 15.

12 M. Proust, *Remembrance of Things Past*, trans. by C. K. Scott Moncrieff, T. Kilmartin, A. Mayor, vol. 3 (Harmondsworth: Penguin, 1983), p. 986.

> [And I, in spirit, who so long had not been, trembling, in her presence, wracked by awe, began again to tremble at her glance (without more evidence that eyes could bring, but darkly, through the good that flowed from her), sensing the ancient power of what love was.]

Recognition is instantaneous, because, as Borges said, 'infinitamente existió Beatriz para Dante'.[13] Time has elapsed, but it does not have to be regained. Beatrice's presence is enough to join past and present without the help of memory, for the 'signs' of anagnorisis are inner motions, which the character knows as he knows himself. Those 'signs' come to life again, ten years after Beatrice's death, resurrected by a 'power' that moves from her. The mystery Proust speaks of is present here, too, the 'virtue' which flows from the Lady being hidden; it is not, however, the mystery that prefaces death, but that of love's might, which radiates in the world and transfixes human beings.

The indelible mark left on the heart by this power replaces all external signs. In order to recognize Odysseus, Penelope must ask him to reveal the 'secret sign' of their bed. In Dante, this has become 'occulta virtù'. And if, as Charles Singleton said, 'recognition "by occult virtue" is common enough in medieval narrative',[14] Dante alone transforms it into a heart-quake. When the 'occulta virtù' becomes 'lofty' through visual power — when it openly explodes — recognition is complete:

> Tosto che ne la vista mi percosse
> l'alta virtù che già m'avea trafitto
> prima ch'io fuor di puerizia fosse (*Purg.*, xxx. 39–42)

> [But on the instant that it struck my sight — this power, this virtue, that had pierced me through before I'd even left my boyhood state.]

Yet, significantly, Dante does not say that he recognized Beatrice, and this is what makes his scene so different, for instance, from the parallel one in the Middle-English *Pearl*.[15] Instead, he manoeuvres Dante the pilgrim to turn to Virgil, who has in the meantime vanished to his confine, and to quote to

---

13 J. L. Borges, *Nueve ensayos dantescos* (Madrid: Espasa Calpe, 1982), p. 152.

14 C. Singleton, *The Divine Comedy* (Princeton, NJ: Princeton University Press, 1970), vol. 2, p. 739. See also Singleton's *Dante Studies 2. Journey to Beatrice* (Cambridge, MA: Harvard University Press, 1958).

15 *Pearl*, 164-68, in *The Poems of the Pearl Manuscript*, ed. by M. Andrew and R. Waldron (London: Arnold, 1978).

him the line of the *Aeneid* in which Dido reveals to her sister Anna that she now feels for Aeneas the same passion she felt for her husband:[16]

Agnosco veteris vestigia flammae (*Aeneid*, iv. 23)

conosco i segni de l'antica fiamma (*Purg.*, xxx. 48)

[I recognize the signs of the ancient flame]

Dante does not recognize Beatrice, but the tokens of his old love for her. He feels the 'gran potenza', then voices it, transforming it into an 'ancient flame'. A few instants earlier, Beatrice had appeared as if bathed in the colour of a 'living flame', the colour of charity but also that which she wears in the *Vita nuova*.[17] When Dante feels and then recognizes in himself the signs of the ancient flame, both images ('fiamma viva' and 'antica fiamma') acquire new poignancy, opposing, as it were, and completing each other beyond time, suspended between old love and present charity, between sight and inner feeling, appearance and recognition. Compared to this line, pronounced in Beatrice's presence and addressed to its own source, Virgil, even the cry of Racine's Phèdre, 'Je reconnus Vénus et ses feux redoutables', nearly pales into pompous insignificance.[18]

We can, and indeed must, go two steps further in this reading of the Virgilian ancient flame. The first step is to remember that the *Aeneid* itself is called 'divina fiamma' by Dante's Statius in *Purgatorio* xxi (l. 95). In quoting one of his lines to Virgil, Dante is therefore paying him double tribute, acknowledging the divine status of the poetry of the *Aeneid*. The final step is to recognize a much more disquieting correspondence, that between this 'antica fiamma' and the 'fiamma antica' of Ulysses in *Inferno* xxvi, the only difference between the two being the inverted position of the adjective 'antica'.

Dante never does things like this by chance. Hence we must ask what the correspondence and inversion might mean. In *Inferno* xxvi Ulysses is a flame — to be precise, the 'greater horn of the ancient flame' (l. 85) in which both he and Diomedes are punished as counsellors of fraud

---

16 *Aeneid*, IV, 23 is, already imitated by Ovid, in *Amores*, II, i., 8.
17 *VN.*, II. 3; XXXIX. 1. On this aspect of the *Vita nuova* and the problem of recognition, see A. C. Charity, 'T. S. Eliot: The Dantean Recognitions', in *The Waste Land in Different Voices* ed. by A. D. Moody (London, Arnold, 1974), pp. 117–56.
18 J. Racine, *Phèdre*, I, iii, 277.

in the eighth *bolgia* of the eighth circle, the same circle as Master Adam and the others of canto xxx — Ulysses is a flame because of his 'ardour' to gain experience of the world and of human vices and human worth. In other words, he is the flame of the unbridled passion for knowledge, 'conoscenza'. On the other hand, Dante's feeling towards Beatrice is a flame because of love, his old passion. Beatrice herself obliquely represents Faith or Theology and, quite explicitly in *Purgatorio* xxx, Wisdom, divine 'sapientia'.[19] Thus, we have Ulysses equalling passion for knowledge and Beatrice equalling love of Wisdom. What Ulysses and Beatrice, the two ancient flames, have in common is the burning desire to apprehend and comprehend — they are two figures of intellectual activity, and hence the two most important characters of the *Comedy*. Where they differ — and this is why the adjective 'antica' precedes 'fiamma' in Beatrice's case, whereas in Ulysses' it follows the noun — is both in the nature and the object of this quest. Ulysses' search for knowledge is active, roaming this world — and possibly the other one as well — in search of experience, both of the vices and virtues of human beings and, when the occasion presents itself, of the 'mondo sanza gente' [the world without people] (*Inf.*, xxvi. 117) and perhaps even of the world of death. Thus, as if he were following the ideas of the radical Averroists of Dante's time,[20] Ulysses thinks there should be no Pillar of Hercules, no limit, to stop human exploration of the truth. Beatrice's love of Wisdom is contemplative rather than active and its object is not this, or any material, world, but divine Wisdom, i.e. God Himself. Since God is infinite, this, too, has no limit, yet rather than producing endless wandering it looks for its own fulfilment — as *Paradiso* xxx among many other Dantean texts proclaims — in simply gazing at him ('che solo in lui vedere ha la sua pace', l. 102).

Beatrice performs only one action in the *Comedy*, her mission to Limbo to ask for Virgil's help in saving Dante lost in the dark wood. Before this action, inspired by the Virgin Mary and by Lucy, Beatrice sat on her throne in the Empyrean, absorbed in contemplation. After that action, recounted in *Inferno* ii, and after guiding Dante through the Heavens, Beatrice returns to contemplation in *Paradiso* xxxi by giving Dante a last smile and look,

---

19 Lines 31 and 68: the green crown worn by Beatrice is compared to 'Minerva's olive fronds', Minerva representing Wisdom.

20 See Maria Corti, *Scritti su Cavalcanti e Dante* (Turin: Einaudi, 2003); Piero Boitani, 'Shadows of Heterodoxy in Hell', in *Dante and Heterodoxy. The Temptations of 13th Century Radical Thought*, ed. by M. L. Ardizzone (Newcastle: Cambridge Scholars, 2014), pp. 60–77.

and then turning to the 'eternal fountain' (*Par.*, xxxi. 93). *Purgatorio* xxx, the canto where she appears to Dante again after ten years, constitutes as it were the hinge of the entire poem, where Dante's past and present join hands and where human and divine meet.

The drama of the reunion, with Beatrice's stern reproaches to Dante and her reconstruction of his life and betrayal, comes in the second section of the canto, where events and themes of the 'vita nova' (i.e. his adolescence and his book) are either implicitly or explicitly recalled, establishing the necessary link with *Inferno* ii and thus creating the myth of Beatrice for the next seven hundred years. The angels try to intercede for Dante by singing Psalm 30, 'In te, Domine, speravi' (*Purg.*, xxx. 83), and thus praying for mercy, with the result that, without moving Beatrice one inch from her inflexible examination of Dante's sins, they make Dante melt into tears. The simile the poet now uses is a crucial example of supreme purgatorial poetry, that is, of a poetry which still employs earthly, and indeed ponderous, terms of comparison, but at the same time points to the lightness of the *Paradiso*.

Dante compares his frozen stance, 'without tears or sighs', when Beatrice utters her harsh words, to the snow which, among the living trees, freezes on the mountains of the Apennines when the northeast wind blows, and then compares his dissolving into 'breath and water', when the singing angels take pity on him, to the snow melting when the warm winds from Africa arrive:

> Sì come neve tra le vive travi
> per lo dosso d'Italia si congela,
> soffiata e stretta da li venti schiavi,
>   poi, liquefatta, in se stessa trapela,
> pur che la terra che perde ombra spiri,
> sì che par foco fonder la candela. (*Purg.*, xxx. 85–90)

[Compare: the snow that falls through growing eaves freezes the spine of Italy in drifts blown and compacted by Slavonian winds. But when the southern lands (where shadow fails) breathe once again, within itself it thaws, then trickles down, as candles melt in flames.]

An accumulation of details and metaphors verging on the baroque but still absolutely precise dominates here. Each thing is, to begin with, designated indirectly: 'vive travi' for live, green trees, which then become actual beams; 'dosso d'Italia', the backbone of Italy, for the vertebrae of the Apennines; 'venti schiavi' for the winds from Schiavonia, namely the

Slav countries; 'terra che perde ombra' for Africa; 'spiri' corresponding to 'breath' and 'winds'. Then the snow drips into itself, i.e. the water from the upper layers penetrates into the snow underneath. And a final simile within the simile, the absolutely simple, normal, common flame melting the candle, concludes the passage. To recount a powerful emotional crisis, and the final act of his conversion, Dante deploys the poet's licence and the scientist's precision.

Yet it is in moving, so to speak, towards the melting snow that the poet refines and lightens the image. Without examining passages in *Paradiso* ii and xxvii as I have done elsewhere,[21] I only point to the moment where Dante employs the melting snow image for the last time in the poem, in *Paradiso* xxxiii: 'così la neve al sol si disigilla' [thus the snow comes unsealed in the sun] (l. 64). In terms of poetry, this is what T. S. Eliot would, on the mystical plane, call 'a condition of complete simplicity / (Costing not less than everything)'.[22]

Purgatorio xxx is in many ways a figural foreshadowing of *Paradiso* xxx. It announces themes and images which the later canto develops and fulfils in the blazing light of the Empyrean. For instance, the theme of resurrection and Doomsday, which in *Purgatorio* xxx appears, as we have seen, in a simile, becomes central in the corresponding canto of *Paradiso*. When Beatrice tells Dante that they have now left the greatest of material spheres and reached the Heaven of pure light, she adds that he will be able to see both heavenly ranks, that of the angels and that of beatified human beings, the latter in such countenance as they will have when standing 'a l'ultima giustizia', on Judgment Day, i.e. with their bodies. The new sight ('novella vista') the pilgrim has acquired upon entering the Empyrean allows him to see the Resurrection of the Flesh, of which Solomon spoke in canto xiv as a future event (*Par.*, xiv. 37–60), as something that has already taken place. Later in the canto, when the mystical rose shines in all its effulgence, Beatrice points to the immensity of the City of God — of the 'convent', she says, of 'white robes' (*Par.*, xxx. 129) — and asks Dante to note how the thrones of the blessed are almost all full. This indicates that Dante, in 1300, thinks Doomsday is about to come, but in fact the expression 'white robes' implies that, from the point of view of the beholder struck by the '*lumen gloriae*', it is already here. For 'white robes' ('bianche stole'), is straight out

---

21 *Dante e il suo futuro*, pp. 169–83.
22 T. S. Eliot, *Little Gidding* V (*Four Quartets* IV), 40–41.

of the Book of Revelation (7: 9), and when Dante uses that word, 'stole', as in *Paradiso* xxv (l. 127), he means both the body and the soul, either of Christ after the Ascension and Mary after the Assumption, or of the blessed after the resurrection on Doomsday. It is a time warp which depends only on the way one looks at it.[23]

The second semantic field in which *Paradiso* xxx fulfils *Purgatorio* xxx is that of Beatrice. We have seen how she acquires Biblical and liturgical connotations when she appears in the Garden of Eden, while retaining key features of her earlier *Vita nuova* incarnation. Peter Dronke has pointed out how the old 'libello' is still present in Beatrice's celebration in *Paradiso* xxx, not only because Dante himself points this out, recalling the first day he saw her 'in this life', but also because the circumstances of both events, the first view of Beatrice and the present one, are inserted within a grand cosmic perspective.[24] He is right, too, in considering Beatrice's praise in *Paradiso* xxx ('loda' being *par excellence* a *Vita nuova* word) not so much a farewell to her as a 'Summa Poetica'. Indeed, while holding on to his love for her (he writes, in one of the poem's most beautiful lines, that he turned his sight to her because forced to do so by love and the disappearance of the triumphing angelic choirs he was beholding — 'nulla vedere e amor mi costrinse', l. 15), and while evoking his own life and poetic career, Dante now transports Beatrice into the sphere of transcendence:

> Se quanto infino a qui di lei si dice
> fosse conchiuso tutto in una loda,
> poca sarebbe a fornir questa vice.
> La *bellezza* ch'io vidi si trasmoda
> non pur di là da noi, ma certo io credo
> che solo il suo fattor tutta la goda.
> Da questo passo vinto mi concedo
> più che già mai da punto di suo tema
> soprato fosse comico o tragedo:
> ché, come sole in viso che più trema,
> così lo rimembrar del dolce riso
> la mente mia da me medesmo scema.
> Dal primo giorno ch'i' vidi il suo viso
> in questa vita, infino a questa vista,
> non m'è il seguire al mio cantar preciso;

23 See A. M. Chiavacci Leonardi, *Le bianche stole. Saggi sul 'Paradiso' di Dante* (Florence: Sismel — Edizioni del Galluzzo, 2010), pp. 3–25, 39–70.

24 P. Dronke, 'Symbolism and Structure in "*Paradiso* 30"', *Romance Philology* 43 (1989), 29–48.

ma or convien che mio seguir desista
più dietro a sua *bellezza*, poetando,
come a l'ultimo suo ciascuno artista.
    Cotal qual io la lascio a maggior bando
che quel de la mia tuba, che deduce
l'ardüa sua matera terminando,
    con atto e voce di spedito duce
ricominciò: 'Noi siamo usciti fore
del maggior corpo al ciel ch'è pura luce...' (*Par.*, xxx. 16–39)

[If all that has, till this, been said of her were now enclosed to form
one word of praise, it would not, even so, fulfil my need. The *beauty* I
saw, transcending every kind, is far beyond us here — nor only us. Its
maker, I think, alone could know its joy. From now on, I'll admit, I'm
overwhelmed, defeated worse than all before — in comic or in tragic
genre — by what my theme demands. As sunlight trembles in enfeebled
eyes, calling to mind how sweet to me her smile was, itself deprives
my mind of memory. Not since the day that I, in our first life, first saw
her face until this living sight, has song in me been cut so cleanly short.
It is, however, right that I stand down — as every artist, at the utmost,
does — and no more trace her *beauty*, forming verse. And so what then
she was I now will leave to clarions far greater than my trumpet sounds,
and draw my vaunting line towards its end. As she then was — a guide
in word and deed, her work all done — she spoke again: 'We've left the
greatest of material sphere, rising to light, pure light of the intellect...']

What has always struck me about this passage is the subtle balance
between open proclamation and the inexpressibility *topos*. On the
one hand, Beatrice's smile is likened to the sun and her beauty said to
transcend the human and to be fully enjoyed only by her Creator, God.
On the other, Dante declares himself vanquished from now on more than
any tragic or comic writer ever was by a 'point' of his theme. Later, he
says that recalling her smile deprives his mind of its very self and that,
although from the first day he saw her he never stopped singing of her, he
must now desist pursuing her beauty in poetry, as every artist does when
he comes to his limit. Indeed he will now leave her — and only in this
sense is this a farewell, a farewell to poetry about Beatrice — 'to clarions
far greater than [his] trumpet sounds', while he proceeds to complete
his 'hard matter': not to a greater poet (it would be ridiculous to think of
Dante relinquishing Beatrice to, say, a Petrarch), but to the trumpet the
angels will play on the Last Day.

It seems obvious to conclude from all this that Beatrice has become the Absolute, a divine figure, and that the poet encounters the same difficulty in talking about her now as he will have in the last canto in writing about God. 'Bellezza', the word he twice employs here for her, only applies, throughout the *Comedy*, to Beatrice, the angels, and perhaps once each to Mary and to the stars. It is a beauty Beatrice herself first predicates on her own figure in *Purgatorio* xxx, and which she herself says in *Paradiso* xxi constantly increases as they climb higher up through the Heavens. It is the beauty of the Bride in the Song of Songs, the 'claritas' of Wisdom.[25]

In this respect Beatrice's *pulchritudo* is not different from that of the Empyrean, essentially represented by the continuous metamorphosis of light — *lumen*, river, pool, rose — and hence basically coinciding, on the formal level, with what Albert the Great calls *resplendentia* and Thomas Aquinas, following the Latin translation of Dionysius, *claritas*.[26] In the *Divine Names*, Dionysius defines *pulchrum* and *pulchritudo* in the following manner: (I have italicized the words which correspond to Dante's description of the Empyrean):

> The sacred writers lift up a hymn of praise to this Good. They call it beautiful, beauty, love (*dilectio*), and beloved (*diligibile*). They give it the names which convey that it is the source of loveliness and is the flowering of grace. But do not make a distinction between 'beautiful' and 'beauty' as applied to the Cause which gathers all into one. For we recognize the difference in intelligible beings between qualities that are shared and the objects which share them. We call 'beautiful' that which has a share in beauty, and we give the name of 'beauty' to that ingredient which is the cause of beauty in everything.

> Supersubstantiale vero pulchrum, pulchritudo quidem dicitur propter traditam ab Ipso omnibus existentibus, iuxta proprietatem uniuscuiusque,

---

25 Sapientia (Vulgate) 6:13. 'Bellezza / bellezze' begins to be used in *Purg.*, xiv. 149: 'chiamavi 'l cielo e 'ntorno vi si gira / mostrandovi le sue bellezze etterne' (angels); then *Purg.*, xxix. 87, where the twenty-four *seniores* sing either to Mary or to Beatrice: 'Benedicta tue / nelle figlie d'Adamo, e benedette / siano in etterno le bellezze tue' (see Judith 13:23 and 15:11; Luke 1:28, 42). Beatrice talks about herself in *Purg.*, xxx. 128: 'e bellezza e virtù cresciuta m'era'. The theological virtues ask Beatrice to unveil her 'second beauty', *Purg.*, xxxi. 138. In *Par.*, vii. 66 'le bellezze etterne' refers to the angels; but in *Par.*, xiv. 134 it is Beatrice's eyes that are called 'vivi suggelli / d'ogni bellezza'. In *Par.*, xxi. 7, Beatrice speaks about her beauty increasing as she and Dante climb through the Heavens. In *Par.*, xxviii. 84, 'sì che 'l ciel ne ride / con le bellezze d'ogne sua paroffia', 'bellezze' must refer to the stars.

26 E. De Bruyne, *Études d'esthétique médiévale*, III, *Le XIIIe siècle* (Bruges: De Tempel, 1946), p. 307.

pulchritudinem et sicut universorum *consonantiae* et *claritatis* causa, *ad similitudinem luminis,* cum *fulgore* immittens universis pulchrificas *fontani radii* ipsius traditiones et sicut omnia ad seipsum vocans unde et callos dicitur et sicut tota in totis congregans.

[But the 'beautiful' which is beyond individual being is called 'beauty' because of that beauty bestowed by it on all things, each in accordance with what it is. It is given this name because it is the cause of harmony and splendour in everything, because like a light it flashes onto everything the beauty-causing impartations of its own well-spring ray.][27]

As he describes the changing features of the Empyrean, Dante the poet asks God himself to grant him enough power to say what he saw:

> O isplendor di Dio, per cu' io vidi
> l'alto trïunfo del regno verace,
> dammi virtù a dir com' ïo il vidi! (*Par.,* xxx. 97–99)

[Splendour of God! Through you I came to see triumph exalting in the realm of truth. Grant me true strength to say what then I saw!]

This kind of invocation becomes frequent, from now on, in *Paradiso,* and culminates in the last canto with the prayer to the 'somma luce' in lines 67–72. But the *incipit* in fact goes back to the conclusion of *Purgatorio* xxxi:

> O isplendor di viva luce etterna,
> chi palido si fece sotto l'ombra
> sì di Parnaso, o bevve in sua cisterna,
> che non paresse aver la mente ingombra,
> tentando a render te qual tu paresti
> là dove armonizzando il ciel t'adombra,
> quando ne l'aere aperto ti solvesti? (*Purg.,* xxxi. 139–45)

[Splendour of living and eternal light! Who would not seem — though pale from studying deep in Parnassian shade, whose wells he drinks — still to be much encumbered in his mind, endeavouring to draw what you

---

27 The English section of this quotations comes from Pseudo-Dionysius, *The Divine Names,* IV, 7, 701 C, in *The Complete Works* (Mahwah, NJ: Paulist Press, 1987), pp. 76–77; the Latin from S. Thomae Aquinatis *In Librum Beati Dionysii De divinis nominibus* (Turin and Rome: Marietti, 1950). M. Ariani has explored Dante's indebtedness to the Dionysian ideas on beauty in his *Lux inaccessibilis. Metafore e teologia della luce nel* Paradiso di Dante (Rome: Aracne, 2000), in particular pp. 327–45.

then seemed, where Heavens in harmony alone enshadow you, as you came forth and showed yourself in air?]

Yet this 'isplendor' is not God's — it is the splendour of Beatrice's 'second beauty', her mouth, which the three theological virtues ask her to unveil. The first line translates Wisdom 7: 26, 'candor lucis aeternae', an attribute of divine Sapientia. But Dante cannot have failed to notice that this line returns at the beginning of the Epistle to the Hebrews (1: 3), where it explicitly refers to Christ. And indeed he has Beatrice heralded, in *Purgatorio* xxx, with 'Benedictus qui venis' (l. 19).[28] What he is saying in this passage at the end of *Purgatorio* xxxi is that the poet who has laboured in his work — grown pale under the shade of Parnassus — or drunk deep of its Castalian spring, would necessarily seem to have a deranged mind if he tried to render the beauty of Beatrice-Wisdom-Christ when it revealed itself by melting into air there, in the Garden of Eden, where the sky, in harmony with it, is but a mere shadow of that beauty. Yet it is just possible to read 'cielo' as 'Heaven' rather than 'sky' for the enormity of Dante's proclamation to become apparent. In that case, while the normal figural reading would have Beatrice foreshadow divine pulchritude, we would find Heaven foreshadowing Beatrice's beauty, and the only consummation devoutly to be wished would be for God himself — as *Paradiso* xxx maintains — to enjoy it.

---

28 That is, the words with which Jesus is greeted upon entering Jerusalem (Matthew 21:9).

31. Beauty and the Beast

Catherine Pickstock

The project of a vertical reading of Dante suggests a 'speculative' — or *all at once* — grasp of the themes of the *Comedy*, as opposed to an horizontal *running-through* its various successive narratives, rhetorical appeals and snatches of dialectic. But if one were seeking a complete reading, one would need to combine a straight read-through with an horizontal succession of the parallel vertical readings.

In order to try to arrive at this combination in microcosm, I will read the three canto Thirty-Ones in chronological succession, but I will at the same time note the ways in which the vertical reading speculatively undercuts this. I will argue that this undercutting seems to require a problematization of the apparent tale of a journey from darkness to light. The reader seems to travel from below to above, but in another and specifically Christological sense, below turns out to be above, and above below. Therefore, the reader is implicitly invited not just to see herself as part of the receptive rose (*Par.*, xxxi. 1, 10, 16–18),[1] but also of the company of seraphic bees who plunge downwards into the rose's heart (*Par.*, xxxi. 7). For to travel towards the divine viewpoint turns out to have shared in it secretly from the outset. And since this is the viewpoint of a creative God, His gaze paradoxically looks downward and outward from Himself, by the force of his nature as love.

This substantive truth of the poem is echoed in formal and literary terms. The poem seems more to be anaphorically resumed or recapitulated,

---

1   I use the following English translation: Dante Alighieri, *The Divine Comedy*, trans. and ed. by Robin Kirkpatrick (London: Penguin Classics, 2006, 2007, 2012).

       http://dx.doi.org/10.11647/OBP.0119.10

than forgotten, as it advances towards its conclusion, like the 'positive remembrance' involved in drinking the waters of Eunoe (*Purg.*, xxxi. 92). Unlike a mere fiction, composed of surrogate signs, it does not dissolve upon completion, because it is 'about itself', in a sense that is stronger than the usual postmodern meaning of fiction understood formalistically. It is *about itself* because it invokes by imaginative means what Dante held to be truths, rather as Plato refers to the city of the *Laws* as the 'true tragedy', because it does not extrinsically represent the high realities, but lives them out, providing a context for their unfolding. In this way, the *Comedy* is closer to liturgy than it is to literature, as it inhabits what it is about. Indeed, Giorgio Agamben, in his short book *Ninfe*, places Dante just prior to the invention of 'literature', and Boccaccio just after. This, he argues, is because the imagination, for Dante, was not yet understood as primarily a portal between the real and the fantastic, but rather, between the corporeal and the intellectual, within a world-view that saw the intellectual as raising things into a higher reality, and as bringing us closer to the realm of really existing intellectual beings, the angels and God.[2] Similarly, at a lower level, the imagination starts the work of making things more real, and offers access to a realm of strange beings — gods, monsters, nymphs — in some degree or other real. If, indeed, the imagination misleads us, then this is somewhat in the sense of conveying us into a really monstrous sphere, a true tragedy, as opposed to one of benign, pastoral or sentimental enchantment.

What it means for Dante to write poetically and imaginatively about the very highest theological matters, and in the mode of secular lyricism, rather than the hymnic, is unresolved. It is however important that he does not just leave the secular repertoire of myth and mythic beings behind. It is almost as if he approaches Christian theology in the mode of what Boccaccio was soon to call a pagan 'poetic theology'.[3] This is a figurative idiom which returns, or bends back upon the human and the human city. In consequence of the poetic, and not theological, discourse of the *Comedy*, one can argue that its prime subject is the political rather than the theological. But it is never, as yet, a question of pure fiction; rather, of alternate dreams and nightmares which offer to us, or invoke, genuine omens of reality. There are questions here which one can only begin to understand, but Dante's translation in *Monarchia* of the Averroist collective intellect into the collective cultural and linguistic mind of the city suggests

---

2   Giorgio Agamben, *Ninfe* (Turin: Bollati Boringhieri, 2007).
3   Giovanni Boccaccio, *La Vita di Dante* (Milan: Per Giovanni Silvestri, 1823), XXII.

that, for him, the political is a crucial threshold between the imaginative and the intellectual or theological realms.[4]

To speak poetically of the theological may be another way of remaining on the margin. And it is also a margin between the private and the particular, on the one hand, and the universal, on the other, as manifest in the role of Beatrice. For Averroes, only the imagination distinguished one human being spiritually from another, given the literal singleness for him of the intellect (as carrying to an extreme the more common Arabic versions of the Aristotelian theory of understanding, as for Avicenna). Even though Aquinas sharply rejected this, he nonetheless insists that the finite act of individual thinking can only be completed in the imagination.[5] Dante would perhaps more naturally be aligned with Aquinas, though there remains here a gesture towards Averroes in his *Monarchia*. In any case, for Dante to remain within a poetic discourse is to remain relatively within the earthly and the civic spheres. His invocation of the Heavens is arguably to refer or tie them mainly to a this-worldly anchorage.

Yet there is another possibility, which is that Dante seeks to write about both domains at once. This would suggest that the *Comedy*, as consciously intended or not, expresses a poetic theology as the most appropriate for a religion of the God-Man and of the Incarnation. As we shall see, a vertical reading of the canto Thirty-Ones tends to bear this out.

In the case of each of the canto Thirty-Ones, I will proceed from a more formal, textual and successive phenomenological analysis to a more allusive, symbolic and theological one.

Inferno xxxi

In *De libero arbitrio* 2, Augustine elaborates a phenomenology and metaphysics of the senses, which culminate in a discussion of the respective democratic thrall of our senses of sight, hearing, touch and taste. Whereas *my* tasting something precludes *your* tasting it at the same moment, and my touching a thing precludes your touching that same point, the senses of vision and hearing are more collectively structured; a thing may be seen and a sound may be heard by more than one person at one

---

4 See Dante, *Monarchia*, I. iii, 9, drawing on Averroes, *De anima*, 3. See also Dante, *Convivio*, IV. xiii. 8.
5 St Thomas Aquinas, *Tractatus de unitate intellectus contra Averroistas* Series Philosophica 12 (Rome: Universitatis Gregorianae, 1957).

particular moment.[6] For Augustine, this hierarchization of the collectivity and exclusivity of the senses, and especially the prioritization of the sense of sight, allows him to build towards a presentation of the transcendence of the Good, and the democratic lure of its contemplation or vision in the light of God. In this context, the collectivity of our sense of sight betokens the Beatific restoration of our vision after the Fall, even though for now the disparity and exclusivity of the compass of our senses is conditioned by human fallenness.

It is striking that the exclusivity and successive aspect of the lower senses, as outlined by Augustine, seems to determine or shape the compass of Dante's sense of sight when he is in Hell and Purgatory. What can be seen is determined not by collectivity and availability, which one could connect with Dante's politicized Averroism of collective understanding; but rather, by exclusivity and limitation. The reader becomes increasingly aware of the layer upon layer (or 'tier to tier', anticipating the redeeming layers of seraphim 'bees' at *Par.*, xxxi. 16) of occlusions, whether physical, such as when Dante's (and so the reader's) view of an object is occluded, blocked from sight in some way; and of confusions or distortions of distance and size, or other kinds of inaccessibility impeding perception or passage; or of temporal interruption, such as when an object or person passes out of view, or is covered over in darkness. What might be momentarily and partially visible from a particular angle is soon lost from sight, or subject to a new perspectival limitation or perturbation, or is revealed to be something quite other than one's initial understanding.

Although the landscape of this domain at first seems hyperbolically static and fixed, bound up in chains and shackles, and held down in deep pits, with an abiding pseudo-eternal or slab-like determinedness, the visions it accords are scarce and fleeting, hard to obtain, and involve effort, machination, struggle and danger, or else are shifting, misleading or Protean. This partiality and precariousness of vision, linked with struggle, is at once a condition of human fault, and the beginning of the cure of such fault. One might say that the landscape is homeopathic in character, and that this applies as much to the Hellish landscape as to that of *Purgatorio*, at least insofar as it is being traversed by Dante, and not just dwelt in by the damned — although there is a sense in which Dante's own giving voice to the damned is in some way salutary for them.

---

6   St Augustine, *De libero arbitrio* 2. 3. 9. 29 ff

Such perspectival limitation is accentuated by the meticulous documentation of physical layerings, until the reader becomes dizzy with a sense of the lack of possibility, caused by a kind of hyper-perspectivalization. Rather than a heightening of subjectivity and sense of human potential or scope, one feels a loss or curtailment of subjective unity:

> Quiv'era men che notte e men che giorno,
> sì che 'l viso m'andava innanzi poco (*Inf.*, xxxi. 10–11)

> [Here it was less than night and less than day, so that our seeing went no way ahead]

The fact that the infernal time is less than both night and day, a kind of intermediate twilight, not yet pitch-black night, is significant: it suggests that there is a murky way through, yielding a sense, as it were, of potential, and neither an absolute confinement or closure, nor any sense of latitude. Some degree of human vision seems still to be available, but what is in fact seen (or heard) cannot be trusted to be true to the reality of its first impression. And yet it *might* still be true, and this inkling of possibility ensures that a hollow kind of yearning issues forth. The faint chance of a foothold means that hope is not altogether extinguished, even in this Hellish place.

There are countless examples of the successive exclusivities of vision, in this canto and others in *Inferno*. One notes fastidious documentation of deictic positionings, of one thing or person in relation to another, of multiple over-layering, with every angle or line or temporal duration specified, every span anchored by a piercing comparator — a crossbow, a sharp edge, a sting or a bite — each giving a keen sense of occlusion or rebarbative difficulty (*Inf.*, xxxi. 82, 5–6, 1–3, respectively; see *Purg.*, xxxi. 85). It is interesting to note that such exactitude and deictic fastidiousness yields not a sense of command over the terrain, or acuity of perception, but rather unclarity and distortion. One can think of the several visual distortions — the towers that turn out to be monsters (*Inf.*, xxxi. 31–32) — and of the way that whichever angle Dante and Virgil look from, they are always 'too far away' (*Inf.*, xxxi. 23, 26). Deictic co-ordination is further confused by low-down things nonetheless being of great height; and by recourse to subjective measurements whose repeated assertion seems to make clarity recede, rather than to disambiguate: numerous measurements of proportion — the size of Hell, of the giants, of Satan — yield a sense of disproportion rather

than accurate comparison of size. The things described seem to be out of
scale, such as the pine-cone, or the comparison of Antaeus with a leaning
tower that appears to fall when a cloud passes behind it (*Inf.*, xxxi. 59, 136,
respectively. See also *Inf.*, xxxi. 64, 83, 84, 113).[7] One might describe this
chronotopic confusion as an asymptotically receding anti-plentitude, later
balanced by Dante's chronotopic comprehensiveness in the *Paradiso*, where
at last he draws his eyes dancingly through every step, 'mo sù, mo giù e
mo recirculando' [now up, now lower, circling all around] (*Par.*, xxxi. 48).

I have so far emphasized visual perturbations, but human hearing is
also subject to distortion. The speech of the giant Nimrod, the constructor
of Babel according to extra-Biblical tradition, is impossible to understand;
he screams an unknown language (*Inf.*, xxxi. 67–68, 79–81) in a hideous
anti-betokening of speaking in tongues at Pentecost's reversal of Babel-
Babylon, yielding for him a perverse unity of language: 'che a lui ciascun
linguaggio / come 'l suo ad altrui, ch'a nullo è noto' [For every tongue, to
him, remains the same as his tongue is to others: quite unknown] (*Inf.*,
xxxi. 80–81). In a similar way, the horn, in the Psalms an emblem of pride,
blasts so loudly that it confounds hearing and leads one backwards and not
forwards (*Inf.*, xxxi. 13–15, 71–75).

A contrast is drawn between Dante's difficult, distorted and juddering
movement through this domain, and its occupants' own physical stasis.
Dante's journey represents their one chance in all eternity to speak to
the living, to extend beyond their domain, to gain a foothold, as it were,
via Dante to the reader, as exploited most notably when Virgil offers to
the giant Antaeus the chance of worldly fame if he will aid Dante and
himself (*Inf.*, xxxi. 115–29). Through his poetic textual delineation of the
giants' fixedness, and their definitive immutable destinies, we espy their
eternal situation: they are not obliterated, but held fast, thonged (*Inf.*, xxxi.
73), in their individual self-destroying forms, as if they were an archival
array of God's judgements, a kind of abiding inverse homeopathy by
which the doomed inhabitants, by *contrapasso*, continually repeat their
self-condemning gestures and are in no way released from them by self-
destruction, but rather held as perpetual contexts for their deployment
('Elli stessi s'accusa' [He stands his own accuser] (*Inf.*, xxxi. 76)). The pit in
which the monsters are held up to their navels is a kind of alchemical still
which outlines their condition more emphatically (*Inf.*, xxxi. 32–33), and

---

7   See Aristotle, *Ethics*, 5.3.1131b16: 'The just is the proportional, the unjust is what violates
the proportion'.

seems to make them more themselves. This is later answered in *Purgatorio* where Beatrice, under her veil and beyond the stream, is said to 'surpass her former self' (*Purg.*, xxxi. 82–84), and in *Paradiso*, where the veil's covering-over paradoxically shows forth the true image (*Par.*, xxxi. 107–08).

A further contrast is drawn between Dante's own struggle to see past the constantly shifting occlusions, despite his relative bodily freedom to roam this landscape, and the disastrous occupants' own hyperopic vision. From their enchained emplottedness, nonetheless, in parody of divine foreknowledge, they can see all that is to come, living with prehending and panoptic vision, as if in hyper-life, but nonetheless in physical delimitedness and as fixedly dead (*Inf.*, xxxi. 127–28). Yet, unlike God, they see not with equanimity, but *with affliction* all that can be seen, via all the passions of life (*Inf.*, xxxi. 71–72), with no release in action or movement. This yields a sense of terrible distillation and compression, of a fixed scope of gigantic and barbaric concentration and unity, and with this, a kind of hideous purity of situation and character.

Whilst the occupants inhabit their own disasters, stand as their own accusers, and are fixed in an abiding position of circular crisis by a reverse homeopathic circuit, it is notable that a genuine, positive homeopathic opportunity seems to arise for Dante from his own passage through this landscape, just as he in turn presents an opportunity to the static inhabitants; as living still, Dante can carry back Antaeus' name (*Inf.*, xxxi. 125–28). Here, where the fixed nature of the co-ordinates of situatedness is harshly thematised,[8] and there seems to be no reachable source of help, or assistance in movement, a 'walking further on' (*Inf.*, xxxi. 112), it seems that movement is no more than a passage into a greater viscosity of torment and fear: 'così forando l'aura grossa e scura / [...] fuggiemi errore e cresciemi paura' [so, boring through that dense, dark atmosphere, [...] false knowledge fled and fear grew yet more great] (*Inf.*, xxxi. 37–39). There seems to be a deictic exclusivity which withdraws help, assistance or mediation, in such a way that movement and release cannot come from without, but only, tormentingly, via recourse to the self-same spot one has been drilled into so definitely, and from the very things or place that cause the need to escape. Succour comes from the repeated crashings of condemnation, and direct appeal to the very sources of torment: so it is

---

8   Erich Auerbach, *Mimesis: The Representation of Reality in Western Literature*, trans. by Willard R. Trask (Princeton, NJ: Princeton University Press, 1953), pp. 167–69.

Antaeus to whom they must appeal for help to get to the next layer down (*Inf.*, xxxi. 100f).

This chilling homeopathic and anaphoric manoeuvre, whilst it issues in a closed circuit which, one might think, would delimit or enchain the wayfarer still more, is nonetheless fundamental to his movement, albeit so slight. And without the redemptive effect of the homeopathic circuit, Dante might not have reached Purgatory at all. So, it is Antaeus, against all odds, who sets the travellers down with emphatic gentleness: 'ma lievemente al fondo […] ci sposò' (*Inf.* xxxi. 142–43) [Yet lightly he set us, lightly […] (*Inf.*, xxxi. 142–43), echoing the tenderness with which Virgil had taken Dante's hand to lead him towards the giants (*Inf.*, xxxi. 28).

Indeed, the canto seems to be structured by such discrete homeopathic detours. It opens directly into a series of perfectly circular travails:

> Una medesma lingua pria mi morse,
> sì che mi tinse l'una e l'altra guancia,
> e poi la medicina mi riporse
>   così od'io che solea far la lancia
> d'Achille e del suo padre esser cagione
> prima di trista e poi di buona mancia (*Inf.*, xxxi. 1–6)

> [The self-same tongue that bit me first so hard that both my cheeks had coloured up, bright red, now offered once again its remedy. So, too (as I have heard the story told), the spear that both Achilles and his father bore would cause a wound that spear alone could cure]

Here, meticulous plotting of fixedness presents one's only chance, as a kind of purification by filth, or a liberation by enchainment, and we find that a backwards step is still nonetheless a step; so Virgil asks Antaeus to carry them and he leans on the giant; here a risk is one's best hope. A cure of hunger increases hunger; a hideous horn clears one's vision, even if it confounds one's hearing; language as fallen also cures, as though in half-anticipation of speaking in tongues or incantatory purification at *Paradiso* xxxi. 97–99.

Just as the usual facets of speech, hearing and sight are mixed up or distorted, so the usual co-ordinates of vertical and horizontal are upset: down in the lowest depths, we find figures of vertiginous height; the giants are hyperbolically tall, being compared with tall and sublime things such as St Peter's pine cone, mountains, fallen ship masts which swing upwards suddenly (*Inf.*, xxxi. 145). The pseudo-immediacy of the homeopathic circuit, together with the plummeting of the high, and the soaring and upward swinging of the low, present a kind of proto-echo, or demonic foretaste of the Gryphon's own twofold nature (*Purg.*, xxxi. 122–23), and of God's own mediation of Himself, and the turning of all to mediation in *Paradiso*, which I shall discuss below.

As such, the giants are like extreme ante-types of Christ, even though they are situated morally just above Judas and Satan, half buried to their torsos (just where the Gryphon's own two natures are joined: *Purg.*, xxxi. 123), yet rising to the skies monumentally above their waists, and compared with massive things, such as Monteriggioni's crown of towers (*Inf.*, xxxi. 41). Moreover, they can be mistaken for the towers of the city (*Inf.*, xxxi. 20, 31–32), and so are like the very pillars of the cosmos. Ambiguities seem to abound: though Dante is more frightened to discover that they are giants, and not civic towers after all, Virgil thinks he should be less so (*Inf.*, xxxi. 39). Is an irony here intended concerning human power and justice? What is more, the half-giant Antaeus, just *because* he is more wedded to the ground (and could not be defeated in wrestling, if he clove to it), failed to join the gigantomachy, or rebellion of the giants against the gods, when in their pride they piled Pelion upon Ossa to reach the heavenly domain (*Inf.*, xxxi. 119–21). It is further suggested that if Antaeus had joined in, the rebellion might have been successful, implying a Christian ambiguity as to which side was in the right — pagan Heaven or pagan earth? And precisely on the Libyan terrain, where the earth-bound Antaeus had *defeated and eaten* monstrous lions (*Inf.*, xxxi. 118), Scipio is later able to defeat Hannibal's elephants (*Inf.*, xxxi. 116–17), which earlier in the canto were said to be wisely left, by shaping nature, bereft of intelligence (unlike the giants) (*Inf.*, xxxi. 49–57). Even this benign monstrosity is defeated by Roman power allied with justice. It is not a god, but a giant, who is linked with this defeat, by Dante, and the same Antaeus seems not totally lost in Hell. He can still gain fame on earth, and is still capable of performing a charitable action — that of setting Dante and Virgil down in the very lowest, Satanic sphere, and doing so lightly (*Inf.*, xxxi. 142). Here, his gigantic paradox is fully revealed. Just because he is so tall, 'che ben cinque alle, / sanza la testa, uscia fuor de la grotta' [rising high (omitting head) five yards above the pit] (*Inf.*, xxxi. 113–14), he can bend right down, not just to the earth, his mother Gaia, to whom he is fatally bound, but even beneath her (*Inf.*, xxxi. 142–43). Here is a kenotic act of charity, but in this case, charity is to commit people for a time to the lowest loss of all, in order that they further learn.

Once more, the logic would seem to be homeopathic in character. Faults and wounds are indeed damages, but in their very nature as privative, they must immediately also start to yield a cure, like the Spear of Pelleus, Achilles' father (*Inf.*, xxxi. 4–6). There may here be a derived link with the name of the Fisher-King Pelles, and Dante may have known of this and its Christological resonance. But this is surely invoked in any case: the bearing of a fault is what cures, as with the idea that the wood of Christ's cross was taken from the tree of good and evil which first precipitated disaster. And in the case of this canto, the healing instrument (which was also the first source of error) is *language*; rebuking words hurt, but also begin to heal, just as it is Antaeus' *name* which Dante will carry back to the living. This is the only way to restore language beyond Babel, a process to which Dante's mythopoesis itself contributes.

All of this is striking, if not exceptional for Christian tradition. Still more striking, perhaps, is the way in which, in this canto, not even Hell seems to be omitted from this homeopathic economy. The earth, her giants, are the foundation, and although this ground has slithered and erred, it remains the foundation. It must be rescued, not perhaps for its own sake, but for the sake of the entirety of reality which it supports. In addition, this rescuing is at one level a self-rescuing, since the giants, as both mythical and Biblical, for all their grotesque horror, point the way back to that foundation, by first plumbing the spiritual depths beneath even the level of their own monstrous but merely chthonic rebellion.

Purgatorio xxxi

Although *Purgatorio* xxxi opens with a physical boundary, and a sense of a goal being held at a distance, that of the span of a river crossing (*Purg.*, xxxi. 1), here a new sense of momentum and acuity is immediately sensed. For there is, right at the outset *direct speech*, a turning at once towards the reader with language, its sharpness of sword-point (*Purg.*, xxxi. 2), its lack of delay or postponement and a sense of immediacy (*Purg.*, xxxi. 1–6).

However, difficulty still remains, for this is the immediacy not of freedom or arrival, but of reproach and further reproach, of relentless fastidious upbraiding; so much so, that it is not Dante's sight or hearing which is impeded this time, but his own attempts to speak in reply (*Purg.*, xxxi. 8–9).

The image of the crossbow and sharp sword continue from *Inferno* into the opening of *Purgatorio*: Dante is confronted by the sharp-edged sword of

Beatrice's opening words (*Purg.*, xxxi. 2), and by the crossbow shot, which had in *Inferno* xxxi been invoked to indicate the span of distance from the monstrous Ephialtes (*Inf.*, xxxi. 83), but which is here presented in the opposite state, drawn up too far, indicating that the force of Dante's reply is pathetically enfeebled; one would need eyes to see it, as no ear could hear such weak speech (*Purg.*, xxxi. 14–15). There is then a suggestion of a lack of 'being at the right distance'; either there is hellish distance from, or else purgatorial proximity to the other. The crossbow, unlike the spear, it seems, does not wound enough to heal, and verbal occlusion still seems to impede expression, rather as it was vision that became blocked by over-layerings in *Inferno*.

Beatrice asks Dante which chains and ditches had restrained him (*Purg.*, xxxi. 25), such that he could not follow after her. So, here, it is not the occlusion of sight or sound, but of his physical passage, or action, which is invoked, and his failure of action upbraided (*Purg.*, xxxi. 55–60). 'Present things with their false pleasures', he replies, had delayed him; again, his voice is weakened, and his mouth is struggling to shape the words (*Purg.*, xxxi. 34). The occlusion of speech and the unclarity of the *Inferno* seem to distend here into Purgatory, and are later echoed in the inexpressible plenitude of delight and beauty at *Paradiso* xxxi. 136–38.

While speech may heal via confession, it was sound that had led him astray (the sound of the sirens (*Purg.*, xxxi. 43–45)), and speech which, though curtailed, feeble and muffled, nonetheless brings purification. One finds in *Purgatory*, then, a continuation of the homeopathic trope, but here the resonance becomes Christological in character. The infernal vertical interpenetration of high into low, and low into high, is intensified, and mingled with a chiasmic interpenetration along a horizontal axis. We find a looking up and a looking down, just as there is height in the depths — giant monsters in Hell, who plummet so far down, only to rise up, are as long and broad as St Peter's pine cone, and swing up like ship-masts. So likewise, in Purgatory, the abject rise up — Dante is compared to an uprooted oak tree (*Purg.*, xxxi. 70); he is drawn down and submerged into the waters (*Purg.*, xxxi. 94, 101–02), so much so, that he swallows the water into his body, as a kind of extreme unction, an inner and outer comprehensive purification and compromise of boundary; the nymphs are elevated as stars in the sky (*Purg.*, xxxi. 106–07); Beatrice, like Christ, was once descended (is she regarded as pre-existent, one wonders? (*Purg.*, xxxi. 108)), and so now Dante looks upward towards her, through the upward gaze of others (*Purg.*, xxxi. 110–11).

At this point of looking upward, we are surprised by an horizontal or lateral interaction, for Dante looks upward towards Beatrice, only to find her not looking down towards him, as we had been expecting — especially after the arrestingly direct speech of the opening lines (*Purg.*, xxxi. 1–6) and her urgings that Dante look upwards (*Purg.*, xxxi. 68–69, 73) — but rather, looking away and across at the two-natured Gryphon (*Purg.*, xxxi. 120) who himself embodies the upper and the lower, as both Christ and man, embodying both Beatrice and Dante together (*Purg.*, xxxi. 122–23). Her unexpected looking-away is later echoed in *Paradiso* xxxi, when Dante is expecting Beatrice to respond to him, but rather 'something else replied' (*Par.*, xxxi. 57–58), and his expectation is finally realized only when she both looks towards him and away from him (*Par.*, xxxi. 92–93) and he no longer feels a sense of unease or strife of absence, articulated in lines 57–58. The shift in *Purgatorio* from vertical mediation, whereby Beatrice points towards upwards intensification, to a shared horizontal gaze upon the mediator, Christ himself, anticipates the paradisal conclusion. As Heather Webb has pointed out, there is a progress towards *seeing with*, besides *gazing at* Beatrice.[9] And the shared gaze is not just directed towards a shared goal, which is God, but also at the shared medium, the God-Man, or incarnate *Logos*, which is the objective *milieu* within which both an interpersonal vertical assistance, and a more eschatological, horizontal and reciprocal exchange of persons, are possible.

Is this interpenetration of high and low, and here to there, and now to then, an acosmic mediation, a kind of pantheistic conflation, inflecting a newly connected-up landscape with a sense of being on the brink of becoming one-in-oneself, and no longer distended through the landscape of boundary and hopelessness? Is there almost no mediation here at all, but mutual interchanging? Or is this rather the paradox of the most extreme distance of inaccessible transcendence being immediately present in hyper-proximity, closer than mere immanence, as it were outside oneself, more oneself than oneself? This will be fully shown to us only in *Paradiso*.

Where Beatrice's direct and exacting gaze towards Dante had been a piercing kind of sight ('alza la barba' [raise your beard], an injunction which he felt as 'il velen de l'argomento' [the venom that her meaning bore] (*Purg.*, xxxi. 68, 74–75)), to see Beatrice now, Dante's own gaze must be sharpened. This is at first described as a purification or *proving*, as the

---

9   Heather Webb, *Dante's Persons: An Ethics of the Transhuman* (Oxford: Oxford University Press, 2016), pp. 191–205.

prickling of a nettle, a sting and a bite (*Purg.*, xxxi. 85–90), again via a homeopathic circuit, which leads almost without delay to inner and outer baptism, obliterating the memory of sin. It seems that evil is a sharp wound, its curing even sharper, and then the very nature of the cured is the most extreme sharpness of all, for it attains to the complete penetration affected by light and knowledge.

Dante's purified and renewed vision seems to be achieved by seeing with the gaze first of the four nymphs, who are versions of the natural virtues of fortitude, temperance, prudence and justice, infused by grace; and then of the three brighter lights of the three theological virtues of faith, hope and charity. One of the first group declares:

> 'Merrénti a li occhi suoi; ma nel giocondo
> lume ch'è dentro aguzzeranno i tuoi
> le tre di là, che miran più profondo'. (*Purg.*, xxxi. 109–11)

> ['We'll lead you to her eyes. Yet to that light, so jubilant, within, those three beyond — their gaze still deeper — will make yours more keen'.]

This leading and sharpening is achieved through dancing. Dante is inserted into the nymphs' dance (*Purg.*, xxxi. 104) — this is a circular dance which nonetheless *leads to* Beatrice and the Gryphon — is it a spiral, then, and not a pure circle? Here, one can suggest that seeing is construed as dancing, prefiguring *Paradiso* xxxi, where dancing becomes seeing, and Dante will 'vola con gli occhi' [fly with wings of sight], and both seeing and dancing become a kind of dynamic purification (*Par.*, xxxi. 97–99).

At this point, more bow imagery enters in: Dante was originally pierced by the arrow of *amor*, as both wounding and healing (*Purg.*, xxxi. 107). And so now, after all, the arrow is presented as akin to the spear. But in seeing the eternal Beatrice, this double effect is not placated or cancelled, but rather increased. His eyes are drawn to hers in hot flames, yet Beatrice's gaze is cool and still, 'pur sopra 'l grifone [li occhi] stavan saldi' [fixed unmoving on the gryphon, never wavering] (*Purg.*, xxxi. 120). The Gryphon is compared with both Dante and Beatrice; it is unchanging, and yet oscillates between divine and human, seen through the transparent medium of a mirror, anticipating the air as Beatrice's veil (*Purg.*, xxxi. 145; see also *Par.*, xxxi. 70–72).

As if indicating a cosmic transition at this point, and drawing the reader sharply into the cosmo-poesis of the poem, as Dante had been brought up sharply by Beatrice's direct speech at the opening of the canto, so the reader is addressed directly, and asked to consider how Dante marvelled at the unchanging nature of the Gryphon and his transmuting 'twyform' image or reflecting kinds (*Purg.*, xxxi. 122–24), anticipating the implicit direct address of the reader at *Par.*, xxxi. 37–42, where the reader is similarly asked to consider his astonishment at coming to 'l'etterno dal tempo' [this eternal realm from time]' (l. 38) and to compare it with the stupefaction of barbarian pilgrims visiting Rome (ll. 31–35). It is interesting to note that being asked to consider the intensity of Dante's emotion is not something a reader can do without in part sensing that emotion herself; for who can bring an emotion to mind without somewhat re-living it? These interludes of direct address, therefore, reflect the idiom of this text as exceeding the extrinsic compass of literature, and indicating its transition to cosmic liturgical 'true tragedy', recalling the moment in the mediaeval liturgy when the Celebrant petitions the prayers of the congregation to assist the felicity of his sacrifice.[10]

And then, as if growing out of Dante's beseeching of the reader to imagine an emotion which is co-ultimate with feeling that emotion, the nymphs beseech Beatrice to turn to Dante. Here the repetition of 'grace' in line 136 suggests that their beseeching is inclining to grace, which is co-ultimate with final vision, and appropriate to the nymphs' own mixed character as super-naturalised natural virtues. Beatrice unveils herself to reveal her mouth as her second beauty (*Purg.*, xxxi. 136–45). Sight and voice thereby meet, and so are synthesised as incoming and outgoing, upward and downward, as both light and sound, all in-gathered.

It is interesting to note that a shift has occurred in the recourse to vocal and optical intermediaries. The intensification of vision which comes by Dante's entering into the dance is not a mediation, nor a recourse to intermediaries, for he may look *for himself*; and yet, equally, his vision is not unmediated, for the nymphs are still needed, and their assistance intensifies his vision (*Purg.*, xxxi. 111). One might construe this as a redeemed version of the *mille-feuille* of over-layerings of *Inferno*, which in that domain had occluded or distorted perception, even as they had been the only mediators. But here, the intermediaries make access sharper, smoother and more apparently immediate.

---

10 See Catherine Pickstock, *After Writing: On the Liturgical Consummation of Philosophy* (Oxford: Blackwell, 1998), pp. 173–74; see also p. 179.

One can discern here the beginnings of a Trinitarian vision, of a God who is immediately present to Himself, and to all else, and yet paradoxically present as an ultimate interpersonal mediation. As mentioned above, Heather Webb has indicated that for God, and for our vision of God, to *see* is to see *with* and *alongside* someone else.[11] Moreover, it is to see with more than one, with many, as in the visionary dance, if God is triune. Not only does genuine dyadic love here give rise by contagion of generosity to the third person, who is (for Richard of St Victor and Thomas Aquinas) *condilectio*,[12] but also, from the outset, the third thing loved by the initial pair is always the objective, spatial and social medium assumed by their encounter, just as no private relationship really exists before a social and political order. The Father and the Son are immediately co-present, and yet, this immediacy is the mediation of the shared 'spirit' of their encounter, the summoning of its desire, which is present from the outset, and yet is further transmitted. For Patristic tradition, spirit is the product of Father and Son, as the bond of their love, and yet also the breath by which the Father utters the Son.

So, the dance exceeds a dyadic gaze, builds upon it, and yet is its pre-condition. The persons of the dance, as it were, generate one another through imitative steps, and it is intrinsic to the dance that there is a 'third' of rhythm, even between two solitary dancers. In this way, a third dancer, and then a fourth, etc. and so on, is always implied. As with the seraphim in *Paradiso* who merge movement with vision (*Par.*, xxxi. 97–99), it would seem that there can be no vision of love without the generation and movement of love, which is at once reciprocal and yet communal, or even collective.

But can we make still more of the role of the nymphs here? As Giorgio Agamben has pointed out, nymphs in mediaeval to renaissance poetry and art were taken as the prime love objects for the imagination. As such, they hovered between human and preternatural, between the character of the elemental spirits of water, wood and field, on the one hand, and the possessors of a subtle matter, more rarefied than ours, on the other. Beatrice has nymphs for her handmaidens, and is herself perhaps a kind of nymph, or akin with them, both as a real woman of the city, and an imagined, ideal woman who is implicitly a pre-existent spirit who has descended from Heaven to aid Dante (*Purg.*, xxxi. 108). Boccaccio's *Comedia delle ninfe*

---

11 Webb, *Dante's Persons*, pp. 191–205.
12 See Richard of St Victor, *On the Trinity*, trans. by Ruben Angelici (Eugene, OR: Cascade Books, 2011), xi, p. 3. See also *Par.*, xxxi. 25–27.

fiorentina was perhaps a gently satirical reference to the *Commedia* itself, which he admired. But as Agamben notes, for Boccaccio, there is already a 'literary' tension between real women, on the one hand, who have the advantage of accessible reality, and idealised personifications — of stars, of attributes, etc. — which lack solidity, but which at least, as Boccaccio advises, 'do not piss'.[13]

Yet for Dante, this tension does not seem to be present. Beatrice is both real and ideal, both embodied and ethereal, without contradiction. Similarly, the four actual nymphs are (after classical mythology), later elevated as stars (*Purg.*, xxxi. 106–07), and yet later still, it would seem, restored after all to a nymph-status in the realm of the borders between the Earthly Paradise and Heaven. It appears that the eschatological horizon of resurrection resolves Boccaccio's dilemma, and sustains Dante's poetic discourse as embodied vision rather than literature; not as a hesitation between the real and the fictional, but as a poetic realisation of heightened reality.

One could suggest that the nymphs are counter-giants. Where the giants in pride try to reach the skies, the nymphs are elevated there (*Purg.*, xxxi. 106–07). As the supernatural version of the natural virtues (spoken of by Aquinas, for whom justice can be elevated to a supernatural virtue), they represent a benign paradox of below and above; natural virtues are only really virtues, even as natural, when moved by grace. There can apparently be justice, for example, without charity, as for the pagans, but this is an illusion. There is no meting out justice without love. Aquinas notes that even the natural virtues are in reality obscurely ordered to the beatific vision.[14] They must become explicitly so ordered so as not to slide into lesser or quasi-virtues. So, one can suggest that the nymphs embody the paradox of a human nature which can only be fulfilled in its nature by surpassing itself, by receiving the gift of conjoining with God. They represent a raising by charity, but also a completion of charity, in the return to the city and the completion of its natural destiny.

The same paradoxical return is represented by Matelda whom Beatrice here invokes unnamed (*Purg.*, xxxi. 92ff), and later names and connects with pure beauty and terrestrial innocence (*Par.*, xxxiii. 118–19). Dante must now pass through her waters of Lethe, where forgiveness is a negative oblivion of past wrong. But later he must *drink* her waters of forgiveness, as positive recollection, the waters of Eunoe (*Purg.*, xxxi. 94). It here seems

---

13 Giovanni Boccaccio, *Elegia di Madonna Fiammetta; Corbaccio*, ed. by Francesco Erbani (Milan: Garzanti, 1988), p. 243 ('tutte son femine, ma non pisciano').

14 See for example St Thomas Aquinas, *Summa Theologiae*, IaIIae, q. 62.

that the written *Comedy* itself becomes one with this drinking, a reaching of the end, which is also a reaching down, and a reaching back, even into the depths of Hell. This is suggested especially by the cosmic summaries or recapitulations which in-gather the whole poem (as, for example, at *Purg.*, xxxi. 106–08 or at *Par.*, xxxi. 80–81), suggesting a clear distinction between Dante's metaphysics and a Buddhistic one, as suggested for him by Christian Moevs.[15] Beatrice may indeed be a kind of Bhoddisatva figure, but for Dante, beyond Buddhism, the reaching back and down belongs to the very eternal essence of God.

Paradiso xxxi

In *Paradiso* xxxi, the themes of occlusion and veiling, of the struggle for mediation, and of drawing together towards a redeemed simultaneity of disparate poles, in a spiral or circular form, are brought to the beginning of a conclusion.

Here, the intervening distances which both sight and sound must traverse to reach their goals become *one with* the poles which they mediate. Immediacy prevails, and yet mediation remains as now paradoxically *itself immediate*, like the sky itself, with both a Christological and a Trinitarian implication, as I have suggested in the foregoing. Thus, a flying multitude of angels does not impede vision, but becomes a diaphanous frame for seeing right through (*Par.*, xxxi. 19–24), beyond even the veiling of the air (*Purg.*, xxxi. 145), which had remained as a carapace at the end of *Purgatorio* xxxi. Just as the horizontal medium, as mere medium, is abolished in Paradise, so also is the vertical medium. There is no longer to be a linear journey, and the traversing of the paradisal realm cannot simply be read as a line of progress. For here, the mediators still lead one onward, and yet the immediate mediacy of the Trinitarian goal points one back again, rendering Beatrice, as Heather Webb has argued, as much the final goal as God, even though, in another sense, she leads through herself towards God. So just as Beatrice was veiled and shown forth by the veil of air at the end of *Purgatorio*, so Beatrice is God's airy veil. But she is an emanatory veil, and as such, remains, like all created things, in the ultimate, just as the Son, as the 'art' of the Father, remains with the Father, and all things are finally gathered up into this filial art.

---

15 Christian Moevs, *The Metaphysics of Dante's 'Comedy'* (Oxford: Oxford University Press, 2005).

The interpenetration of the axes in *Purgatorio*, mentioned above, here reaches a new intensity of combination. The complete absence of occlusion seems here to be thematised: the spiralling descent of the multitude did not get in the way of what was above, and the white rose, because God's light is penetrative (*Par.*, xxxi. 22; see also ll. 13–15); the faces that are won to love are adorned by others' light, rather than shaded or occluded from the light (l. 49). And at lines 76–79, Beatrice is unimaginably higher than, and more distant from Dante, yet, as visible, she is as close as can be, and not mixed with any medium (*Par.*, xxxi. 77–78).

The Christological vertices, or the drawing together of axes and dimensions, here reaches a higher pitch. The low is exalted, just as in Hell there are massive giants. Beyond the highest point, there is a pure unity of above and below, goal and grace.

But is it the case that in Paradise there is no more mediation? Are the figures of envoy and substitution of *Inferno* and *Purgatorio* pushed aside, in favour of unmediated simultaneity? Are there no veils in Paradise?

If there is no more medium, that is because *all is now medium*, or veil, as reflecting the paradoxes both of the Trinity and of the Incarnation. To reach the goal is to reach a roundel of exchange, and to reach the top is also to return to the starting point. All, both horizontal and vertical, is finally resumed, in-gathered, rendering the progress and the exchanges along the way, the goal itself, when all things are finally seen in another, more final light. Beatrice has descended to Hell to rescue Dante (*Par.*, xxxi. 80–81). The fusion of an arrow shot by one, and an arrow shot towards one, means only that the flight in the middle persists (see also *Purg.*, xxxi. 107). The seraphim are at the goal, i.e. God, and yet they do not stop at the goal, but continuously fly around it (*Par.*, xxxi. 130–32), rather as the nymphs' circular dance nonetheless follows a spiralling line towards Beatrice in *Purgatorio* xxxi (l. 104). So also, Dante's own gaze does not stop fixed at a single point, but is drawn up and then down, and circles all about (*Par.*, xxxi. 43–48).

This continued circular motion at the goal recalls the mediaeval Canon of the Mass, in which the worshipper does not reach the altar of God once and for all, but rather travels around it, encircling it — '*et circumdabo altare tuum, domine*' [I will compass thine altar, O God][16] — combining singing, circling and seeing, all in one. The synthesis of a goal, and the movement

---

16 I. B. Botte and C. Mohrmann, *L'ordinaire de la Messe*. Textes et Études Liturgiques 2 (Leuven: Peeters, 1953), pp. 70–71.

towards the goal, or of medium, is one and the same with the liturgical roundel which we inhabit, distended through our passage through fallenness, where everything oscillates successively, occluding us, and falling short of us, all the way to the paradisal synthesising vertices, where everything is veiled and unveiled at once, without contradiction, and to a greater clarity. Indeed, such veilings or over-layerings, and comings-in-between, which might in *Inferno* or *Purgatorio* have veiled the passage of one's sight, in *Paradiso*, cause an *intensification of vision*:

> Né l'interporsi tra 'l dispora e 'l fiore
> di tanta moltitudine volante
> impediva la vista e lo splendore:
>   ché la luce divina è penetrante
> per l'universo secondo ch'è degno,
> sì che nulla le puote essere ostante. (*Par.*, xxxi. 19–24)

> [Nor, interposed between the flower and the height, did all that multitude in flight impede that radiance or the faculties of sight. Divine light pierces through the universe — to be received, as fit, in all degrees — in such a way that nothing can oppose.]

Crucially, things interposed between one thing and another are seen in *Paradiso* not as an occlusion, but as 'adornment', providing an accentuation or increased keenness, through delightful enflowering, of what is seen: the faces won to love are 'ornati' [arrayed] in others' light (*Par.*, xxxi. 50).

In a similar manner, Veronica's veil tells us only 'more clearly', as it were adorning and accentuating, and not covering over, the truth of Jesus's face, the true God (*Par.*, xxxi. 106–08), and problematizes the mundane distinction between thing and medium. The veil, it seems, remains, even in the reality which lies concealed beneath it, which is shown as its essential emanation. As seemingly in the case of Veronica, to remove the veil is to restore it, for it is not an extrinsic layer, but the right concealment through which the real and the true are given, or shown as themselves. When the Croatian pilgrim views the Veronica, at *Paradiso* xxxi. 103–08, his concern is with the veracity of what is shown forth, its accuracy of representation: 'was this the way, true God, you looked on earth?' (*Par.*, xxxi. 108). The emphasis here is on the veil or covering singularly reconstruing an exactitude of image. The more the veil reveals, the more it remains a veil, and the pilgrim's own response to the image that is displayed to him (*Par.*, xxxi. 106) becomes part of the veil's own exactness of image, since the onlooker's response to the image is perforce part of Christ's own automatic image-making, which is continuous with his presence; just as God's impress is at one with his reality, instigated here through the pilgrim's response. The image of the true God, paradoxically as accurate and shown-forth, must be veiled. The veiled story of the transmission of the *vera icon*, then, is also the truest, and the most allegorically iconic of the icon, just as Christ's impress of an image of himself belongs to his image, which is to convey or transmit.[17]

Because the high and the low are synthesised, descent through sin in the end ascends in and through the descent of grace. The seraphim flying around, as pure medium, are also pure height as pure descent, indicated by their descent like 'a swarm of bees', into the rose of the Church (*Par.*, xxxi. 1–7), in order to pollinate themselves (*Par.*, xxxi. 10–12). Some commentators speak of a reversed figure of speech here, whereby the Church is pollinated by the seraphim with divine grace,[18] rather than the seraphim drawing pollen from the Church, as it were in the mode of real bees drawing pollen from a flower.

But one could argue, alternatively, that the figure remains natural, and that the bees remain founded in the literal, in accordance with the patterns of Biblical allegory which Dante applied to his own composition.[19] Rather, it is the theological metaphysics that is reversed; the seraphim are presented as depending upon the Church (*Par.*, xxxi. 10). Perhaps this is because Christ is higher than the angels, and all of the cosmos depends upon him and exists through him, and the Church as his bodily extension. But beyond that, the Church is also Mary-Ecclesia, and comprises all beseeching and redeemed subjectivities (*Par.*, xxxi. 100–01). This would seem to suggest that if the cosmos holds together in Christ (as for St Paul), then it also holds together through human assent and active reception. Another inversion is therefore on display. The movement 'beyond beatitude', yet defining of it, as for Pseudo-Dionysius, a share in the creative power of God, is at one with the circling around, and the movements downward and backward,

---

17 On the variable traditions of the Veronica, and the theological ironies of this variation in relation to the unmediated exactitude of the image, with detailed reference to material culture, see B. A. Windeatt, '"*Vera Icon?*": The Variable Veronica of Medieval England', *Convivium Supplementum* (2018), 3-15. See also Suzanne Conklin Akbari, *Seeing Through the Veil: Optical Theory and Medieval Allegory* (Princeton, NJ: Princeton University Press, 2004).

18 *Paradiso: Commentary*. ed. and trans. by Charles S. Singleton. Bollingen Series LXXX (Princeton, NJ: Princeton University Press, 1991), pp. 512-13.

19 G. A. R. Clifford, *Transformations of Allegory*. Concepts of Literature Series (London: Routledge and Kegan Paul, 1974).

spanning the course of the whole *Comedy* (whose soteriological course is summarised at *Par.*, xxxi. 80–81), the very book we hold in our hands, and indeed spanning our own selves, addressed (directly at *Par.*, xxxi. 40, and implicitly throughout, as privy to Dante's perceptions and affections), and drawn into that book, like the bees themselves, the creatures closest to God.

In this way, one can observe a zig-zagging movement. Like the Gryphon, as the ultimate beyond ultimate, so God's light, as the highest, penetrates completely down to the very lowest point, so that all becomes diaphanous, or veil-like. The light is three-fold in character; it is not just the source, but also the flowing, or flowering-out, and the medium (*Par.*, xxxi. 71–72). The zig-zag implies a Trinitarian ontology whereby the summit is not an end-point, but eternally an ecstatic going-out, 'mirroring eternal rays, to form a crown or aureole around' (ll. 71–72). The vertical height of arrival is compared with the horizontal pilgrimage of barbarians to Rome, or Croatian pilgrims to see Veronica's veil (*Par.*, xxxi. 31–35). Equivalently, Dante's own eyes now dance; they stroll and fly — in reaching their destination, they enter into the most perfect movement, which is circular (*Par.*, xxxi. 46–48). Just as the seraphim, in flying around, obtain to the Beatific vision, so this vision is not statically held back, chained, thonged or covered over, but is itself defined as movement, and an infinitely fast or instantaneous journey. Arrival and sharply piercing are now contemporaneous and immediate, as everything has become the diaphanous medium (*Par.*, xxxi. 46–48).

Comparably, Beatrice's heavenly crown does not simply descend upon her, but has to be made from rays of light coming to meet her, and radiating outwards; as if the rays make her, or she is part of the rays, which then disperse outward again (*Par.*, xxxi. 71–72). One might say that Beatrice is an active receiver of emanating descending light, rather as for the Albertine tradition, and echoing Aquinas's recension of Avicenna's view of the active disposition of matter towards the reception of form. One might place this image of Beatrice's crown of constitutive refracting light beams in the tradition of Robert Grosseteste's considerations of light as the super-form.[20] Equally, to receive light is to receive something active, whose

---

20 See *Robert Grosseteste. De luce, seu de incohatione formarum*, trans. by Clare Riedl, Medieval Philosophical Texts in Translation No. 1 (Milwaukee, WI: Marquette University Press, 1942); *Robert Grosseteste and His Intellectual Milieu*, ed. by J. Flood, J. R. Ginther, J. W. Goering (Turnhout, Belgium: Brepols publishers, 2013); Albert the Great, *Summa Theologiae*, I. 6, 26. 2–3; 10. 59–60; *Commentary on Dionysius' Mystical Theology*, trans. by Simon Tugwell, O. P., 10. 59–60; Simon Tugwell, *Albert and Thomas: Selected Writings* (New York: Paulist Press, 1988); Aquinas, *Quaestiones Disputatae de Potentia Dei*, q. 5 a. 1 ad 5 and *Summa Contra Gentiles* III, 20 [5].

motion continues in and beyond one's reception of it, and is intensified by another's gaze (*Par.*, xxxi. 140–42), as mirroring eternal rays (*Par.*, xxxi. 71).

Dante and Bernard go back to talking near the end of the canto. The final vision here is of Mary, and so of the God-bearer (*Par.*, xxxi. 100–01). A tension arises between looking at Mary and trying to speak of her (*Par.*, xxxi. 136–38). Sight here surpasses description, yet speaking of this difficulty is itself a — sublime — description. Mary is the brightest, and interestingly, here, occlusions again seem to outdo one another, in a curious redeeming echo of the agonistic infernal landscape in which one thing occludes another, but here it is an outdoing of brightness and not of darkness and shadow:

> Io levai li occhi; e come da mattina
> la parte orïental de l'orizzonte
> soverchia quella dove 'l sol declina,
>   così, quasi di valle andando a monte
> con gli occhi, vidi parte ne lo stremo
> vincer di lume tutta l'altra fronte. (*Par.*, xxxi. 118–23)

> [I raised my eyes. And, as when morning dawns, the orient horizon in new light defeats the part in which the sun goes down, so too, as though my eyes were travelling from valley up to mountain peak, I saw the rim outdo, in brightness, every other part.]

In Mary's sphere, moreover, there is still a multiplicity where each angel is equal but different in effulgence (*fulgore*) and art. Although there is a vision of Mary and angels at the end, each one actively has his art, 'ciascun distinto di fulgore e d'arte' [in blaze and chosen deed all differing] (*Par.*, xxxi. 130–32). Language, games, songs and voice remain, even at this point, where one might think that sight was all that one needed. Rather, a synaesthesia of seeing and dancing, and seeing and singing, and singing as a continuation and intensification of movement, as dancing, seems to draw all human ecstatic expression into one perfect instantaneous mediation. The final vision here is of descending grace, of a human smile upon play (*Par.*, xxxi. 92–93). Again, as in *Purgatorio*, Beatrice's mouth combines sight and speech. Beyond the sight of her face, there is the sight of her smiling mouth, and so a return to utterance.

Likewise, the descent of creation remains. Speech is not a surrogate sign which must vanish, but remains in the ultimate, as expressive art, and is exalted, as all becomes medium. Dante's own art 'about' these things is itself an aspect of what it is about — the indispensability of the imagination, as the mediating realm, which Dante both sees, and sees by partially producing. The burning of desire and care remain for Bernard, and are not cancelled out in the ultimate. And again, as for the nymphs in *Purgatorio*, Dante looks through the gaze of others, and here especially through Bernard's gaze, but no longer with their looking on his behalf, or for his sake, but as an adornment, making it more ardent (*Par.*, xxxi. 142). And so, right at the end, it is the look of the other which becomes a new kind of medium. If poles and medium are now as one, then the pole of looking or speaking can itself act as medium.

The final implication of the three canto Thirty-Ones, read together, as in the foregoing, could be seen as the shift from the mediation of objective properties via an objective middle to interpersonal mediation. There seems to be nothing outside the personal interplay of connections and objects, as they are also subjects, and *vice versa*. People see through and by one another, as poles to be seen, and as middles to be traversed, all one, and all as kinship and gift, as *condilectio*, and all as adornment. They overlap, assist, intensify and adorn one another, but not as successive perspectives of exclusivity, or ciphers, as before, one gaze at a time, ceding place to another, as if by a competitive *agon*, vying for presence. The 'right distance' to sustain relationship has been found at last. Here, finally, one sees particular individuals. Just as the angels are 'distinct in radiance and art' (*Par.*, xxxi. 132), so we see the personal faces of Beatrice, Bernard and Mary. To see them is not just to see a final goal, but also to see the final medium which is all there is to see. The canto concludes with Dante's particular gaze, carried and intensified by Bernard's, as a borrowing of heat and ardour. He has now joined those 'won to love — adorned with others' light' ('a carità süadi / d'altrui lume fregiati', *Par.*, xxxi. 49–50), carried, as we are as readers, by their return gaze. And not Mary alone, but Mary as the creative ambience of angels.

The chronological story of the three vertically-compared canto Thirty-Ones is one of inversions, and speculative synthesis, of below becoming above, and above below, where even Beatrice has left her footprint in the depths of Hell (*Par.*, xxxi. 81); of over there coming nearby, over here, and yet remaining infinitely distant (*Par.*, xxxi. 74–75); and of a final end-point still comprising movement, and movement-around (*Par.*, xxxi. 46–48, 71–72); of servitude and freedom (*Par.*, xxxi. 85–86); a story of the false and yet finally salvific compass of giants, and of the true reaching upwards of nymphs, which also hurls back downwards, in order to be re-woven together in the labyrinth of gazes and adornments. Above all, it is a story of monsters, of the false yet true monsters, the giants and the true monster, Christ, who assumes even our distorted nature; and still more ultimately, a story of mediation between the false monsters and the true. The key mediators are female — Beatrice, the four nymphs, the three personified theological virtues, and the Heavenly Queen herself. By their height of beauty (*Par.*, xxxi. 134), physical and spiritual, refracted 'ne li occhi a tutti li altri santi' [in all the eyes of all the saints] (*Par.*, xxxi. 135), they lure the false monsters towards the truth; they even beguile downwards the divine into a saving hybridity. By this double action, they render the monstrous tame.

The vertical story of the canto Thirty-Ones is therefore the story of Beauty and the Beast; the instigation of redeeming homeopathy by a union of opposites.

32. Particular Surprises: Faces, Cries and Transfiguration

David F. Ford

In their introduction to the first volume of *Vertical Readings in Dante's 'Comedy'*, George Corbett and Heather Webb describe this project as 'an experiment with a clear aim: to see what would happen when we asked scholars to read all the same-numbered canto sets of the poem vertically'.[1] This chapter is a variation on the other experiments so far, though perhaps more in line with the chapters on the canto Thirty-Ones, Thirty-Threes and Thirty-Fours. Mine is a reading by a Christian theologian whose main work is in contemporary theology, both as a scholar of it and a contributor to it, and who within that field has a special interest in hermeneutics and the interpretation of scripture — mainly the Bible but also other scriptures. Given the immense range of hermeneutical and contemporary theological possibilities opened up by the canto Thirty-Twos, I have set quite strict limits for myself, focusing on those three cantos with little reference to other parts of the *Comedy*, taking one of the many biblical references (the Transfiguration of Jesus) as my primary text within those cantos, and selecting just a couple of theological topics for attention with an eye more on contemporary discussions than on historical theology (where most of the theological scholarship has, understandably, been concentrated).

---

1 *Vertical Readings in Dante's 'Comedy': Volume 1*, ed. by George Corbett and Heather Webb (Cambridge: Open Book Publishers, 2015), p. 1, http://dx.doi.org/10.11647/OBP.0066

     http://dx.doi.org/10.11647/OBP.0119.11

Purgatorio xxxii: Transfiguration

I begin in the middle of the middle canto:

> Però trascorro a quando mi svegliai,
> e dico ch'un splendor mi squarciò 'l velo
> del sonno, e un chiamar: 'Surgi: che fai?'
>   Quali a veder de' fioretti del melo
> che del suo pome li angeli fa ghiotti
> e perpetüe nozze fa nel cielo,
>   Pietro e Giovanni e Iacopo condotti
> e vinti, ritornaro a la parola
> da la qual furon maggior sonni rotti,
>   e videro scemata loro scuola
> così di Moïsè come d'Elia,
> e al maestro suo cangiata stola;
>   tal torna' io, e vidi quella pia
> sovra me starsi che conducitrice
> fu de' miei passi lungo 'l fiume pria.
>   E tutto in dubbio dissi: 'Ov' è Beatrice?'
> Ond' ella: 'Vedi lei sotto la fronda
> nova sedere in su la sua radice.
>   Vedi la compagnia che la circonda:
> li altri dopo 'l grifon sen vanno suso
> con più dolce canzone e più profonda'.
>   E se più fu lo suo parlar diffuso,
> non so, però che già ne li occhi m'era
> quella ch'ad altro intender m'avea chiuso.
>   Sola sedeasi in su la terra vera,
> come guardia lasciata lì del plaustro
> che legar vidi a la biforme fera. (*Purg.*, xxxii. 70–96)

[So I speed on to when I came awake, and say how splendour tore apart sleep's veil and this cry: 'Rise! What are you doing there?'. When brought to see the budding apple flowers which make the angels greedy for their fruit, and makes in Heaven perpetual marriage feast, Peter and James and John were overcome but, waking once again, they heard that word which shattered greater sleeps than theirs had been, and saw the school they'd sat in two souls short — since Moses and Elijah both had gone — their teacher with his robe now much transformed. So, too, I woke, and saw, above me there, the one who in compassion led my steps along the river sometime earlier. And, full of doubt, I said: 'Where's Beatrice?' At which, 'See there', she said, 'beneath the leaves — new — she's seated at the root of that. And see the company that encircles her! The rest behind the Gryphon go on high, singing a deeper, ever sweeter song'.

And if her speech flowed further on than this, I do not know. My eyes were set, by now, on her. She'd closed my mind to other thoughts. Alone, she sat upon that one true earth as guard, left there to watch the chariot which, as I'd seen, the two-form beast had tied.][2]

In the story of the Transfiguration of Jesus in the gospel of Luke, his three disciples, Peter, James and John, 'were weighed down with sleep' (*gravati erant somno*, Luke 9:32, Vulgate), and in *Purgatorio* xxxii this is taken as a point of connection with Dante falling asleep and being awakened. Other biblical transfiguration themes of splendour, seeing, being overcome, hearing the voice of God, the presence and then disappearance of Moses and Elijah, the command to rise, and the transformation of Jesus' clothing are present straightforwardly; but there are also surprising elements woven in. Two are especially striking.

One is the introduction to the analogy with the Transfiguration in lines 73–75. The mention of angels and Heaven echoes the passage that precedes the Transfiguration story in each of the gospels (for example, Luke 9:26–27) but this is given a very different context by references to the Song of Songs and the book of Revelation on the themes of love and marriage. Are the 'budding apple flowers' those of the Song of Songs 2:3–7, with its apples and apple trees, feasting and awakening, traditionally understood as an allegory of Christ and the 'tree' of his cross?:

> As an apple tree among the trees of the wood,
> so is my beloved among young men.
> With great delight I sat in his shadow,
> and his fruit was sweet to my taste.
> He brought me to the banqueting house,
> and his intention towards me was love.
> Sustain me with raisins,
> refresh me with apples;
> for I am faint with love.
> O that his left hand were under my head,
> and that his right hand embraced me!
> I adjure you, O daughters of Jerusalem,
> by the gazelles or the wild does:
> do not stir up or awaken love
> until it is ready!

---

2 Dante Alighieri, *The Divine Comedy 2: Purgatorio,* trans. and ed. by Robin Kirkpatrick (London and Harmondswith: Penguin Books, 2007), p. 305.

The 'perpetual marriage feast' in Heaven recalls the marriage feast of the Lamb who has died and been raised, Jesus himself, in the book of Revelation (19:6–9; cf. 21:1–14). His bride is the Church of the Saints, identified with the Holy City, the New Jerusalem, in the context of nothing less than the new Creation — 'a new Heaven and a new earth' (Revelation 21:1). So Dante has cast himself analogously in the role not only of the disciples closest to Jesus at the Transfiguration but also as the lover in the Song of Songs, allegorically identified with God, and as a participant in the most comprehensive and surprising transformation of all, the renewal of both Heaven and earth.

Comparably daring is the second surprise. In the Transfiguration story there is a dramatic transition when the disciples emerge from the cloud, from which the voice of God had addressed Jesus as 'my Son, my beloved' (Luke 9:35), and then suddenly 'Jesus was found alone' (9:36).[3] But here it is Beatrice who is found alone by Dante (l. 94) — a further example of Dante's breathtakingly audacious figural representation of her.

This central trope of the Transfiguration and its intertexts resonates backwards and forwards in canto xxxii. Our imagination and theological understanding are prepared for the Transfiguration through the earlier part. There is repeated emphasis on sight and seeing, beginning with the opening lines:

> Tant' eran li occhi miei fissi e attenti
> a disbramarsi la decenne sete,
> che li altri sensi m'eran tutti spenti. (*Purg.*, xxxii. 1–3)

> [My eyes were now so fixedly intent to free themselves from that decade-long thirst that every sense but sight had been eclipsed.]

The sun, which also figures in Matthew's Transfiguration narrative, is mentioned no less than four times (ll. 11, 17, 52, 56). The lead-in to finding Beatrice alone is an intensity of seeing:

> già ne li occhi m'era
> quella ch'ad altro intender m'avea chiuso. (*Purg.*, xxxii. 92–93)

> [My eyes were set, by now, on her. She'd closed my mind to other thoughts.]

---

3   There are variant readings of Luke 9:35, but the Vulgate has *dilectus*, beloved, which is also the undisputed reading in the parallel passages in Matthew (Vulgate *dilectus*) and Mark (Vulgate *charissimus*).

But above all there is the choreography of facing, one of the pervasive and theologically important features of the *Comedy*.[4] In his Transfiguration, the face of Jesus is transformed (Luke 9:29) and shines like the sun (Matthew 17:2) as he converses with Moses and Elijah. And at the beginning of *Purgatorio* xxxii there is 'the holy smile' (l. 4) of Beatrice. My favourite theological essay on the *Comedy* is that of Peter Hawkins, 'All smiles. Poetry and Theology in Dante's *Comedy*', in which, after a delightful survey of smiling in the *Comedy*, he concludes that 'the smile is not only Dante's signature gesture but perhaps his most original and indeed useful contribution to medieval theology — and indeed to the Christian tradition itself [...]. It is the gesture that moves us from *Inferno* to *Paradiso*, from the human to the divine, and from time to eternity'.[5]

Here it is Beatrice's smile as the lure of Dante's desire year after year. His face must be forced away from it to attend to anything 'less' (l. 7). When Dante is awakened from sleep he first sees Matelda — 'quella pia [...] che conducitrice / fu de' miei passi lungo 'l fiume pria' [the one who in compassion led my steps along the river sometime earlier] (ll. 82–84) — but immediately asks about Beatrice and, when directed to her, concentrates on her alone.

Only when Beatrice reassures him about being with her both now and forever (ll. 100–03), and then directs his gaze towards the chariot, with an instruction to write down later what he sees, does he obediently give 'la mente e li occhi ov' ella volle' [eye and mind to where she said I should] (l. 108). There follows an allegorical plunge into church history. This has its own choreography of facing, in stark contrast with that between Jesus and his disciples or between Dante and Beatrice. It culminates in the 'puttana sciolta' [loose-wrapped whore] with 'le ciglia intorno pronte' [flickering

---

4 I have been fascinated by this for years. See especially David F. Ford, *Self and Salvation: Being Transformed* (Cambridge: Cambridge University Press, 1999) on Dante pp. 25, 80, 120 and (on Beatrice's smile), p. 275.

5 Peter S. Hawkins, 'All Smiles. Poetry and Theology in Dante's *Comedy*', in *Dante's Commedia: Theology as Poetry*, ed. by Vittorio Montemaggi and Matthew Treherne (Notre Dame, IN: University of Notre Dame Press, 2010), pp. 36–59: 'Despite the degree to which Dante is associated with the infernal, it is his creation of a "smile of the universe", radiant throughout Purgatory and Paradise, that shows his spin on the ancient religion he inherited. To be told that God the Trinity smiles upon himself; to see Gregory smiling at his former error; to catch the delight in Mary's eye, which spreads like lightening throughout the heavenly rose; to consider that the resurrection of the body might mean the raising up of one's own distinctive smile; or to imagine seeing God face-to-face as an encounter with holiness that does not require eyes averted and lips closed tight but rather entails the spontaneity of a smile returning a smile — to entertain these possibilities requires a "new life" for the Christian imagination, one that did not take place in Dante's fourteenth century and is now (sadly) long overdue' (pp. 53–54).

lashes quick to look around], turning her 'occhio cupido e vagante' [wandering and cupidinous eye] on Dante and being whipped by the giant for this (ll. 148–56). There is something comparable in the aftermath to the Transfiguration, as Jesus and the disciples come down the mountain and plunge into a drama of demon-possession, leading to Jesus speaking of his own betrayal (Luke 9:37–45). Another commonality is the way in which the texts note the protagonists seeing things that cannot be understood or spoken about at the time but need to be witnessed later: 'And they kept silent and in those days told no one any of the things they had seen' (Luke 9:36; cf. Mark 9:9–10, Matthew 17:9).

Inferno xxxii: Frozen Faces; Embraced and Eaten by Hatred

This vivid, allegorical engagement with the corruption and sin of the church and Christian history sends us back to the choreography of facing in *Inferno* xxxii. There we have no allegory, only a realistic plain sense, reaching after what Dante calls harsh, rough, rawly rasping language (*Inf.*, xxxii. 1). This describes extreme face to face distrust, hatred, anger, violence, suffering.

There is no frank and open facing between the sinners, or between Dante and the sinners; rather, Dante underlines the difficulty of genuine facing repeatedly:

> Ognuna in giù tenea volta la faccia. (*Inf.*, xxxii. 37)
>
> [And each one kept his face bent down.]

> pur col viso in giùe (*Inf.*, xxxii. 53)
>
> [Still gazing downwards]

> latrando lui con li occhi in giù raccolti. (*Inf.*, xxxii. 105)
>
> [He barked but kept his eyes held firmly down.]

But there are two distinctive images in this canto that contrast with the sorts of facing that are to come in the *Purgatorio*, and above all in the *Paradiso*.

The dominant one is the frozen face. Dante vividly evokes this surprising feature of the depths of Hell: not heat but cold. Here the shadows are 'livide [...] / dolenti ne la ghiaccia' [fixed in ice lead-blue] (l. 34) with teeth chattering, tears frozen solid, ears lost to frostbite.

> Poscia vid' io mille visi cagnazzi
> fatti per freddo; onde mi vien riprezzo,
> e verrà sempre, de' gelati guazzi. (*Inf.*, xxxii. 70–72)

[And then I saw a thousand mongrel faces bitten by frost. (I shiver remembering — and always will — to see a frozen puddle.)]

Among these faces, smiling is unimaginable, as is any gracious interaction. Instead, even more horrific than the frozenness is the second, gruesome surprise: how they interact with each other, and how Dante relates to them. In a parody of love and Eucharistic communion, they embrace in fixed, violent hatred and cannibalistic consumption.

> Con legno legno spranga mai non cinse
> forte così; ond' ei come due becchi
> cozzaro insieme, tanta ira li vinse.
>   [...]
> Ch'io vidi due ghiacciati in una buca,
> sì che l'un capo a l'altro era cappello;
>   e come 'l pan per fame si manduca,
> così 'l sovran li denti a l'altro pose
> là 've 'l cervel s'aggiugne con la nuca:
>   non altrimenti Tideo si rose
> le tempie a Menalippo per disdegno,
> che quei faceva il teschio e l'altre cose.
>   'O tu che mostri per sì bestial segno
> odio sovra colui che tu ti mangi,
> dimmi 'l perché'. (*Inf.*, xxxii. 49–51, 125–35)

[To wood wood never has been clamped so hard as these two were; and, overwhelmed with ire, each butted each like any pair of goats. [...] But then I saw two frozen in one single hole, one head a headpiece to the one below. As bread is mangled by some famished mouth, so too the higher gnawed the lower head, precisely where the nape and brainstem meet. The dying Tydeus in this same way, in loathing, chewed the brows of dead Menalippus, gnawing the skull and everything besides. 'O you who by so bestial a show make known your hatred for the one you eat, now tell me — why?']

Even Dante himself is drawn into the violence, with an ambivalent, or rather multivalent, confession that poses sharply the philosophical and theological puzzle about human and divine freedom in the *Comedy*:

> se voler fu o destino o fortuna,
> non so; ma, passeggiando tra le teste,
> forte percossi 'l piè nel viso ad una. (*Inf.*, xxxii. 76–78)

> [And whether by intention, chance or fate (well, I don't know!) pacing among these heads, hard in the face of one, I struck my foot.]

It certainly seems quite intentional when Dante 'lo presi per la cuticagna' [grasped him tight against the scalp] (l. 97) and later 'tratti glien' avea più d'una ciocca' [yanked out several tufts] (l. 104). I will return later to this question of freedom, which relates to my theme of surprise.

Paradiso xxxii: Transfiguration in Abundance

For now, let us follow the interplay of facing into *Paradiso* xxxii. It is implicit throughout, as those in the rose of Heaven are pointed out to Dante in a series of gracious introductions. Within the rose, presided over by the Virgin Mary, the Hebrew women and men, such as Eve, Rachel, Sarah, Rebecca, Judith, Ruth, Adam and Moses, who came before Christ, come together with the Christian saints, such as John the Baptist, Peter, John the Evangelist, Francis, Benedict, Augustine,[6] Lucy and Anne. This echoes the Transfiguration's bringing together of Peter, James and John with Moses and Elijah. The surprise here is the presence of Beatrice alongside Rachel.

The first explicit mention is of the Christian saints 'quei ch'a Cristo venuto ebber li visi' [who turned their countenance to Christ now come] (l. 27). Dante is also told to note the faces of the children, as the mystery of their salvation and ranking is explored. Then there is a double climax of facing.

The first is a rich yet mysterious evocation of the way God, presented here as king in his kingdom, through his 'tanto amore e [...] tanto diletto' [great love, his pure delight] (l. 62) and his 'lieto aspetto' [translated variously as 'look of happiness' (Kirkpatrick); 'glad sight' (Mandelbaum); 'own eyes' bliss' (Binyon) and 'happy image' (Huse)] (l. 64) creates everything and distributes grace:

---

6 One of the puzzles of the *Comedy* is why Augustine's massive theological presence in Western Christianity is not reflected in his role in the poem — he is simply mentioned here in passing.

> Lo rege per cui questo regno pausa
> in tanto amore e in tanto diletto,
> che nulla volontà è di più ausa
>   le menti tutte nel suo lieto aspetto
> creando, a suo piacer di grazia dota
> diversamente; e qui basti l'effetto. (*Par.*, xxxii. 61–66)

[The king, through whom this kingdom is at peace, in such great love, and in such pure delight, that nothing in our wills dare aim so high, creating, in his look of happiness, all minds, bestowed, as he best pleased, his grace in different ways. The outcome says enough.]

I will return later to this interweaving of love, delight, daring, creativity, happiness and the differentiation of grace.

The second, more extended climax, evokes the face of Mary. Dante's adoration of Mary takes up and carries further his adoration of Beatrice; it is also his primary way into the adoration of Jesus Christ. And facing is central to this core set of relationships in contemplation, adoration, joy, wisdom, grace and love:

> Riguarda omai ne la faccia che a Cristo
> più si somiglia, ché la sua chiarezza
> sola ti può disporre a veder Cristo. (*Par.*, xxxii. 85–87)

[Return now. See that face resembling Christ closer than all. For that bright light alone can make you wholly fit to look on Christ.]

One might debate whether Christology or Mariology is more central to the *Comedy*, but our cantos leave no doubt about the theological, conceptual priority of Jesus Christ, while perhaps giving imaginative and affective priority to Beatrice in *Purgatorio* xxxii and to Mary in *Paradiso* xxxii. In *Purgatorio* xxxii the 'binato' [two-formed] (l. 47) Gryphon symbolises Christ as human and divine, and the embracing framework is that of sin and salvation culminating in Jesus Christ, but the drama that grips the reader is between Dante and Beatrice. In *Paradiso* xxxii Christ is likewise central to the reality described, with all history pivoting around his coming or having come, and the light of Mary's face enabling looking on Christ; but what I have called the second climactic facing, that of Mary, is both longer and more intense.

Dante sees 'happiness rain down on her' ('sopra lei tanta allegrezza / piover', ll. 88–89), so 'that nothing I had ever seen before had brought my wondering eyes to such a poise, nor shown so much to me of how God looks' ('che quantunque io avea visto davante, / di tanta ammirazion non mi sospese, / né mi mostrò di Dio tanto sembiante' (ll. 91–93). The effect on the 'beata corte' [happy court] (l. 98) of the angel Gabriel's singing is that 'ogne vista sen fé più serena' [their faces showed the more serene] (l. 99). Gabriel, in his delight, is noted by Dante, who asks:

> 'qual è quell'angel che con tanto gioco
> guarda ne li occhi la nostra regina,
> innamorato si che par di foco?'
>   Così ricorsi ancora a la dottrina
> di colui ch'abbelliva di Maria,
> come del sole stella mattutina. (*Par.*, xxxii. 104–08)

> ['which is that angel who, with such delight, looks at our Queen and gazes in her eyes so deep in love he seems to be on fire?' I went, in this way, back to learn from him of one who drew his beauty from Maria, as, from the sun, the morning star draws light.]

This is transfiguration in abundance, being multiplied, shared — a contagion of light, love, beauty and delight; Bernard in his comments immediately sets it in the proper theological hierarchy of Gabriel, Mary and Jesus:

> 'perch' elli è quelli che portò la palma
> giuso a Maria, quando 'l Figliuol di Dio
> carcar si volse de la nostra salma'. (*Par.*, xxxii. 112–14)

> ['For he it is who carried down the palm to Mary when the only Son of God chose to take on the weight of human form'.]

Then, after Bernard has directed Dante's eyes to other saints in the rose, he prepares him for the ultimate facing of the Trinitarian God that is to come in the final canto:

> 'e drizzeremo li occhi al primo amore,
> sì che, guardando verso lui, penètri
> quant' è possibil per lo suo fulgore'. (*Par.*, xxxii. 142–44)

> [And turn your eyes towards the Primal Love, so that, in looking there, your eye should pierce as far as possible His dazzling light.]

But note the form of the preparation: it is 'praying for the gift of grace'] from Mary ('credendo oltrarti / orando grazia conven che s'impetri', ll. 146–47). Our third vertical canto ends with a colon, on the verge of Bernard's prayer to Mary. There will be more to say on this later.

The Soundtrack:
Cries, Song, Conversation, Prayer

Before I come to my culminating set of theological issues I want to recapitulate briefly our three cantos. I have concentrated on the visual. What about the soundtrack that accompanies these dramas of facing? Before I begin with the *Inferno* it is worth making an obvious point: the *Comedy* is a verbal creation, to be read and heard, and all its visual vividness is evoked by words, by auditory and imaginative means.

Hell is noisy as well as nasty, and the opening of *Inferno* xxxii longs for a harshness of language to match it. The problem is that this is no 'impresa [...] / da lingua che chiami mamma o babbo' [task for tongues still whimpering 'Mum!' or 'Dad!'] (ll. 7–9). So Dante turns to the Muses for inspiration, 'sì che dal fatto il dir non sia diverso' [so fact and word may not too far diverge] (l. 12).

What he portrays is the polar opposite of children crying out to loving parents. There are cries of pain and outrage:

> forte percossi 'l piè nel viso ad una.
> Piangendo mi sgridò: 'Perché mi peste?' (*Inf.*, xxxii. 78–79)

> [hard in the face of one, I struck my foot. It screeched out, whiningly: 'Why stamp on me?']

Conversation turns into interrogation, even accompanied by torture. Exchanges are full of insult, anger, hatred and cruelty:

> quando un altro gridò: 'Che hai tu, Bocca?
> non ti basta sonar con le mascelle,
> se tu non latri? qual diavol ti tocca?'
>   'Omai', diss' io, 'non vo' che più favelle,
> malvagio traditor; ch'a la tua onta
> io porterò di te vere novelle'. (*Inf.*, xxxii. 106–11)

[Another yelling now: 'What's with you, Big Mouth? Not satisfied to
castanet cold jaws? You bark as well. What devil's got to you?' And then
I said: 'I'd have you speak no more. You're vile, you traitor. I'll augment
your shame, I'll carry in your name a true report'.]

There is a clear contrast with *Purgatorio* xxxii, where, as Dante and Statius
proceed, 'temprava i passi un'angelica nota' [Our steps were measured to
the angel song] (l. 33). The first address there is a cry of blessing on the
Gryphon. Then Dante is overwhelmed by a hymn:

> Io non lo 'ntesi, né qui non si canta
> l'inno che quella gente allor cantaro,
> né la nota soffersi tutta quanta. (*Purg.*, xxxii. 61–63)

> [I did not understand (it's not sung here) the hymn these people sang,
> nor could I bear in full the beauty of its harmonies.]

Such singing, like smiling, was absent from Hell. After Dante sleeps and is
awoken by a cry of 'Surgi' ['Rise!'] (*Purg.*, xxxii. 72), the sight of Beatrice is
accompanied by 'più dolce canzone e più profonda' [a deeper, ever sweeter
song] (l. 90).

But we are still in the *Purgatorio*, and here in the Earthly Paradise where
the first sin occurred, and the signs and sounds of hope and salvation are
interwoven with reminders of sin and suffering. The allegory of Christian
history is violent in action and imagery, and at its centre is a heartfelt cry
from the Heavens at the corruption of the church: 'O navicella mia, com'
mal se' carca!'['My little ship, what ill load weighs you down!'] (l. 129).

In *Paradiso* xxxii there is still a reminder of sin when Ruth is introduced
as: 'colei / che fu bisava al cantor che per doglia / del fallo disse "*Miserere
mei*"' [the one who bore the mother of the man who sang, mourning his fault,
the '*Miserere mei*'] (ll. 10–12). But this is sin forgiven, people reconciled with
God. The primary focus is on Mary, full of grace, to whom Gabriel sings,
and the main sound besides singing — as in the case of the mother of Mary,
St Anne, 'tanto contenta di mirar sua figlia, / che non move occhio per
cantare osanna' [so happy as she wonders at her child she does not move
her eyes to sing 'Hosannah'] (ll. 134–35) — is that of gracious introductions,
conversation shot through with wonder, delight and desire, and the wise
instruction of Bernard leading into the final line: 'E cominciò questa santa
orazione' [And so he now began his holy prayer] (l. 151).

Grace and Surprise

Now for some theological ruminations. I noted earlier the remark from *Inferno* xxxii: 'se voler fu o destino o fortuna, / non so' [And whether by intention, chance or fate / (well, I don't know!)] (ll. 76–77) and its connection with Dante's understanding of freedom. Set that alongside the lines from *Paradiso* xxxii:

> Dentro a l'ampiezza di questo reame
> casüal punto non puote aver sito,
> se non come tristizia o sete o fame:
>   ché per etterna legge è stabilito
> quantunque vedi, sì che giustamente
> ci si risponde da l'anello al dito;
>   e però questa festinata gente
> a vera vita non è *sine causa*
> intra sé qui più e meno eccellente. (*Par.,* xxxii. 52–60)

[Within the broad expanse of all this realm there cannot be a single point that's chance, nor any hunger, thirst or misery. For all that you may see here is decreed by God's eternal law. Hence, right and fit, all corresponds as finger to a ring. And so it is that, not without good cause, these children — sped too soon to this true life — are in their excellences less and more.]

If, in addition, one remembers Dante's assertion that human freedom is 'the greatest gift bestowed by God, on human nature'[7] one begins to grasp how complex this matter is, of which both the historical and contemporary theology of human and divine freedom are evidence.

But for now I will take as a key point of convergence between Dante's position in the *Comedy*, and a range of mainstream Christian thinkers in recent decades, the principle that human freedom and divine freedom are directly, not inversely related. In other words, the more involved we

---

7   Dante states this in *Paradiso* v. 19–22: 'Lo maggior don che Dio per sua larghezza / fesse creando, e a la sua bontate / più conformato, e quel ch'e' più apprezza, / fu de la volontà la libertate' [the greatest gift that God, in spacious deed, made, all-creating — and most nearly formed / to His liberality, most prized by Him — was liberty in actions of the will]. For a discussion of this freedom with relevant quotations, see Patrick Boyde, 'Aspects of Human Freedom', in *Perception and Passion in Dante's* Comedy (Cambridge: Cambridge University Press, 1993), pp. 193–214.

are in loving God, living in line with God's free love for us, the more free we are. This, of course, contradicts those concepts of human freedom, or autonomy, which see human and divine freedom as in competition with each other. Heaven, for Dante, is the realm where God's freedom is seen in full harmony with human freedom. I do not want to undertake here the lengthy task of justifying this theology (with which I am in agreement) but to take off from it, and in particular to reflect on the next six lines, which have already been quoted:

> Lo rege per cui questo regno pausa
> in tanto amore e in tanto diletto,
> che nulla volontà è di più ausa
>   le menti tutte nel suo lieto aspetto
> creando, a suo piacer di grazia dota
> diversamente; e qui basti l'effetto. (*Par.*, xxxii. 61–66)

[The king, through whom this kingdom is at peace, in such great love, and in such pure delight, that nothing in our wills dare aim so high, creating, in his look of happiness, all minds, bestowed, as he best pleased, his grace in different ways. The outcome says enough.]

Grace can be seen as God's freely given love in action, and one of Dante's characteristic ways of describing grace coming together with human freedom is as love marked by delight, joy, happiness, beatitude. Smiling and singing are, as we have heard, among his favourite incarnate images of this. God's own 'look of happiness' is at the heart of creation, and human beings are fulfilled when this is mutual, in joyful adoration of God and delight in each other and in creation. And God, being infinitely free, is free to surprise us continually.

I want to dwell for a while on this theme of surprise. The *Comedy* is itself a massive surprise, and is full of surprises, within which I include its structure, its language and imagery, its plot and characters, its meetings and conversations, many philosophical and theological thoughts, its interpretations of scripture and other texts, the various turns, renewals, transformations and reorientations, and more. The most obvious indicator of the theme is Dante's repeated bewilderment and amazement as he travels through Hell, Purgatory and Heaven, and the need for him to expand his capacities of heart, mind and imagination in order to cope with one new thing after another. One of his achievements as a poet is to portray Heaven as a place of progressive astonishment. In *Paradiso* xxxii this is focused first on understanding the place of the children, and next on Mary, full of grace ('*gratïa plena*', l. 96), with the passage just quoted explaining the first but also relevant to the second. I want to highlight just two aspects of that passage.

One is the note of daring. 'Che nulla volontà è di più ausa' [nothing in our wills dare aim so high] (l. 63) is not only testimony to the transcendence of God's love, delight and creativity. It also implies that our wills might dare to aim quite high. We can, by God's grace, act in love, take delight, and stretch our minds, and Dante through the *Comedy* takes part in such daring creativity.

The second is the note of diversity, as given by God who 'a suo piacer di grazia dota / diversamente' [bestowed, as he best pleased, his grace / in different ways] (ll. 65–66). People are radically diverse, each unique, and we have no divine overview of them. How, then, are we to respond to them in all their otherness? The *Comedy* is a pedagogy of response to others, and Dante the poet dares to aim quite high — perhaps, at times, too high — in his judgements on them.

I now take a leap to our own situation of diversity, and in particular the theological daring that contemporary religious diversity requires. The logic of Dante's audacity in relation to his predecessors and contemporaries is that we who come after him might be inspired by his daring even when differing from his conclusions. God must be allowed to go on springing surprises, and if Dante does not allow his sources to have the last word so neither should Dante be allowed to have it now. Honouring Dante is not just a matter of repeating him, but of doing today things analogous to what he did in his day. So just as Dante was steeped in several cultural, philosophical, cosmological, political and religious traditions, and improvised audaciously on them all, so he can help inspire a comparably daring improvisation today. At a time when some in Italy are agitating for his removal from the school syllabus because of Mohammed being placed in Hell, and other negative references to Islam (including, many agree, the identification of the dragon in *Purgatorio* xxxii with Islam), what might be a creatively Dantean surprise in the area of interreligious relations? I would suggest two points for now.

First, between Christians and Muslims, their two scriptures, Bible and Qur'an, must be part of the engagement. Dante is a master of intertextuality, brokering the fruitful interplay of texts and exploring their levels, and it would be fascinating to transfer some of his art to reading the Qur'an and the Bible alongside each other, and even to bring the *Comedy* as a biblically-shaped poem into dialogue with Muslim poetry inspired by the Qur'an. We have seen how the Transfiguration of Jesus, for example, resonates through our three cantos, together with many other scriptural texts. Peter Hawkins gives a consummate biblical analysis of *Purgatorio* xxxii, showing how it is part of a 'massive turn to scripture' at the end of the *Purgatorio*, one that stretches from Eden in Genesis to the Book of Revelation and ranges through the whole of the canon in between.[8] Hawkins also offers one of the most apt images of Dante's daring in dealing with the Bible, a quality from which the interplay between the scriptures of the two most numerous religions of the twenty-first century could greatly benefit. He suggests the inadequacy of Luca Signorelli's portrayal of Dante in the San Brizio Chapel of Orvieto Cathedral, and adds:

> Perhaps only a moving picture would do, for then we would see him as he really is over the long course of the *Commedia* — less a scholar safely ensconced within his library and more an aerialist of the afterlife, a tightrope walker who negotiates the perilous high wire he has himself strung out between God's Book and his own poem. Part of the excitement of watching him making his high-flying moves is the realization that he is always performing without a net, as if inviting the disaster that never quite befalls him. But, perhaps the most thrilling aspect of his artistry is the sustained *balance* of his entire act, the way his reckless daring is so artfully concealed. One simply cannot stop marveling at the sureness of his footing, the careful measure of each bold step forward, the confident way he holds on to the air.[9]

For our interreligious situation one might hope for a comparable artistry combined with the sort of respect, generosity and love towards the contemporary non-Christian other that Dante accords to Virgil but not to Mohammed.

A second point is the diversity of grace, if God 'a suo piacer di grazia dota / diversamente' [bestowed, as he best pleased, his grace / in different ways] (*Par.*, xxxii. 65–66). A combination of trusting the God of love, joy and

---

8 Peter Hawkins, *Dante's Testaments. Essays in Scriptural Imagination* (Stanford: Stanford University Press, 1999), pp. 180–228.

9 Hawkins, *Dante's Testaments*, pp. 70–71.

compassion, together with an understanding of grace that is differentiated, particular and part of the mystery of how God is 'best pleased', might suggest a more positive attitude than Dante's to Muslims and others whom Dante confidently judges to be in Hell. At the least, Karl Barth's maxim that the Christian is one who, in the light of Christ, is permitted to hope for the best for all people, might be adopted, leaving Dante with more surprises than he might have anticipated. Inter-faith engagement needs an eschatology of surprise, as well as the agnosticism that is its necessary accompaniment, since by definition surprises are not known in advance. The practical effect of this should be alertness and openness to grace coming through new events, people, texts, and ideas, and so on.

Moving on from inter-faith relations, and still relevant to it, though of far wider relevance too, is the question, posed by the closing lines of *Paradiso* xxxii, about prayer for grace. It is easy to protest that, if all in Heaven is really 'per etterna legge [...] stabilito' [decreed / by God's eternal law] (l. 55), then why does Bernard need to pray for Dante and beg for 'grazia da quella che puote aiutarti' [grace from her who can assist] (l. 148)? The answer leads us to the heart of the mystery of divine surprise.

Prayer is an alignment of human freedom with the freedom of God in radical intimacy with God. The freedom to pray is itself a gift of grace, and the free acknowledgement of this utter dependence on God is a recognition not only of the non-competitive relationship between divine and human freedom but also of the fact that the second is created by the first. And communion with a God of surprises opens the way to full and active participation in creating those surprises, which includes the writing of prayer and praise such as that which Dante puts into the mouth of Bernard in the final canto, and which leads into the ultimate surprise of the beatific vision.

It is a stupendous thought, that human beings might, in prayerful humility and yet in reality, receive the life, light and love, indeed the very Spirit, of the God of Jesus Christ, who does new things, renews old things, and is endlessly creative. Yet that is standard Christian teaching and Dante fully accepted it. In fact, if anything he appears to 'over-accept' it, entering into it with such wholehearted conviction that his *Comedy* claims the authority of scripture, he himself is assured of his place in Heaven, and 'his lady' Beatrice is his guide and the revealer of matters never before the subject of poetry.

Cadenza: In the Fitzwilliam Museum…

Finally, a cadenza. In the Fitzwilliam Museum in Cambridge, in Holy Week of 2015, as part of the King's College Holy Week programme, the poet Micheal O'Siadhail gave for the first time a reading from a work still in progress, called *The Five Quintets*.[10] This is a poem on something of the scale of the *Comedy*, consisting of five long poems on each of five themes: 'Making' (the arts), 'Dealing' (economics), 'Steering' (politics), 'Finding' (the sciences) and 'Meaning' (philosophy and theology). Each poem shows the influence of Dante, and explores how major areas of life and thought have developed in the past few centuries, as well as what is happening now, and how the future might be shaped. Here in conclusion (with the author's permission) is one of the poems from the five long cantos of 'Making'. It consists of four sonnets in the form of a conversation between the poet and Dante: the first and third sonnets are in the poet's voice; the second and fourth are in Dante's.

Dante Alighieri

1

My Dante, tend *nel mezzo del cammin*
Forgotten bulbs your times again unearth;
Your gift to see a flowering unforeseen,
To rake the soil for Europe's lush rebirth.
A rich pre-modern mind allows you mix
Rife thoughts retrieved with things so up-to-date
In science, art or purse and politics,
The cosmos in your seedbed city state.
You're lily-signed Firenze's exiled son –
Why is that place assailed by so much strife? –
Who'll name and face dead figures one by one,
Descending and ascending afterlife.
By conscious metaphor and fact combined
You parallel the purpose of God's mind.

2

Ah yes, the middle of the way and yet
Recall the years I yearned, a troubadour
For Beatrice since Mayday when we met

---

10 O'Siadhail has been working on this for nearly a decade and it is due for publication in 2018 (by Baylor University Press in the USA).

One fateful moment in 1284.
I break new ground and graft a Comedy –
I'm politician, poet citizen;
Though love can shape a tongue in Tuscany,
I end an exile, never home again.
With Virgil I will climb hell's deepest ice
To reach the doorway of the dead and weep
Till Beatrice, unknotting nerves in me,
Redeems my guilt and, braving paradise,
I dare allow my sacred poem to leap
From where we are to where we're made to be.

3
You're polymath and eager pioneer
Who doubling back becomes a daring scout,
Defining our modernity's frontier
By summing up what somehow opens out.
A fluke of birth, a lucky *floruit,*
As banished and uncoddled by soft fame,
You blame defectors' sham and counterfeit;
Unhampered your cold hell will name and shame.
But more! As certain as the second thief,
This day in paradise you too are shown
The smile whose warmth unzips the lily's leaf,
The light eternal in itself alone.
You're stretching still my mind and my desire
To walk our daring God of love's high wire.

4
But seven centuries beyond my theme,
You've chosen to pursue the selfsame path
And summing up an era work the seam
Between the modern and its aftermath.
You've climbed from hell to heaven's vertigo.
I'll be your guide! Though dazzled in that gaze,
Allow flawed words their spill and overflow,
For God delights in lily-gilding praise.
Imagine all we've done or left undone,
Our broken longings longing still for more,
Completed in the glory of one glance
And as both stars and atoms dance and dance,
Our lives unreel around one loving core
Where all our wills and all desires are one.

33 and 34. Ice, Fire and Holy Water

Rowan Williams

'Freezing Fires' and Heavenly Motion

The end of the *Inferno* is shaped around images of stasis; nothing really *moves* in Hell, despite appearances. The homely image of a windmill (*Inf.*, xxxiv. 4–6) evokes not only wind itself but flowing water. But for all the ferocity of the wind in Hell, its function is not to move, certainly not to grind wheat for nourishment, but to freeze: it blows in order to prevent motion, to turn flowing water to ice and to fix the damned in glassy immobility ('come festuca in vetro', *Inf.*, xxxiv. 12). We have already encountered in *Inferno* xxxiii (ll. 91ff) the excruciating image of tears freezing as they flow, a kind of foretaste of the universal ice of the ninth circle. And the wind that keeps all things in their deathly stillness, in the cold that literally threatens to make Dante lose his voice (*Inf.*, xxxiv. 22ff), is the effect of the beating of Satan's featherless bat-like wings, the three pairs of 'grand' ali' (l. 46) that agitate the air around him. Satan is himself immobilised in the ice: he is in some degree a parodic version of the unmoved mover of Paradise, the agitation of his wings causing only immobility and silence. It is worth noting that the cessation of movement and the cessation of *speech* go together in Hell, as the description of Dante's sense of suspension between life and death (*Inf.*, xxxiv. 25–27) suggests: speech is a form of intelligent or purposive motion, and the wordless bliss of Heaven is not a cancellation of such motion but a kind of growth from and beyond it, as we shall see when we look at the culminating images of the *Purgatorio* and *Paradiso*.

    http://dx.doi.org/10.11647/OBP.0119.12

The contrast between the stasis and frozenness of Hell and the fluid motion of grace is very clearly signalled in the closing sections of the *Purgatorio*. The two rivers described in *Purgatorio* xxviii (ll. 121ff), Lethe and Eunoe, flow directly at the prompting of God. The water does not come from condensation produced by ice from mist; it is not the result of any cyclical process within creation. Whereas in Hell, grief is eternally fixed in frozen tears, so that destructive and painful remembrance can never be taken away, the waters of Purgatory flow (as a pure act of divine giving) to enable both forgetting and restoration, the forgetting of sin and the restoring (presumably) of the otherwise buried merit of good that has been done. The Earthly Paradise that is being described here is quintessentially a place where waters flow (*Purg.*, xxviii. 25–33 and xxix. 7 etc.): the descriptions of Dante's encounter with Beatrice are shot through with the imagery of water flowing, immersion in water, even the melting of ice. When Dante hears the angelic choir singing 'In you, O Lord, have I hoped', the ice which has been constricting his heart melts into 'breath and water' (*Purg.*, xxx. 82–99); the whole sequence of events up to the end of the *Purgatorio* describes his immersion in and drinking from the two rivers that will liberate him for Heaven. Beatrice teases him (*Purg.*, xxxiii. 94ff) about his forgetfulness of his failures after drinking from Lethe (his forgetfulness actually indicates that there *is* something he needs to forget), and urges him on to drink from Eunoe (ll. 127–38). He rises from the *santissima onda* (l. 142), made ready for the transition to Heaven, and the language, echoing the familiar liturgical use of *unda* for the waters of baptism, makes it plain that what is happening is a recapitulation of the reality that baptism effects, swallowing the memory of evil and failure. Less insistently flagged but clearly in the conceptual landscape, the restoration of 'breath', *spirito* (*Purg.*, xxx. 98), points us to biblical language about 'water and the (Holy) Spirit', as in, for example, the third chapter of St John's Gospel: it is baptism that releases both the divine spirit that adopts us into divine life and prosaically restores breath to the hoarse and constricted voice of the poet.

Thus the climax of the *Purgatorio* is depicted against the background of living water, the streams flowing in and from the Earthly Paradise like the biblical Tigris and Euphrates flowing from Eden (*Purg.*, xxxiii. 112). Everything here is very deliberately opposed to the frigidity of Hell: water flows; the ice that paralyses the heart and constrains the voice melts; the water of the two rivers is both for drinking and for immersion. But the same kind of contrast is also at work in the final canto of the *Paradiso* in connection with the imagery of wind and wings. The invocation of the Mother of God gives *ali* to the soul that wishes to rise and is humble enough to seek aid from her prayers (*Par.*, xxxiii. 15); yet the *proprie penne* of the mind cannot, even when lifted by grace, rise to the mysteries of the ultimate depths of the Trinitarian life (l. 141, and compare *Par.*, xxxii. 146 where St Bernard warns Dante of the fragility of *l'ali tue*). Similarly, if we take the language of *Paradiso* xxxii. 89 as it stands, the implication seems to be that there is a wind that blows in Heaven which brings all things together, *quasi conflati insieme*, mysteriously uniting substance and accidents in intelligible form, and showing them in one single and simple moment of enlightenment (Dante may here be thinking of Gregory the Great's phrase about St Benedict seeing all things as if gathered into one in the light of God[1]). The wind stirred by the Devil's wings is a force that keeps things rigorously apart, unrelated in their icy stillness; what it is in Heaven that causes the substances of the universe to be *conflati* is a power that interweaves and connects all things. And (though this is a little more speculative) where the *Inferno* uses the image of a huge ship's sails for Satan's wings (*Inf.*, xxxiv. 46–48), the *Purgatorio* itself begins (i. 1–3) with the image of a ship in full sail. *Paradiso* ii opens with another evocation of a journey on board ship towards our final destiny in the vision of Heaven; and there is a possible indirect echo in *Paradiso* xxxiii. 94–96, with Dante's evocation of Neptune's amazement at the sight of a fleet under sail as an analogy for his own wonder at the way the heavenly wind gathers the apparently fragmentary elements of creation together.

Frozen Speech and Heavenly Inarticulacy

We have already noted the convergence for Dante of speech with movement; hence the trajectory of the *Inferno* towards one kind of silence, and of the *Paradiso* towards a wordless intensity that is both supremely free movement and the ultimate stillness of universal harmony. Throughout most of the *Inferno*, the sinners are famously loquacious — autobiographical, minatory, complaining, defiant, or simply destroyed by grief (like Ugolino in canto xxxiii). It is only at the end that we find absolute silence, in Satan and the three traitors in his three mouths. Satan and Judas silence each other: Judas's head is inside the devil's mouth; but Brutus too hangs without a

---

1 Gregory the Great, *Dialogues*, II.35.

word ('non fa motto', *Inf.*, xxxiv. 66) even though his head hangs free. The traitors have betrayed language itself: treason (which we have hitherto seen in dreadful but slightly less extreme shapes, as with Fra Alberigo earlier in canto xxxiii) is designated here in the depths of the pit as the ultimate sin, because it is a rebellion against the dependability of words and relations, an offence against that implicit promise that is made in all intelligible speech, that words can be relied on. Betrayal constitutes a sort of suicide of language, and so an unravelling of created reality itself as a system of intelligible relatedness. Satan, the root and paradigm of all treason, is speechless because he has directly turned his back on the living truth: he can have nothing to say that can be understood, and his silence is like a black hole at the centre of Hell, holding all its inhabitants as a sort of magnetic centre. And this is why, after the deathly stasis of the *Inferno*, the journey through Purgatory is, from one point of view, a recovery of convivial speech. In contrast to the traitors, who cannot even speak of the memory of their guilt, who are even further beyond penitence than the rest of the damned, Purgatory makes possible a truthful acknowledgement of sin, the voicing of human failure in a healing communal life: when Dante, struggling to articulate ('a pena ebbi la voce che rispuose', *Purg.*, xxxi. 32), confesses his turning away from truth, Beatrice commends him for neither being silent nor denying his guilt: by the climax of his conversation with her in canto xxxiii, Dante, having drunk from the waters of Lethe, has 'forgotten' not only the memory of his abandonment of the vision Beatrice represents, but also the obscuring of truthful speech by over-ambitious speculation. He must learn to hear naked words ('nude [...] parole', ll. 100–01) from Beatrice, which will show him the distance between what he can grasp and the truth to which her contemplation looks: he must become completely receptive to the active reality he confronts, although this leaves him with a stronger-than-ever sense of incapacity to grasp what Beatrice is telling him (ll. 76–84).

So in Purgatory, there is a skilfully evoked tension between speech and listening; this is not the dead and despairing silence of Hell, but a chastening of fluent and confident speech that arises from the most extended efforts of the mind, a silence on the far side of mental and spiritual action and attention to what has been spoken and shown by the grace-filled interlocutor. The poet's speech is presented as halting, uncertain of itself. When the mind is so closely held by what it contemplates that it cannot formulate an impression of it (indeed it is what the mind contemplates that literally and actively 'impresses'), there will be no subsequent words that can carry what has been communicated. And so in Paradise, this tension is again brought into focus at a point of climax: as sight takes over from speech, memory itself is 'outraged' ('cede la memoria a tanto oltraggio', *Par.*, xxxiii. 57), almost 'violated'. When you wake from a dream, you may know you are changed, that something has imprinted itself, even though nothing can be remembered. What has been experienced is still *present* in or to the mind in some sense, but cannot be summoned up as an object for mental examination (ll. 55–61). All that Dante can do is to pray that something may surface in the memory by God's gift, so that it may be left for posterity ('per tornare alquanto in mia memoria / e per sonare un poco in questi versi', ll. 73–74). The active mind at its supreme stretch of activity has to yield to vision; vision 'impresses' and leaves a lasting mark, but does not lend itself to easy, let alone adequate, speech; however, the 'outraged' memory may still be able to find some words to point to what has been encountered.

What Dante is bringing into view here is the transforming role of *interruption* in the encounter with God: speech is neither simply affirmed nor simply denied in its active relation to Him, but stretched, broken and re-established. Between the silence of utter shame and emptiness or self-evacuation in Hell and the silence of self-excess and ecstasy in Heaven, the poet's imaginative language exists: it seeks to give linguistic form to what has impressed itself upon the mind, but — precisely because it is stumbling in the wake of an action beyond its own comprehension or capacity — it will necessarily convey only 'un poco' [a little] (*Par.*, xxxiii. 69, 74). The more we try to speak, the more we fall short, failing to make sense even more dramatically than babies at the breast (ll. 106–08). In other words, we are warned by the poet that what we are reading is baby-talk, but also alerted that the reason it is baby-talk is not a shortage of things to say but an abundance, informed directly by the action of what is spoken about upon the receptive mind. Just as — in Beatrice's playful response to Dante's forgetfulness (*Purg.*, xxxiii. 94–97) — the fact of oblivion paradoxically shows that there was something to be forgotten, so the fact of inarticulacy shows that there is something to talk about, even if in bare fact we *cannot* adequately talk about it. The point echoes that made by St Thomas Aquinas, following Pseudo-Dionysius when he argues that it is the crudest or 'less noble' metaphors for God that may be most communicative in some circumstances because we know they cannot literally apply.[2]

The language of interruption reminds us sharply that the entire narrative of the *Commedia* is about an interruption. Dante is really alive on earth but temporarily, imaginatively in the next world: what leads up to the climactic vision at the end of the *Paradiso* is a sequence of events and encounters out of due time, breaking into Dante's earthly life. The rationale of the whole narrative structure is this ultimate vision and its articulation in inarticulate words. In this sense, the whole poem that is the *Commedia* is the fruit of interruption: the poetic voice when turned upon its highest and most demanding subject, at the end of the *Paradiso*, demonstrates its authenticity by its own awkward and imperfect character, and the preceding narrative will show how and why this is so.

The point about interruption is ironically reinforced by the apparently bizarre episode, in *Inferno* xxxiii, that introduces a living person, Alberigo (ll. 121–27). If Dante is really on earth and only transiently, interruptively, in the next world, Alberigo, alive at the time of writing is only apparently alive on earth, as his eternal destiny is already fixed and he is 'really' in Hell; what now inhabits his body on earth is assumed to be some diabolical presence. Alberigo is a betrayer, one who has undermined the significance of the language we share; his fate foreshadows the climactic vision of the three great traitors in Satan's mouth. In a sense he *cannot* as a breaker of his word survive in human society on earth. He has already denied the convivial reality for which humanity is created and has shut himself off from grace — so we may as well imagine him in Hell and his body on earth preserved as a fictive covering only. Alberigo informs Dante that this punishment is not unique to him (mentioning the case of Branca Doria, also still 'alive' on earth): it is the natural penalty for those who break away from truth. Thus the fatally corrupted speech of the traitor like Alberigo is set over against the broken and remade speech of the believing poet: the traitor's plausible fluency takes him from earth to Hell, the poet's awkward witness to the active truth that has overtaken and impressed itself upon him allows him to survive in Hell, Purgatory and Paradise while still living out his time on earth. Dante's sojourn in the afterlife is like the sleep that overtakes him in *Purgatorio* xxxii (ll. 64–69), which is, significantly, compared with the sleep or trance that overtakes the apostles Peter, James

---

2   Aquinas, *Summa Theologiae*, Ia, q. 1, a. 9, ad 3.

and John as they are about to witness Christ's Transfiguration in the gospel narrative of Luke (9:32): just as the apostles wake up and see clearly the transfigured face of Jesus, so Dante wakes and sees Beatrice's handmaid, pointing him towards Beatrice herself among her heavenly companions (ll. 76–78). The sleep is an interval of grace as well as simply an interruption, a suspension of ordinary consciousness that will show itself in what is said after the episode and in the new capacity for clear sight that is given to the poet, but will escape anything like detailed description, however hard the poet tries. Or to put it another way again, the word-breaker like Alberigo treats words as cheap, to be discarded at will in the service of the greedy ego; the poet recognises words as monumentally weighty and even costly to bring forth, revealing among other things just how far short of reality the words of the still not-fully-redeemed self always are.

So in addition to the conversation about movement and stasis between the concluding cantos of the three sections, there is a conversation about speech itself. As we have seen, speech is tied up with motion: the lack of one accompanies the lack of the other. Hell is thus silent as well as frozen; and the ultimate silence and frozenness have to do with the primordial sin, the betrayal of the truth and in particular of pledged loyalty, truth in the sense of 'troth', we might say. When words are used to obscure reality and to break covenant, they damn us. So deeply is this true that the traitor still alive on earth is already dead in his or her sins, having resigned their life to the diabolical power of falsehood. Meanwhile, the poet struggling to find words for the excess of truth and reality or life that is encountered in the territories of the afterlife has to recognise that the best he or she can do is to allow grace to 'displace' the usual functioning of the mind — not in the way in which a demon displaces the soul of the living traitor, but with the same transforming effect that a dream exhibits. Something is changed, we live in another element, and so the words will not work exactly; but it is a work of sustained exactitude to say where and how they stop working. In this territory, image and metaphor operate, struggling to give form to what has been 'impressed', and the mind, so far from being simply arrested, journeys a literally unimaginable distance ('più e più intrava', *Par.*, xxxiii. 53). Something is seen and absorbed at ever-increasing depth, with language unsuccessfully trying to keep up.

And that is why we can trust what the poet says, because the language faithfully embodies its own challenge and struggle, breaking and healing repeatedly, but not being in any way frozen (note the unfreezing image yet again at *Par.*, xxxiii. 64, 'Così la neve al sol si disigilla', to describe the inner unloosing or releasing that is given in the trance of loving sight). Language, repeatedly challenged and purified, purged of the darker and more guilty memories which threaten to immobilise it, emerges from Purgatory ready to take the imprint of the divine mystery. Hell is the state in which the sinful, treasonous human attempt to reduce language to what we want and what will serve our distorted desires culminates at last in the ice of the ninth circle. Water — holy, baptismal water — flows again in Purgatory, rising simply at God's will, so that it is always flowing in the direction of our healing, so to speak, and its flowing becomes a potent metaphor for the renewal of speech.

The Movement of Love and the Fixity of Contemplation

The silence of Hell is necessarily a silencing or negating of *relation*. There is an anecdote in the fifth or sixth century *Sayings of the Desert Fathers* in which Hell is described as a place where no-one ever sees another's face; and Dante's Hell has at its centre a complex picture of relation dissolved, presented precisely in an image of faces turned away from each other. It is clear that — as has often been observed — Dante wants to present the central circle of Hell as a parodic version of the ultimate reality of Heaven: Hell is the radical denial of relation, faces that do not engage with each other, Satan's three faces all looking in different directions, and the faces of the arch-traitors either hidden or with their heads hanging downwards, out of Satan's sight. The supreme reality in Heaven is the vision of greater and greater 'involution', interdependence — first in the gathering together of all created things into a 'simple light' ('un semplice lume', *Par.*, xxxiii. 90), which kindles fire in the mind ('la mente mia [...] accesa', ll. 97–99), then in the climactic vision of the three circles, each three-coloured ('tre giri / di tre colori', ll. 116–17), two mirroring one another, the third infusing fire into the other two (ll. 118–20). Is Dante saying that each of the *giri* is of a different colour, or that each is three-coloured? There is a good case for the latter, especially as two are compared to 'iri' [rainbows] (l. 118): Satan's three faces are of different colours, and it would be appropriate for the three dimensions of the Trinitarian life to appear as the opposite of this. If so, the image is a visualisation of the fact that, in the Trinity, according to orthodox Catholic teaching, nothing is exclusively the property of any one divine person. This unsurpassable divine reality is *circulazion* (l. 127), the eternal movement of each into the other, in absolute contrast to the multidirectional, fundamentally fractured faces of Satan; as if, while God knows and loves what God is and turns his gaze on his own life, Satan cannot and will not see himself: there is nothing there to see, no substantial good that can be contemplated with joy. The 'circles' of Heaven might be more appropriately rendered 'circular motions', 'orbits', to capture the movement implied in the use of *giri*. Again the contrast is being drawn between the simple stasis of Hell and the endlessly stable, even still, movement of Heaven.

The human image is either occluded or defaced in Hell: Satan consumes human bodies. But within the circling motion of the Trinitarian life, a human form is to be seen — *la nostra effige* (l. 131), our image. In some sense this is 'coterminous' with the circling orbits, but grasping how this might be or what language might express the coincidence of the two forms is, says Dante famously, like a geometer trying to calculate a circle's area without having the mathematical tools (ll. 133–35). The point is unmistakable, though: the focal contrast between Heaven and Hell is this ultimate *visibility* in Heaven of the human face and form, as opposed to its destruction in Hell. And if this is what characterises Heaven, there is always an invitation to engagement, and so to movement. As Robin Kirkpatrick puts it pithily in his notes on this canto, 'Dante is concerned to make action rather than being the ground of existence' — or perhaps we should say that he refuses to understand being without reference to action and relation.[3] At the end of the *Paradiso*, Dante's mind or imagination is fully aligned with the 'turning' of the universe by love; his desire now moves in rhythmic unity with the sheer motion of divine self-knowing and self-loving, enacted and embodied in the created world and supremely in the created yet ultimately revealing form of Jesus. The description of lightning striking the mind so as to bring God's will to inhabit that mind (ll. 140–41) picks up the recurrent imagery of fire and kindling, the spark, *favilla*, of human intelligence (l. 71) brought to a flame by God's lightning stroke, yet more unable than ever to find words for it (l. 142). What is left is the movement of longing that is activated by divine love.

Dante finds his mind, he tells us, *messo* (l. 132), set or arrested, like the mind of the baffled geometer which *s'affige* (l. 133) on the mystery:

---

3 Dante Alighieri, *The Divine Comedy 3: Paradiso*, trans., ed. with comm. by Robin Kirkpatrick (Harmondsworth: Penguin, 2007), p. 480.

the vision begins as bewildered, near-obsessive concentration on the strangeness of what is seen, and this intensity of bafflement has to be displaced or lifted to another plane by the divine 'percussion' of the *fulgore* (l. 140) that is sent from God (Augustine's language in *Confessions* IX.25 about the 'blow' by which we experience encounters with God may be in the far background here). But the language of being 'fixed' at this juncture of the poem's argument recalls the way the same imagery is used at the beginning of the canto, where we are told how God's eternal purpose or counsel is 'fixed' ('fisso', l. 3) in Mary. The paradox inbuilt into this language is that, while it might appear to the unwary reader to echo the immobility that characterises Hell, it actually designates a fixity of dependable relationship, within which the creature can move and even decide with the freedom that it is designed for. Throughout the history of creation, divine love realises itself in and through the liberty of the creature, neither substituting for it nor being absorbed into it. God's will for Mary is that she shall so display the nobility of human nature that its maker will not disdain to become 'made' as a result of her consent. The eternal self-consistency of God is now able to express itself, embody itself in humanity because the fixed purpose of God generates in Mary a fixed resolve of love in return. Similarly, at the end of the canto, with a neat twist on the same theme, the inexhaustible vitality of mobile interpenetration in the Trinitarian life produces a stillness in the contemplating mind, an acceptance of how permanently inadequate the created mind will be for reflecting the intense mobility of divine life. Mary is kindled into the motion of love by the stability of divine purpose; Dante is brought to stillness, even stupefaction, by the motion of divinity. But in both instances, what is happening is love moving itself eternally and moving creatures in their proper motions of harmony. The poem ends with just this evocation of the love that moves the heavenly bodies in perfection, a love with which the *disio* and *velle* (l. 143) of the creature are at last perfectly aligned — both fixed and free.

The ascent from Hell to Heaven, then, is the progression from the absolute self-assertion of the damned — above all, the traitors who believe that they can remake the world of language according to their selfish will — to the absolute self-renunciation of Heaven, where 'naked' words are used stumblingly and awkwardly both to evoke and to frame the silence of contemplation when God's self-gift breaks through into the created mind. The damned end up incapable of moving or being moved, deprived of speech and of the other active uses of the senses; all they know is pain, pure passivity. Their attempt at active assertion has brought them to complete impotence and they can only be acted upon by that which ceaselessly devours, de-realises, them. The blessed are likewise in a state in which they are purely 'acted upon', but acted upon by the direct presence of love, so that they are liberated to move as they are meant to do, in love and in wonder — *fissi* and *messi* in the face of God's mystery, but, precisely *because* of this, also caught up into that created echo or reflection of divine movement that is the circulation of love and mutual service among finite beings, from stars to molluscs. Hell is where wings flap furiously but nothing is moved except empty air. Heaven is where wings fail but are caught up by the breath of grace.

Conclusion

The *Commedia* thus enacts what it describes, leading us from illusory action and the denial of language towards true action — action enabled by grace — and the proper transcendence of language; from the silence that is simply meaning evacuated and cancelled (the lies that lead to the devouring mouth of Satan) to the silence that follows the most intense and concentrated efforts to speak truly. The gracious stillness at the end of the *Paradiso* has to be won by the diverse and passionate 'movements' of the whole poem; to arrive at this paradoxical condition of being fixed within the divine freedom, we have to make the journey that the *Commedia* describes, tracing the downward trajectory that leads to faceless and impotent silence, rediscovering the possibility of speech that atones or amends.[4] And beyond this, the amending and amended speech of the penitent becomes informed and transformed by divine agency — which bestows not only grace of verbal or metaphoric form but the stumbling gracelessness of uncertainty and acknowledged inadequacy, now rendered as another embodiment of grace; so that the final silence is achieved as a triumphant surrender, not a conquest or a theophany but a being-at-home with infinite action, mediated through a created face. Robin Kirkpatrick catches this superbly in his note on the end of the *Paradiso*: this is 'the face that defines and makes possible

---

4 I have in mind, naturally, Geoffrey Hill's great essay on 'Poetry as "Menace" and "Atonement"', in *Collected Critical Writings*, ed. by Kenneth Haynes (Oxford: Oxford University Press, 2008), pp. 3–20: 'in the constraint of shame the poet is free to discover both the "menace" and the atoning power of his own art' (p. 19).

all expression and speech from childhood on'; and it is also a moment of 'proliferation', a deeply generative moment of creativity made possible by mutual regard, the shared taking of time.[5] Contemplating God is the supreme example of taking time in attending to the other; the human face at the heart of the Trinity is a sign of how the God who becomes incarnate renders all human faces worthy of contemplation — and so too renders all human speech worthy of listening, even the tragic and lost voices of the sinners Dante has spoken with and spoken for in the earlier parts of the *Commedia*.

In a way that is familiar from the practice of so many poets of faith (think of Herbert, Hopkins and Eliot), the contemplative vision is figured and gestured to not simply by an absolute silence but by the use of words that slip behind and beneath themselves to let us know that the speaker acknowledges the failure of lyrical elegance as a response to the divine interruption. When Herbert, in poems like 'The Collar' or 'Grief', allows the flow of thought or metre to be sharply interrupted either by the voice of God or by the poet's own cry of hopelessness, when, as in 'Dialogue', he in turn interrupts the divine speech in order to admit his own defeat, or, as in 'Deniall', defers a satisfying rhyme scheme until the very last line, he is deliberately breaking the lyrical and technical finish of the poem's surface so as to indicate the irruptive presence of the God who cannot be called up by skill and rhetorical command. Dante does not break the flow of his scheme, but lets us know, in both the intricacy of his metaphor and the acknowledged inadequacy of the 'fit' of his words to what has been shown, that he is making no claim to a comprehensive telling of the mysteries of grace. Words exhibit grace as they *move*: that is a part of what poetry of any sort is about. Words that have to do with the unimaginable divine have to move more than most, to move out of their own light, out of their own confidence. And in the echo chamber of the imagery of the *Commedia*'s three movements, especially in these concluding passages, we have a trajectory of movement and speech released; a mobile and fragile enacting of how the stillness-in-motion of Heaven all at once inhabits, disturbs and 'fixes' human speech.

5　Kirkpatrick, *Paradiso*, pp. 479–80.

Bibliography

For the default editions and translations of Dante's works, see 'Editions Followed and Abbreviations'.

Agamben, Giorgio, *Ninfe* (Turin: Bollati Boringhieri, 2007).

Agresti, Alberto, *Dante e Vanni Fucci. Nota letta all' Accademia Pontaniana nella tornata del 24 aprile 1892* (Naples: Tipografia della Regia Università, 1892).

Albert the Great, *Summa Theologiae, Opera Omnia*, E. Borgnet (ed.), 38 vols (Paris: Vives, 1890–1899).

—, *Commentary on Dionysius' Mystical Theology*, Simon Tugwell, O. P. (trans.), in S. Tugwell, *Albert and Thomas: Selected Writings* (New York: Paulist Press, 1988).

—, *Albert and Thomas: Selected Writings*, trans. by Simon Tugwell (New York: Paulist Press, 1988).

Alighieri, Dante, *Commedia*, ed. by Anna Maria Chiavacci Leonardi, 3 vols (Milan: Mondadori, 1991–1997).

—, *Inferno, Purgatorio, Paradiso*, trans. ed., with comm. by Robin Kirkpatrick, 3 vols (Harmondsworth: Penguin, 2006–2007).

—, *The Divine Comedy*, trans. by Allen Mandelbaum (Berkeley, CA: University of California Press, 1980–1984).

—, *The Divine Comedy*, trans. and comm. by Charles Singleton (Princeton, NJ: Princeton University Press, 1970–1976).

—, *Purgatorio*, ed. by Natalino Sapegno (Florence: La Nuova Italia, 1968).

—, 'Dispute with Forese Donati — I', in *Dante: Lyric Poems: New Translation*, trans. by Joseph Tusiani, http://www.italianstudies.org/poetry/cn13.htm

—, *Vita nuova*, trans. by Barbara Reynolds (Harmondsworth: Penguin Books, 1969).

—, *Epistole, Ecloge, Questio de situ et forma aque et terre*, ed. M. P. Stocchi (Padua: Antenore, 2002).

Andrew M. and R. Waldro, eds, *The Poems of the Pearl Manuscript* (London: Arnold, 1978).

Aquinas, Thomas, *Summa Theologiae*, ed. by Thomas Gilby, 61 vols (Cambridge: Cambridge University Press, 2008).

—, *In Librum Beati Dionysii De divinis nominibus* (Turin and Rome: Marietti, 1950).

—, *Tractatus de unitate intellectus contra Averroistas* Series Philosophica 12 (Rome: Universitatis Gregorianae, 1957).

—, *Quaestiones disputatae*. 10th edn, ed. by Raimondo Spiazzi (Turin: Marietti, 1949).

—, *Summa contra gentiles*. Ed. by P. Marc, C. Pera, and P. Caramello (Turin: Marietti, 1961).

Aristotle, *The Complete Works of Aristotle*. Ed. by Jonathan Barnes (Princeton: Princeton University Press, 1984).

Ariani M., *Lux inaccessibilis. Metafore e teologia della luce nel 'Paradiso' di Dante* (Rome: Aracne, 2000).

Armour, Peter, *Dante's Griffin and the History of the World: A Study of the Earthly Paradise (Purgatorio, cantos xxix–xxxiii)* (Oxford: Clarendon Press, 1989).

—, 'Paradiso XXVII', in *Dante's Divine Comedy, Introductory Readings III: Paradiso*, ed. by Tibor Wlassics (Charlottesville, VA: University of Virginia Press, 1995), pp. 402–23.

—, 'Canto XXIX. Dante's Processional Vision', in *Lectura Dantis. Purgatorio*, ed. by Allen Mandelbaum *et al.* (Berkeley and Los Angeles, CA and London: University of California Press, 2008), pp. 329–40.

Ascoli, Albert R., *Dante and the Making of a Modern Author* (Cambridge: Cambridge University Press, 2008).

Atturo, Valentian, 'Dalla pelle al cuore. La "puntura" e il "colpo della pietra", dai trovatori a Petrarca', *Studi romanzi* 8 (2012), 85–101.

Auerbach, Erich, *Mimesis: The Representation of Reality in Western Literature*, trans. by Willard R. Trask (Princeton, NJ: Princeton University Press, 1953).

Augustine, *Confessions*, trans. by William Watts, Loeb Classical Library, 2 vols (Cambridge, MA: Harvard University Press, 1970).

—, *Homilies on the Gospel of John*, ed. by Philip Schaff (Grand Rapids, MI: Eerdmans, 1983).

—, *On the Free Choice of the Will, On Grace and Free Choice, and Other Writings*, ed. and trans. Peter King (Cambridge: Cambridge University Press, 2010).

Baldelli, Ignazio, 'Le "fiche" di Vanni Fucci', *Giornale storico della letteratura italiana* 174 (1997), 1–38.

Baldwin, C. S., *Medieval Rhetoric and Poetic* (Gloucester, MA: Peter Smith, 1959; 1st edn 1928).

Barański, Zygmunt G., 'Dante's Biblical Linguistics', *Lectura Dantis* 5 (1989), 105–43.

—, 'Funzioni strutturali della retrospezione nella *Commedia*: l'esempio del canto XXVII del *Purgatorio*', in his *'Sole nuovo, luce nuova': Saggi sul rinnovamento culturale in Dante* (Turin: Scriptorium, 1996), pp. 221–53.

—, 'Language as Sin and Salvation: A *Lectura* of *Inferno* XVIII' (Binghamton, NY: Centre for Medieval and Renaissance Studies, 2014).

—, ed., '"Libri poetarum in quattuor species dividuntur". Essays on Dante and "Genre"', *The Italianist* 15 (1995).

Bargetto, Simona, 'Memorie liturgiche nel XXVII Canto del *Purgatorio*', *Lettere italiane* 49 (1997), 185–247.

Barnes, John C. and Jennifer Petrie (eds), *Dante and the Human Body* (Dublin: Four Courts Press, 2007).

Barolini, Teodolinda, *The Undivine Comedy: Detheologizing Dante* (Princeton, NJ: Princeton University Press, 1992).

Basile, Bruno, 'Canto II. La luna e l'ordine del cosmo', in *Lectura Dantis Romana. Cento canti per cento anni*, ed. Enrico Malato and Andrea Mazzucchi, vol. III (Rome: Salerno Editrice, 2015), pp. 61–84.

Bausi, Francesco, *Dante fra scienza e sapienza: esegesi dal canto XII del Paradiso* (Florence: Leo S. Olschki, 2009).

Bellomo, Saverio (ed.), *Theologus Dantes: Thematiche teologiche nelle opere e nei primi commenti* (forthcoming).

Beltrami, Pietro G., 'Metrica e sintassi nel canto XXVIII dell'*Inferno*', *Giornale storico della letteratura italiana* 162 (1985), 1–26.

Bemrose, Stephen, *Dante's Angelic Intelligences* (Rome: Edizioni di storia e letteratura, 1983).

Bernard, Philippe, 'Le cantique des trois enfants (Dan. III, 52–90): Les répertoires liturgiques occidentaux dans l'antiquité tardive et le haut moyen age', *Musica e storia* 1 (1996), 232–76.

Bezzola, Reto R., 'Paradiso XXVII', *Letture dantesche*, vol. III, *Paradiso*, ed. by Giovanni Getto (Florence: Sansoni, 1964), pp. 551–66.

Bigongiari, Dino, 'The Pageant on the Top of Purgatory; Virgil's Departure; the Appearance of Beatrice', in *Readings in the 'Divine Comedy': A Series of Lectures*, ed. by Anne Paolucci (Dover, DE: Griffon House, 2006), pp. 312–25.

Boccaccio, Giovanni, *La Vita di Dante* (Milan: Per Giovanni Silvestri, 1823).

—, *Elegia di Madonna Fiammetta; Corbaccio*, ed. by Francesco Erbani (Milan: Garzanti, 1988).

Boethius, *Theological Tractates; The Consolation of Philosophy*, eds H. F. Stewart and E. K. Rand, trans. S. J. Tester (Cambridge, MA: Harvard University Press, 1973).

Boitani, Piero, *Dante e il suo futuro* (Rome: Edizioni di Storia e Letteratura, 2013).

—, *Riconoscere è un dio. Scene e temi del riconoscimento nella letteratura* (Turin: Einaudi, 2014).

—, 'Shadows of Heterodoxy in Hell', in *Dante and Heterodoxy. The Temptations of 13th Century Radical Thought*, ed. by M. L. Ardizzone (Newcastle: Cambridge Scholars, 2014), pp. 60–77.

Borges, J. L., *Nueve ensayos dantescos* (Madrid: Espasa Calpe, 1982).

Botte, I. B., and C. Mohrmann, *L'ordinaire de la Messe*. Textes et Études Liturgiques 2 (Leuven: Peeters, 1953).

Botterill, Stephen, 'Purgatorio XXVII', in *Dante's Divine Comedy, Introductory Readings II: Purgatorio*, ed. by Tibor Wlassics (Charlottesville, VA: University of Virginia Press, 1993), pp. 398–410.

—, 'From *deificari* to *trasumanar*? Dante's *Paradiso* and Bernard's *De diligendo Deo*', in his *Dante and the Mystical Tradition. Bernard of Clairvaux in the* Commedia (Cambridge: Cambridge University Press, 1994), pp. 194–241.

Boyde, Patrick, 'Aspects of Human Freedom', in his *Perception and Passion in Dante's 'Comedy'* (Cambridge: Cambridge University Press, 1993), pp. 193–214.

Blasucci, Luigi, 'La dimensione del tempo nel *Purgatorio*', in his *Studi su Dante e Ariosto* (Milan and Naples: Ricciardi, 1969), pp. 37–59.

Boitani, Piero, 'La creazione nel *Paradiso*', *Filologia e critica* 33.1 (2008), 3–34.

Borzi, Italo, 'L'analisi dell'anima: amore e libertà (*Purgatorio* XVII)', in *Verso l'ultima salute. Saggi danteschi* (Milan: Rusconi, 1985), pp. 139–76.

Brand, Benjamin, 'The Vigils of Medieval Tuscany', *Plainsong and Medieval Text* 17 (2008), 23–54.

Brown, Jennifer N., 'The Chaste Erotics of Marie d'Oignies and Jacques de Vitry', *Journal of the History of Sexuality* 19 (2010), 74–93.

Brundage, James A., *Law, Sex, and Christian Society in Medieval Europe* (Chicago, IL: University of Chicago Press, 1987).

Bynum, Caroline Walker, *The Resurrection of the Body in Western Christianity, 1200–1336* (New York: Columbia University Press, 1995).

Cacciaglia, Norberto, '"Per fede e per opere" (una lettura del tema della salvezza nella *Divina Commedia*)', *Critica Letteraria* 30.2–3 (2002), 265–74.

Cachey, Theodore J. Jr., 'Cosmology, Geography and Cartography', in *Dante in Context*, ed. by Zygmunt G. Barański and Lino Pertile (Cambridge: Cambridge University Press, 2015), pp. 221–40.

—, 'Cartographic Dante: A Note on Dante and the Greek Mediterranean', in *Dante and the Greeks*, ed. by Jan M. Ziolkowski (Washington, D.C.: Dumbarton Oaks Research Library and Collections, 2014), pp. 197–226.

—, 'Title, Genre, and Metaliterary Aspects of Dante's *Commedia*', in *Cambridge Companion to the Divine Comedy*, ed. by Zygmunt G. Barański and Simon Gilson (Cambridge: Cambridge University Press, forthcoming).

—, 'Una nota sugli angeli e l'Empireo', *Italianistica. Rivista di letteratura italiana* 44.2 (2015), 149–60.

Campbell, Tony, 'Portolan Charts from the Late Thirteenth Century to 1500', in *The History of Cartography, Volume one, Cartography in Prehistoric, Ancient, and Medieval Europe and the Mediterranean*, ed. by J. B. Harley and David Woodward (Chicago, IL: University of Chicago Press, 1987), pp. 371–463.

Calì, Pietro, 'Purgatorio XXVII', in *Dante Commentaries*, ed. by David Nolan (Dublin: Irish Academic Press, 1977), pp. 93–113.

Camozzi Pistoja, Ambrogio, 'Il veglio di Creta alla luce di Matelda — Una lettura comparativa di *Inferno* XIV e *Purgatorio* XXVIII', *The Italianist* 29.1 (2009), 3–49.

Casagrande, Gino, '"I s'appellava in terra il sommo bene" (*Par*. XXVI. 134)', *Aevum* 50 (1976), 249–73.

Casey, Edward S., *The Fate of Place. A Philosophical History* (Berkeley, CA: University of California Press, 1998).

Cestaro, Gary, *Dante and the Grammar of the Nursing Body* (Notre Dame, IN: University of Notre Dame Press, 2003).

Charity, A. C., 'T. S. Eliot: The Dantean Recognitions', in *The Waste Land in Different Voices*, ed. by A. D. Moody (London: Arnold, 1974), pp. 117–56.

Chiavacci Leonardi, A. M., *Le bianche stole. Saggi sul 'Paradiso' di Dante* (Florence: Sismel — Edizioni del Galluzzo, 2010).

Ciavorella, Giuseppe, 'La creazione, gli angeli e i "moderni pastori" (*Paradiso* XXIX)', *Letteratura italiana antica* 13 (2012), 181–207.

Ciacci, Otello, 'La teoria dell'amore: Canto XVII del *Purgatorio*', in *Nuove interpretazioni dantesche* (Perugia: Volumina, 1974), pp. 75–95.

Clark, Joy Lawrence, 'Dante's Vergil: A Poet's Type of Exile' (doctoral thesis, Boston University, 2006).

Clarke, K P, 'Humility and the (P)arts of Art', in *Vertical Readings in Dante's 'Comedy': Volume 1*, ed. by George Corbett and Heather Webb (Cambridge: Open Book Publishers, 2015), pp. 203–21, http://dx.doi.org/10.11647/OBP.0066

Clifford, G. A. R., *Transformations of Allegory*. Concepts of Literature Series (London: Routledge and Kegan Paul, 1974).

Cogan, Marc, *The Design in the Wax* (Notre Dame, IN and London: University of Notre Dame Press, 1999).

Conklin Akbari, Suzanne, *Seeing Through the Veil: Optical Theory and Medieval Allegory* (Princeton, NJ: Princeton University Press, 2004).

Consoli, Domenico, 'Mitriare', *Enciclopedia dantesca*, ed. by Umberto Bosco, 6 vols (Rome: Istituto della Enciclopedia Italiana, 1970–1978), III, p. 979.

Contini, Gianfranco, 'Sul xxx dell'*Inferno*', in his *Un'idea di Dante* (Turin: Einaudi, 2001 [1970]), pp. 159–70.

—, 'Alcuni appunti su *Purgatorio* 27', in his *Un'idea di Dante*, pp. 171–90.

—, 'Un esempio di poesia dantesca (Il canto XXVIII del *Paradiso*)', in his *Un'idea di Dante*, pp. 191–213.

Cook, William R., and Ronald Herzman, 'St. Eustace: A Note on *Inferno* XXVII', *Dante Studies* 94 (1976), 137–39.

Coppa, Aldo, 'La mirabile processione', in *L'Eden di Dante*, ed. by Anonio d'Elia (Cosenza: Giordano, 2012), pp. 109–66.

Corbett, George, *Dante and Epicurus: A Dualistic Vision of Secular and Spiritual Fulfilment* (Oxford: Legenda, 2013).

—, and Heather Webb, eds, *Vertical Readings in Dante's 'Comedy': Volume 1* (Cambridge: Open Book Publishers, 2015), http://dx.doi.org/10.11647/OBP.0066

—, and Heather Webb, eds, *Vertical Readings in Dante's 'Comedy': Volume 2* (Cambridge: Open Book Publishers, 2016), http://dx.doi.org/10.11647/OBP.0100

Cornish, Alison, 'The Sufficient Example: *Paradiso* 28', in her, *Reading Dante's Stars* (New Haven, CT and London: Yale University Press, 2000), pp. 108–18.

Corti, Maria, *Percorsi dell'invenzione. Il linguaggio poetico e Dante* (Turin: Einaudi, 1993).

—, *Scritti su Cavalcanti e Dante* (Turin: Einaudi, 2003).

Crashaw, Richard, 'To the Infant Martyrs', Poetry Foundation, http://www.poetryfoundation.org/poem/181069#poem

Cristaldi, Sergio, 'Simboli in processione', in *Lectura Dantis Romana. Cento canti per cento anni. II. Purgatorio*, vol. 2, ed. by Enrico Malato and Andra Mazzucchi (Rome: Salerno Editrice, 2014), pp. 867–97.

Cróinín, Dáibhí Ó. and Immo Warntjes, eds, *Computus and its Cultural Context in the Latin West, AD 300–1200: Proceedings of the 1st International Conference on the Science of Computus in Ireland and Europe, Galway, 14–16 July, 2006* (Turnhout: Brepols, 2010).

Davies, Oliver, 'Dante's *Commedia* and the Body of Christ', in *Dante's Commedia. Theology as Poetry*, ed. by Vittorio Montemaggi and Matthew Treherne (Notre Dame, IN: University of Notre Dame Press, 2010), pp. 161–79.

De Bruyne, E., *Études d'esthétique médiévale*, III, *Le XIIIe siècle* (Bruges: De Tempel, 1946).

D'Elia, Antonio, *La cristologia dantesca logos-veritas-caritas: il codice poetico-teologico del pellegrino* (Cosenza: Pellegrini, 2012).

Di Cesare, Michelina, 'Il sapere geografico di Boccaccio tra tradizione e innovazione: l'imago mundi di Paolino Veneto e Pietro Vesconte', in *Boccaccio geografo, Un viaggio nel Mediterraneo tra le città, I giardini e…il 'mondo' di Giovanni Boccaccio*, ed. by Roberta Morosini and Andrea Cantile (Florence: Maura Paglia Editore, 2010), pp. 67–88. Donne, John 'The Sunne Rising', in *Metaphysical Lyrics & Poems of the Seventeenth Century, Donne to Butler*, ed. by Herbert J. C. Grierson (Oxford: Clarendon, 1921); Bartleby.com, http://www.bartleby.com/105/3.html

Donno, Daniel J., 'Moral Hydrography: Dante's Rivers', *Modern Language Notes* 92 (1977), 130–39.

Dragonetti, R., 'Dante et Narcisse ou les faux monnayeurs de l'image', in *Dante et les mythes. Tradition et rénovation, Revue des Etudes Italiennes* (Paris: Didier, 1965), pp. 85–146.

Dronke, Peter, 'The Phantasmagoria in the Earthly *Paradiso*', in *Dante and Medieval Latin Traditions* (Cambridge and New York: Cambridge University Press, 1986), pp. 55–81.

—, 'Symbolism and Structure in *"Paradiso 30"'*, *Romance Philology* 43 (1989), 29–48.

Duhem, Pierre, *Medieval Cosmology: Theories of Infinity, Place, Time, Void, and the Plurality of Worlds*, ed. and trans. by Roger Ariew (Chicago, IL: University of Chicago Press, 1985).

Durling, Robert M., 'Additional Note 11, "Dante and Neoplatonism"', in *The Divine Comedy of Dante Alighieri*, ed., trans. and notes by Robert M. Durling and Ronald L. Martinez, 3 vols (Oxford: Oxford University Press, 1996–2011), III, pp. 744–49.

—, 'Deceit and Digestion in the Belly of Hell', in *Allegory and Representation: Selected Papers from the English Institute*, ed. by Stephen J. Greenblatt (Baltimore, MD and London: Johns Hopkins University Press, 1989), pp. 61–93.

—, and Ronald L. Martinez, *Time and the Crystal: Studies in Dante's* Rime petrose (Berkeley and Los Angeles, CA: University of California Press, 1990).

Edson, Evelyn, *Mapping Time and Space: How Medieval Mapmakers Viewed their World* (London: British Library, 1999).

—, *The World Map, 1300–1492: The Persistence of Tradition and Transformation* (Baltimore, MD and Santa Fe, NM: Johns Hopkins University Press, 2007).

—, with E. Savage-Smith, *Medieval Views of the Cosmos* (Oxford: Bodleian Library, 2004).

Elliott, Dyan, *Spiritual Marriage. Sexual Abstinence in Medieval Wedlock* (Princeton, NJ: Princeton University Press, 1993).

Emerson, Ralph Waldo, 'Merlin', in *Poems by Ralph Waldo Emerson* (Boston, MA: Phillips, Sampson and Co., 1846).

Eybel, Emiel, 'Young Priests in Early Christianity', *Jahrbuch für Antike und Christentum. Lettere italiane*, Supplementary volume 22 (1995), 102–20.

Farinelli, Franco, 'L'immagine dell'Italia', in *Geografia politica delle regioni italiane*, ed. by Pasquale Coppola (Turin: Einaudi, 1997), pp. 33–59.

Featherstone M., and G. Nedungatt, eds, *The Council in Trullo Revisited* (Rome: Pontificio Istituto Orientale, 1995).

Fedrigotti, Paolo, '"La verità che non soffera alcuno errore e la luce che allumina noi ne la tenebra". L'intonazione anagogica della *Divina Commedia* ed il suo fondamento cristico', *Divus Thomas* 115.3 (2012), 17–44.

Fels, John, and Denis Wood, *The Natures of Maps: Cartographic Constructions of the Natural World* (Chicago, IL: University of Chicago Press, 2008).

Fergusson, Francis, *Dante's Drama of the Mind, A Modern Reading of the Purgatorio* (Westport, CT: Greenwood Press, 1981).

Ferrante, Joan M., *The Political Vision of the Divine Comedy* (Princeton, NJ: Princeton University Press, 1984).

Ferzoco, George, *Il murale di Massa Marittima. The Massa Marittima Mural*, 2nd edn (Florence: Consiglio Regionale della Toscana, 2005).

Fido, Franco, 'Writing Like God — or Better? Symmetries in Dante's 26th and 27th Cantos of the *Commedia*', *Italica* 53 (1986), 250–64.

Flood, J., and J. R. Ginther, J. W. Goering, eds, *Robert Grosseteste and His Intellectual Milieu* (Turnhout, Belgium: Brepols publishers, 2013).

Ford, David F., *Self and Salvation: Being Transformed* (Cambridge: Cambridge University Press, 1999).

—, 'Dante as Inspiration for Twenty-First-Century Theology', in *Dante's 'Commedia': Theology as Poetry*, ed. by Vittorio Montemaggi and Matthew Treherne (Notre Dame, IN: University of Notre Dame Press, 2010), pp. 318–28.

Fortuna, Sara, and Manuele Gragnolati, '"Attaccando al suo capezzolo le mie labbra ingorde": corpo, linguaggio e soggettività da Dante ad *Aracoeli* di Elsa Morante', *Nuova corrente* 55 (2008), 85–123.

Foster, Kenelm, *The Two Dantes* (London: Darton, Longman & Todd, 1977).

Francesconi, Giampaolo, 'Infamare per dominare. La costruzione retorica fiorentina del conflitto politico a Pistoia', in *Lotta politica nell'Italia medievale. Giornata di studi, Roma, 16 febbraio 2010*, ed. by Isa Lori Sanfilippo (Rome: Istituto storico italiano per il Medio Evo, 2010), pp. 95–106.

Frasso, Giuseppe, '*Purgatorio* XVI–XVIII: una proposta di lettura', in *Contesti della Commedia. Lectura Dantis Fridericiana 2002–2003*, ed. by Francesco Tateo and Daniele Maria Pegorari (Bari: Palomar, 2004), pp. 65–79.

Freccero, John, 'The Dance of the Stars. *Paradiso* X', in *Dante, The Poetics of Conversion*, ed. by Rachel Jacoff (Cambridge, MA: Harvard University Press, 1986), pp. 221–44.

Galbreath, Donald L., *Papal Heraldry* (London: Heraldry Today, 1972).

Getto, Giovanni, *Canto XXVI. Lectura Dantis Scaligera, Paradiso* (Florence: Le Monnier, 1971).

Ghisalberti, Alessandro, '*Paradiso*, canto VII. Dante risponde alla domanda: perché un Dio uomo', in *Lectura Dantis Scaligera 2009–2015*, ed. by Ennio Sandal (Rome and Padua: Antenore, 2016), pp. 141–58.

Gigante, Claudio, '"Adam sive Christus"; creazione, incarnazione, redenzione nel canto VII del *Paradiso*', *Rivista di studi danteschi* 8.2 (2008), 241–68.

Gilson, Etienne, *Dante and Philosophy*, trans. David Moore (New York and Evanston, IL and London: Harper Row, 1963; originally *Dante et la philosophie*, Paris: Vrin, 1939).

Goullet, Monique, Guy Lobrichon and Eric Palazzo, eds, *Le pontifical de la curie romaine au XIIIe siècle* (Paris: Cerf, 2004).

Gragnolati, Manuele, *Experiencing the Afterlife: Soul and Body in Dante and Medieval Culture* (Notre Dame, IN: University of Notre Dame Press, 2005).

—, *Amor che move: linguaggio del corpo e forma del desiderio in Dante, Pasolini e Morante* (Milan: Il Saggiatore, 2013).

Harper, John, *The Forms and Orders of Western Liturgy from the Tenth to the Eighteenth Century* (Oxford: Oxford University Press, 1991).

Havely, Nick, *Dante's British Public* (Oxford: Oxford University Press, 2014).

Hawkins, Peter S., *Dante's Testaments: Essays in Scriptural Imagination* (Stanford, CA: Stanford University Press, 1999).

—, 'Virtuosity and Virtue: Poetic Self-Reflection in the *Commedia*', *Dante Studies* 98 (1980), 1–18.

—, 'All Smiles. Poetry and Theology in Dante's *Comedy*', in *Dante's Commedia: Theology as Poetry*, ed. by Vittorio Montemaggi and Matthew Treherne (Notre Dame, IN: University of Notre Dame Press, 2010), pp. 36–59.

Herzman, Ronald, and William Stephany, 'Dante and the Frescoes at Santi Quattro Coronati', *Speculum* 87 (2012), 95–146.

Hill, Geoffrey, 'Poetry as "Menace" and "Atonement"', in *Collected Critical Writings*, ed. by Kenneth Haynes (Oxford: Oxford University Press, 2008), pp. 3–20.

Honess, Claire E., and Matthew Trehrene, eds, *Reviewing Dante's Theology*, vols 1 and 2 (Oxford: Peter Lang, 2013).

—, and Matthew Treherne, eds, *Se mai continga... Exile, Politics and Theology in Dante* (Ravenna: Longo editore, 2013).

Housley, Norman, *The Italian Crusades: the Papal-Angevin Alliance and the Crusades against Christian Lay Powers, 1254–1343* (Oxford: Clarendon Press, 1982).

Hugh of St Victor, *Didascalicon*, trans. by Jerome Taylor (New York: Columbia University Press, 1961).

Jacoff, Rachel, 'Our Bodies, Our Selves: The Body in the *Commedia*', in *Sparks and Seeds. Medieval Literature and its Afterlife: Essays in Honor of John Freccero*, ed. by Dana Stewart and Alison Cornish, Binghamton Medieval and Early Modern Studies, 2 (Turnhout: Brepols, 2000), pp. 119–38.

—, '*Paradiso* 23: Circular Melody', in *California Lectura Dantis: 'Paradiso'*, ed. by Allen Mandelbaum, Anthony Oldcorn, and Charles Ross (Berkeley, CA: University of California Press, forthcoming).

—, 'Dante, Geremia, e la problematica profetica', in *Dante e la Bibbia*, ed. by Giovanni Barblan (Florence: Olschki, 1988), pp. 113–23.

—, 'At the Summit of Purgatory', in *Lectura Dantis. Purgatorio*, ed. by A. Mandelbaum, A. Oldcorn, C. Ross (Berkeley and Los Angeles, CA and London: University of California Press, 2008), pp. 341–52.

Kantorowicz, Ernst H., *The King's Two Bodies: A Study in Political Theology* (Princeton, NJ: Princeton University Press, 1957).

Keen, Catherine M., '"A Local Habitation and a Name": Origins and Identity in *Purgatorio* XIV', *L'Alighieri* 49 (gennaio-giugno 2017), pp. 69–89.

—, 'The Patterning of History: Poetry, Politics and Adamic Renewal', in *Vertical Readings in Dante's 'Comedy': Volume 2*, ed. by George Corbett and Heather Webb (Cambridge: Open Book Publishers, 2016), pp. 55–76, http://dx.doi.org/10.11647/OBP.0100

Lansing, Richard, 'Narrative Design in Dante's Earthly Paradise', *Dante Studies* 112 (1994), 101–13.

Ledda, Giuseppe, ed., *Le teologie di Dante* (Ravenna: Angelo Longo, 2015).

Le Goff, Jacques, *The Birth of Purgatory*, trans. by Arthur Goldhammer (Chicago, IL: University of Chicago Press, 1981).

Lieberknecht, Otfried, *Dante's Historical Arithmetics: The Numbers Six and Twenty-eight as 'numeri perfecti secundum partium aggregationem' in Inferno XXVIII*, paper given at the 32nd International Congress on Medieval Studies, 8–11 May 1997, Western Michigan University (Kalamazoo), http://www.lieberknecht.de/~diss/papers/p_np_txt.htm

Lombardi, Elena, *The Syntax of Desire. Language and Love in Augustine, the Modistae, Dante* (Toronto: University of Toronto Press, 2007).

—, *The Wings of the Doves: Love and Desire in Dante and Medieval Culture* (Montreal: McGill-Queen's University Press, 2012).

—, 'Plurilingualism *sub specie aeternitatis*. Language/s in Dante's *Commedia*', in *Dante's Plurilingualism. Authority, Vulgarization, Subjectivity*, ed. by M. Gragnolati, S. Fortuna and J. Trabant (Oxford: Legenda, 2010), pp. 133–47.

—, '"Che libido fe' licito in sua legge". Lust and Law, Reason and Passion in Dante', in *Dantean Dialogues. Engaging with the Legacy of Amilcare Iannucci*, ed. by M. Kilgour and E. Lombardi (Toronto: University of Toronto Press, 2013), pp. 125–54.

Mandelstam, Osip, 'Conversation about Dante', trans. by Jane Gray Harris and Constance Link, in *The Poets' Dante: Twentieth-Century Reflections*, ed. by Peter S. Hawkins and Rachel Jacoff (New York: Farrar, Straus and Giroux, 2001), pp. 40–93.

Marietti, Marina, 'I moderni pastori fiorentini (*Paradiso* XXIX 103–26). La parola di Beatrice nel Primo Mobile', *Letteratura italiana antica* 7 (2006), 249–55.

Marletta, Debora, 'Aspects of Dante's Theology of Redemption. Eden, the Fall, and Christ in Dante with respect to Augustine' (doctoral thesis, University College London, 2011).

Mastrobuono, A. C., *Dante's Journey of Sanctification* (Washington, D.C.: Regnery Gateway, 1990).

Mazzucchi, Andrea, 'Le "fiche" di Vanni Fucci (Inf. XXV 1–3). Il contributo dell'iconografia a una disputa recente', *Rivista di studi danteschi* 1 (2001), 302–15.

Mellone, Attilio, *La dottrina di Dante Alighieri sulla prima creazione* (Nocera: Convento di Santa Maria degli Angeli, 1950).

—, 'Emanatismo neoplatonico di Dante per le citazioni del *Liber de causis*', *Divus Thomas* 54 (1951), 205–12.

—, 'Il concorso delle creature nella produzione delle cose secondo Dante', *Divus Thomas* 56 (1953), 273–86.

Miles, Margaret R., *Carnal Knowing: Female Nakedness and Religious Meaning in the Christian West* (Boston, MA: Beacon, 1989).

Minnis A. J., and A. B. Scott, eds, with David Wallace, *Medieval Literary Theory and Criticism, c. 1100-c. 1375* (Oxford: Clarendon Press, 1988).

Mocan, Mira, *L'arca della mente, Riccardo di San Vittore in Dante* (Florence: Olschki, 2012).

Moevs, Christian, *The Metaphysics of Dante's 'Comedy'* (Oxford: Oxford University Press, 2005).

—, 'Miraculous Syllogisms: Clocks, Faith and Reason in *Paradiso* 10 and 24', *Dante Studies* 117 (1999), 59–84.

Montemaggi, Vittorio, *Reading Dante's 'Commedia' as Theology: Divinity Realized in Human Encounter* (New York: Oxford University Press, 2016).

—, '"La Rosa che il verbo divino carne si fece": Human Bodies and Truth in the Poetic Narrative of the *Commeda*', in *Dante and the Human Body*, ed. by John C. Barnes and Jennifer Petrie (Dublin: Four Courts Press, 2007), pp. 159–94.

—, 'Dante and Gregory the Great', in *Reviewing Dante's Theology*, ed. by Claire Honess and Matthew Treherne (Bern: Peter Lang, 2013), vol. 1, pp. 209–62.

—, and Matthew Treherne, eds, *Dante's Commedia: Theology as Poetry* (Notre Dame, IN: University of Notre Dame Press, 2010).

Muessig, Carolyn, 'Paradigms of Sanctity for Medieval Women', in *Models of Holiness in Medieval Sermons. Proceedings of the International Symposium (Kalamazoo, 4–7 May 1995)*, ed. by Beverly Mayne Kienzle (Louvain-la-Neuve: Fédération International des Instituts d'Études Médiévales, 1996), pp. 85–102.

Mulcahey, M. Michèle, *'First the Bow is Bent in Study...'. Dominican Education before 1350* (Toronto: Pontifical Institute of Mediaeval Studies, 1998).

Muresu, Gabriele, 'La *rancura* di Guido da Montefeltro (*Inferno* XXVII)', in his, *L'orgia d'amor: Saggi di semantica dantesca (quarta serie)* (Rome: Bulzoni, 2008), pp. 51–91.

—, 'Virgilio, la corona, la mitria (*Purgatorio* XXVII)', *Rivista di letteratura italiana antica* 8 (2007), 223–61.

Murray, Alexander, 'Purgatory and the Spatial Imagination', in *Dante and the Church: Literary and Historical Essays*, ed. by Paolo Acquaviva and Jennifer Petrie (Dublin: Four Courts Press, 2007), pp. 61–92.

Nardi, Bruno, *Dante e la cultura medievale* (Bari: Laterza, 1949).

—, 'Il mito dell'Eden', in *Saggi di filosofia dantesca* (Milan: Società anonima editrice Dante Alighieri, 1930), pp. 347–74.

Paravicini-Bagliani, Agostino, *Le chiavi e la tiara: immagini e simboli del papato medievale* (Rome: Viella, 1998).

Pertile, Lino, *La puttana e il gigante. Dal 'Cantico dei Cantici' al Paradiso Terrestre di Dante* (Ravenna: Longo, 1998).

—, '"La punta del disio": storia di una metafora dantesca', *Lectura Dantis* 7 (1990), 3–28.

Perugi, Maurizio, 'Arnaut Daniel in Dante', *Studi danteschi* 51 (1978), 59–152.

Pickstock, Catherine, *After Writing: On the Liturgical Consummation of Philosophy* (Oxford: Blackwell, 1998).

Picone, Michelangelo, 'Dante argonauta. La ricezione dei miti ovidiani nella *Commedia*', in *Ovidius redivivus. Von Ovid zu Dante*, ed. by M. Picone and B. Zimmermann (Stuttgart: M&P Verlag für Wissenschaft und Forschung, 1994), pp. 173-202.

—, '*Purgatorio* 27: Passaggio rituale e *translatio* poetica', *Medioevo romanzo* 12 (1987), 389–402.

Pirovano, Donato, 'A la riva del diritto amore: *Paradiso* XXVI', in his, *Dante e il vero amore. Tre letture dantesche* (Pisa: Fabrizio Serra Editore, 2009), pp. 91–126.

Poole, Kevin R., ed. and trans., *The Chronicle of Pseudo-Turpin. Book IV of The Liber Sancti Jacobi (Codex Calixtinus)* (New York: Italica Press, 2014).

Proust, M., *Remembrance of Things Past*, trans. by C. K. Scott Moncrieff, T. Kilmartin, A. Mayor (Harmondsworth: Penguin, 1983).

Pseudo-Dionysius, *The Divine Names*, in *The Complete Works* (Mahwah, NJ: Paulist Press, 1987).

Quadlbauer, Franz, *Die antike Theorie der 'Genera dicendi' im lateinischen Mittelalter* (Vienna: Herman Böhlaus, 1962).

Quondam, Amedeo, 'Corona', *Enciclopedia dantesca*, ed. by Umberto Bosco, 6 vols (Rome: Istituto della Enciclopedia Italiana, 1970–1978), II, pp. 212–13.

Richard of St Victor, *On the Trinity* trans. by Ruben Angelici (Eugene, OR: Cascade Books, 2011).

Rigo, Paola, 'Prenderò il cappello', in Eadem, *Memoria classica e memoria biblica in Dante* (Florence: Olschki, 1984), pp. 135–63.

Robert Grosseteste, *De luce, seu de incohatione formarum*, trans. by Clare Riedl, Medieval Philosophical Texts in Translation No. 1 (Milwaukee, WI: Marquette University Press, 1942).

Romano, Andrea, '"S'aperse in nuovi amori l'etterno amore". Appunti sull'idea di Dio in Dante', *La Panarie. Rivista Friulana di Cultura* 152 (2007), 55–58.

Ryan, Christopher, *Dante and Aquinas. A Study of Nature and Grace in the* Comedy (London: UCL Arts and Humanities Publications, 2013).

—, 'Virgil's Wisdom in the *Divine Comedy*', *Medievalia et Humanistica* II (1982), 1–38.

Sanguineti, Edoardo, *Interpretazione di Malebolge* (Florence: Olschki, 1961).

—, 'Il Canto xxx del *Purgatorio*', in *Letture dantesche*, vol. 2, ed. by G. Getto (Florence: Sansoni, 1965), pp. 605–23.

Schiaffini, Alfredo, 'A proposito dello stile comico di Dante', in *Momenti di storia della lingua italiana* (Rome: Studium, 1953), pp. 47–51.

Schneyer, Johann-Baptist, *Repertorium der lateinischen Sermones des Mittelalters für die Zeit von 1150–1350*, 11 vols, Beiträge zur Geschichte der Philosophie und Theologie des Mittelalters. Texte und Untersuchungen, 43 (Münster: Aschendorff, 1969–1990).

Scott, John A., *Understanding Dante* (Notre Dame, IN: University of Notre Dame Press, 2004)

—, *Dante's Political Purgatory* (Philadelphia, PA: University of Pennsylvania Press, 1996).

—, 'The Rock of Peter and *Inferno*, XIX', *Romance Philology* 23 (1970), 462–79.

Şenocak, Neslihan, *The Poor and the Perfect. The Rise of Learning in the Franciscan Order, 1209–1310* (Ithaca, NY: Cornell University Press, 2012),

Singleton, Charles S., 'The Poet's Number at the Center', *Dante Studies* 80 (1965), 1–10.

—, *Dante Studies 2. Journey to Beatrice* (Cambridge, MA: Harvard University Press, 1958).

Soskice, Janet, 'Monica's Tears', *New Blackfriars* 83. 980 (October 2002), 448–58.

Sowell, Madison U. 'Dante's Nose and Publius Ovidius Naso: A Gloss on *Inferno* 25.45', *Quaderni d'italianistica* 10 (1989), 157–71.

Spitzer, Leo, 'Speech and Language in *Inferno* XIII', in *Representative Essays*, ed. by Alban K. Forcieone, Herbert Lindenberger and Madeline Sutherland (Stanford, CA: Stanford University Press, 1988), pp. 143–71.

Steinberg, Justin, *Dante and the Limits of the Law* (Chicago, IL: University of Chicago Press, 2015).

—, 'Dante's Justice? A Reappraisal of the *contrapasso*', *L'Alighieri* 44 (2014), 59–74, https://rll.uchicago.edu/sites/rll.uchicago.edu/files/SteinbergContrapasso.pdf

Taddei, Ilaria, 'La notion d'âge dans la Florence des XIVe et XVe siècles', *Mélanges de l'Ecole française de Rome. Moyen-Age* 118 (2006), 149–59

Tavoni, Mirko, 'Guido da Montefeltro dal *Convivio* a Malebolge (*Inferno* XXVII)', in *Qualche idea su Dante* (Bologna: Il Mulino, 2015), pp. 251–94

Took, John, *Conversations with Kenelm: Essays on the Theology of the 'Commedia'* (London: Ubiquity Press, 2013).

Valerio, Sebastiano, 'Lingua, retorica e poetica nel canto XXVI del *Paradiso*', *L'Alighieri* 44 (2003), 83–104.

Van Dijk, S. J. P., *Sources of the Modern Roman Liturgy; The Ordinals by Haymo of Faversham and Related Documents (1243–1307)*, 2 vols (Leiden: Brill, 1963).

Vinsauf, Geoffroi de, '*Poetria nova*, lines 970–1037', in *Les arts poétiques du XIIe et du XIIIe siècle*, ed. by Edmond Faral (Paris: Champion, 1971), pp. 227–29.

Von Balthasar, H. U., *The Glory of the Lord. A Theological Aesthetics*, vol. III, *Studies in Theological Style: Lay Styles*, trans. by A. Louth, F. McDonagh, B. McNeil, J. Saward, M. Simon, and R. Williams (San Francisco, CA: Ignatius Press, 1986).

Webb, Diana, 'St James in Tuscany: The Opera di San Jacopo of Pistoia and Pilgrimage to Compostela', *Journal of Ecclesiastical History* 50 (1998), 207–34.

Webb, Heather, *The Medieval Heart* (New Haven, CT: Yale University Press, 2010).

—, *Dante's Persons: An Ethics of the Transhuman* (Oxford: Oxford University Press, 2016).

Wei, Ian, *Intellectual Culture in Medieval Paris. Theologians and the University, c.1100–1320* (Cambridge: Cambridge University Press, 2012).

Windeatt, B. A., '"*Vera Icon*?": The Variable Veronica of Medieval England', *Convivium Supplementum* (2018), 3-15.

Index

This book need not end here...

At Open Book Publishers, we are changing the nature of the traditional academic book. The title you have just read will not be left on a library shelf, but will be accessed online by hundreds of readers each month across the globe. OBP publishes only the best academic work: each title passes through a rigorous peer-review process. We make all our books free to read online so that students, researchers and members of the public who can't afford a printed edition will have access to the same ideas.

This book and additional content is available at:
https://www.openbookpublishers.com/product/623

Customize

Personalize your copy of this book or design new books using OBP and third-party material. Take chapters or whole books from our published list and make a special edition, a new anthology or an illuminating coursepack. Each customized edition will be produced as a paperback and a downloadable PDF. Find out more at:

http://www.openbookpublishers.com/section/59/1

Donate

If you enjoyed this book, and feel that research like this should be available to all readers, regardless of their income, please think about donating to us. We do not operate for profit and all donations, as with all other revenue we generate, will be used to finance new Open Access publications.

http://www.openbookpublishers.com/section/13/1/support-us

Like Open Book Publishers

Follow @OpenBookPublish

Read more at the Open Book Publishers **BLOG**

You may also be interested in...

Vertical Readings in Dante's Comedy
Volume 1
Edited by George Corbett and Heather Web

https://doi.org/10.11647/OBP.0066
http://www.openbookpublishers.com/product/367

Vertical Readings in Dante's Comedy
Volume 2
Edited by George Corbett and Heather Web

https://doi.org/10.11647/OBP.0100
http://www.openbookpublishers.com/product/499

Love and its Critics
From the Song of Songs to Shakespeare
and Milton's Eden
By Michael Bryson and Arpi Movsesian

http://dx.doi.org/10.11647/OBP.0117
http://www.openbookpublishers.com/product/611

Lightning Source UK Ltd.
Milton Keynes UK
UKOW06f2217231117
313200UK00001B/11/P